CRITICAL GAMING: INTERACTIVE HISTORY
AND VIRTUAL HERITAGE

Digital Research in the Arts and Humanities

Series Editors
Marilyn Deegan, Lorna Hughes, Andrew Prescott and Harold Short

Digital technologies are becoming increasingly important to arts and humanities research, expanding the horizons of research methods in all aspects of data capture, investigation, analysis, modelling, presentation and dissemination. This important series will cover a wide range of disciplines with each volume focusing on a particular area, identifying the ways in which technology impacts on specific subjects. The aim is to provide an authoritative reflection of the 'state of the art' in the application of computing and technology. The series will be critical reading for experts in digital humanities and technology issues, and it will also be of wide interest to all scholars working in humanities and arts research.

Critical Gaming: Interactive History and Virtual Heritage

ERIK CHAMPION
Curtin University, Australia

Routledge
Taylor & Francis Group

LONDON AND NEW YORK

First published in paperback 2024

First published 2015 by Ashgate Publishing

Published 2016
by Routledge
4 Park Square, Milton Park, Abingdon, Oxon OX14 4RN

and by Routledge
605 Third Avenue, New York, NY 10158

Routledge is an imprint of the Taylor & Francis Group, an informa business

British Library Cataloguing in Publication Data
A catalogue record for this book is available from the British Library

The Library of Congress has cataloged the printed edition as follows:
Champion, Erik.
  Critical gaming : interactive history and virtual heritage / by Erik Champion.
    pages cm. – (Digital research in the arts and humanities)
   Includes bibliographical references and index.
   ISBN 978-1-4724-2290-3 (hardback) – ISBN 978-1-4724-2291-0 (ebook) –
   ISBN 978-1-4724-2292-7 (epub) 1. Humanities–Data processing. 2. Humanities–
Interactive media. 3. Computer games–Design. I. Title.

AZ105.C56 2015
001.30285–dc23
                                                          2015004740

ISBN: 978-1-472-42290-3 (hbk)
ISBN: 978-0-367-59821-1 (pbk)
ISBN: 978-1-315-57498-1 (ebk)

DOI: 10.4324/9781315574981

Contents

List of Figures

List of Abbreviations

AI	artificial intelligence
AR	augmented reality
BDI	Belief-Desire-Intention intelligent agents
CRPG	computer role-playing game
DH	digital humanities
EEG	electroencephalography
GSR	galvanic skin response
HCI	human–computer interaction
HMD	head-mounted display
NPC	non-playing character
NQC	non-questing character
VE	virtual environment
VR	virtual reality

Key Terms

Artificial intelligence (AI): 'The ability of a computer or other machine to perform those activities that are normally thought to require intelligence' (http://www.thefreedictionary.com/artificial+intelligence).

Apophenia: the game-player's perception of meaning, events or relationships in a computer game not intended by the game designer (after Tynan Sylvester).

BDI: Belief-desire-intentions agent, theory of AI research, particularly designed for AI agents that plan and execute plans. The BDI agent has beliefs about the world, itself and others. Desires motivate the agent. Intentions are what the agent has chosen to do.

Biofeedback: represents a real-time two-way feedback loop between the machine and the user. The user reacts to an action initiated by the system, and the system can then react based on the participants' physical/emotional reaction (and so forth).

Causal mechanics: the game mechanics of a virtual world which appear to dictate cause and effect from the player's perspective, or the designed mechanics which specifies cause and effect from the designer's perspective.

Computer game: an engaging challenge that offers up the possibility of temporary or permanent tactical resolution without harmful outcomes to the real-world situation of the participant.

CRPG: a computer role-playing game.

Cultural presence: a visitor's overall subjective impression when visiting a virtual environment that people with a different cultural perspective occupy or have occupied that virtual environment as a 'place'. Such a definition suggests that cultural presence is not just a feeling of 'being there', but cultural presence is also a sense of being in a foreign time or not-so-well understood place.

Cultural significance: following the Burra Charter 2013 (Australia ICOMOS Incorporated): 'Cultural significance means aesthetic, historic, scientific, social or spiritual value for past, present or future generations. Cultural significance is embodied in the place itself, its fabric, setting, use, associations, meanings, records, related places and related objects.'

Diegetic: the fictional world created by the game or film. For virtual environments designed for digital history and virtual heritage, the world is not necessarily fictional – it could be counter-factual or accurate – but it is still imagined or experienced based on the digital environment. Hence, an imagined world might be more appropriate than a fictional world.

Digital history: can be described as the visualization of historical resources using digital technology.

Game-based historical learning: the focused use of real-time rendering engines, game editors, game platforms, game peripherals and/or game-style interaction metaphors to help the public enhance their awareness of historical issues and heritage sites. Generally, the term implies that the virtual environment experience is best achieved by playing, but that what is learnt through such game-play is designed to be perceived as being culturally or scientifically significant and authentic. This technology may also help scientists communicate on, collaborate with each other or otherwise evaluate various hypotheses on the validity, construction, significance, use, maintenance or disappearance of historical and heritage-based sites, artefacts and cultural beliefs.

Hackathon: a collaboration between designers, programmers and content specialists over a short-term period of one or more days to design software products and prototypes. The end goal can be specific user requirements, to explore how data can generate new forms of information and interaction, or to educate and help facilitate future collaboration between different groups of people with different backgrounds and skills.

Head-mounted display (HMD): a dual-digital display that sits on the head; typically the display changes according to the movement of the user's head, and the display generally can support stereoscopic imagery (which affords an illusion of spatial depth). Some HMD displays are see-through, so can provide augmented reality.

Hermeneutic richness: the depth of interpretation available to understanding oneself or others through artefacts and other cultural remains

'Indiana Jones' dilemma: popular films such as *Indiana Jones* and *Lara Croft: Tomb Raider* have popularized archaeology, but they are actually violent action films and do not promote careful and deferential approaches to archaeological relics and heritage sites. This raises a dilemma; how should archaeology best make use of this popularization while distancing itself from the vandalism, sensationalism, violence and shoddy scholarship?

Intangible heritage: UNESCO defines this as follows: 'The "intangible cultural heritage" means the practices, representations, expressions, knowledge, skills – as well as the instruments, objects, artefacts and cultural spaces associated therewith – that communities, groups and, in some cases, individuals recognize as part of their cultural heritage.'

Interactive history: a shortened form of the more unwieldy phrase 'interactive digital history', it can be seen as the development of digital resources that teaches historical learning through interactive media.

Lovelace Test: Ada Lovelace, an early (or even the earliest) computer programmer, believed that in order to pass the test of human intelligence, a machine should originate an idea that it wasn't specifically designed for. Selmar Bringsjord and others named the Lovelace Test after Ada Lovelace: an artificial agent, designed by a human, passes the test only if it originates a 'program' that it was not engineered to produce and can reproduce that program, and in such a way that the developers of the agent cannot explain how.

Machinima: the practice or technique of producing animated films by using computer game engines.

Memes: similar to Dawkins' theory of the selfish gene, a meme is an element of a culture or of human behaviour which is passed from one person to another without any claim to individual ownership, generally through imitation (see also http://plato.stanford.edu/entries/evolution-cultural).

Mimesis: the representation or portrayal of action and behaviours that together form a dramatic enactment.

MMORPG: an online real-time role-playing game that is played by a very large number of people. Also known as massively multiplayer online role-playing games.

Mod: many computer games now come with editors that allow users to modify the game or import their own 'levels', 3D assets, characters or scripts. These new or modified game levels are called mods.

Monomyth: particularly associated with Joseph Campbell's theory of the Hero's Journey, this can be seen as a schema or framework of patterns that describes myths from around the world in terms of universal themes and stages of progression, revolving around a hero who is called upon to do extraordinary things.

Muthos: the arrangement of the incidents or the organization of events that form the overall plot structure of the narrative.

Narrative: a succession of events meaningfully experienced, told or recalled.

NPC: a character in games that is not controlled by a player – usually an acronym for non-playing character or non-playable character.

Serious games: serious games are games designed to train or educate users. Related terms are game-based learning, edutainment and eduventures.

Simulation dream: the dream of creating a complex simulation of a story world, which creates its own fascinating emergent stories as powerful as those that a human designer/storyteller might create (after Tynan Sylvester).

Story richness: the percentage of interactions in a game that are of interest to the player (after Tynan Sylvester).

Thatcamps: 'THATCamp, The Humanities and Technology Camp, is an open, inexpensive meeting where humanists and technologists of all skill levels learn and build together in sessions proposed on the spot' (see http://thatcamp.org).

Virtual heritage: the attempt to convey not just the appearance but also the meaning and significance of cultural artefacts and the associated social agency that designed and used them through the use of interactive and immersive digital media.

Visualization: the process of representing information visually and non-visually, with the aid of computer technologies.

World Gestalten: Mark Wolf (2014) defined this as 'the structure or configuration of details together implies the existence of an imaginary world, and causes the audience to fill in the missing pieces of that world, based on the details that are given'.

Acknowledgements

I'd like to thank the anonymous reviewers for their painstaking comments, as well as Ashgate Publishing and especially Lianne Sherlock and Dymphna Evans for their patience and assistance. Jakub Majewski was gracious enough to provide feedback on an earlier draft of Chapter 6 and his feedback is greatly appreciated.

During my time writing this book, Professor Ruth Tringham of the University of California, Berkeley kindly offered me the chance to visit and discuss many of the issues that I have tried to extend further here. There have also been many colleagues in the wide and sometimes chaotic field of virtual heritage who have continually inspired and contributed to the ideas I have tried to articulate here. They include Laia Tost, Lon Addison, Sarah Kenderdine, Eric Fassbender and members of ICOMOS, UNESCO and the wider digital heritage community. Thank you all.

For the first case study mentioned in Chapter 3, I would like to thank Associate Professor Sachiyo Sekiguchi of Bunkyo University, Japan. For the second case study, I would like to thank Mark Hurst and Andrew Dekker, and my supervisors Professor Ian Bishop and Professor Bharat Dave (who sadly passed away in 2014). I would also like to thank FAMSI, Dr Ed Barnhart (Director of the Maya Exploration Center), Professor Dennis Tedlock (State University of New York at Buffalo), Professor Peter Murphy of La Trobe University and the many Mayanists who volunteered so much wonderful material. For the third case study, Taoism touch-based games, I would like to thank Li Wang, the participants of the experiment (and participants of the initial pilot study and this study), the Chinese musicians and scholars involved with the project and the staff at Auckland School of Design, Massey University.

For the 'Wild Divine' and 'Half-Life 2' project and our ongoing explorations into biofeedback mentioned in Chapter 8, I would like to thank Andrew Dekker, University of Queensland, and thanks to the Wild Divine company for providing us with access to its SDK.

I would like to thank the following for permission for use of their photographs and illustrations:

Figure 1.1 Digital Sarcophagus – Cat Scans of Pausiris Mummy is courtesy of Associate Professor Paul Bourke, University of Western Australia.
Figure 1.2 EU CHESS Project is courtesy of Fraunhofer IGD and the Acropolis Museum. I would particularly like to thank Jens Keil of Fraunhofer IGD.
Figure 2.2 'Tribal Trouble' – A Hybrid Strategy-Combat-Resource Game is courtesy of Sune Hagen, Oddlabs, Denmark.

Introduction

Critical Gaming: Interactive History and Virtual Heritage can be seen as a collection of chapters designed to provoke thought and discussion, or it can be seen and used as separate chapters that may help class debate in courses dealing with the digital humanities, game studies (especially in the areas of serious games and game-based learning) or aspects of virtual heritage. While there are very few books in this intersecting area, the range of topics that could be investigated and debated is huge. So instead I have concentrated on questions in areas that appear to be central to the intersection of these three areas, have not currently been debated to any great extent or are topics that would suit either individual reflection or classroom discussion and debate.

My primary target groups of readers are those academics and students who wish to investigate how games and virtual environments can be used in teaching and research to critique issues and topics in the humanities. In particular, I want to investigate re-occurring broad issues in the design, playtesting and evaluation of serious games/playful learning/game-based learning for interactive history and for virtual heritage.

Chapter 1, 'Digital Humanities and the Limits of Text', provides a reasoned argument for the preponderance of text-based research in the digital humanities, but argues for the importance and relevance of non-text-based projects and three-dimensional media that augments rather than replaces text. It also proposes ways of improving classroom knowledge via spatial media.

Chapter 2, 'Game-based Learning and the Digital Humanities', asks if there should there be a manifesto and singular definition of 'game'? Should we be more open-minded in defining games and applying them totally or in part to historical and heritage-based simulations? Do definitions of 'games as systems' or as 'procedural rhetoric' offer enough guidance in developing and evaluating historical simulations and virtual heritage projects? In answering this question, the chapter includes suggestions gleaned from three case studies.

Chapter 3, 'Virtual Reality', focuses on intersections between virtual reality, games and digital humanities. Is virtual reality still relevant? I argue that the increasing power and superior accessibility of computer games has already absorbed much of traditional virtual reality. Has virtual reality merged into games and is it within the financial and technical reach of non-expert users? If so, which virtual reality techniques have become mainstream and accessible? What is the future of virtual reality and how will it affect digital humanities – are there specific areas we should focus on?

Chapter 4, 'Game-based History and Historical Simulations', surveys games used for history and historical learning. Which theories can help us design and critique for history and heritage-based projects? Serious games research typically use modified computer games as virtual learning environments. Virtual heritage projects typically aim to provide three-dimensional interactive digital environments that aid the understanding of new cultures and languages rather than merely transfer learning terms and strategies from static prescriptive media such as books. As an intersection between the two fields, game-based historical learning aims to provide ways in which the technology, interactivity or cultural conventions of computer gaming can help afford the cultural understanding of the self, of the past or of others with mindsets quite different from our own. A small part of this chapter stemmed from a chapter in 2007 on game-based historical learning (Champion, 2008).

Chapter 5, 'Virtual Heritage and Digital Culture', covers definitions and major issues in virtual heritage. I propose six general aims for virtual heritage and I suggest three key concepts: inhabited place making, cultural presence and cultural significance. I also suggest objectives that a scholarly infrastructure should undertake to improve the field. For those interested, I wrote a more general overview of history and heritage (but with less discussion on games), which was published in *The Oxford Handbook of Virtuality* (Champion, 2014).

Chapter 6, 'Worlds, Roles and Rituals', explores the nature, purpose and attributes of worlds, role-playing and rituals. Why are definitions of 'world' so difficult to find? How can worlds be realized via digital simulations? Can role-playing in computer games be developed further? Who should be able to read and interpret and perform rituals and why? Part of this chapter was initially published as an essay in the *International Journal of Role Playing* (Champion, 2009) and the passage has been considerably modified.

Chapter 7, 'Joysticks of Death, Violence and Morality', is a theoretical attempt to outline types of violence in computer games and develop a short framework for types of interaction in virtual heritage projects. What is violence, how is it portrayed in games and are there particular issues in virtual simulations? This chapter sketches out both factors leading to violence in digital heritage projects and reasons involving their widespread occurrence. Finally, I will suggest alternatives to violent interaction when applied to digital heritage projects.

Chapter 8, 'Intelligent Agents, Drama and Cinematic Narrative', discusses Selmer Bringsjord's ideas on interactive narrative and whether we can provide alternatives that help develop dramatically compelling interactive narrative. Why has storytelling been so difficult? Why is the *Star Trek* Holodeck so widely cited when no one has come close to building anything remotely similar?

Chapter 9, 'Biofeedback, Space and Place', discusses ways in which biofeedback and brain-controlled interfaces and theories of empathy and embodiment can be used to develop games and simulations for history and heritage-based games. How can we better integrate new research into the body and the brain and recent technologies that incorporate the senses or further integrate recent technologies with the environment? Part of this chapter is based on an *International Journal of Architectural Computing* article (Champion and Dekker, 2011) and the case study of 'Ravensholm' was briefly reported in a DiGRA 2007 conference paper available on the Internet (Dekker and Champion, 2007).

Chapter 10, 'Applying Critical Thinking and Critical Play', summarizes the arguments and findings of the chapters and proposes a quick way of validating critical theories about gaming. Can game-related projects and teaching leverage critical thinking skills? It includes a sample checklist to determine whether a critical position and argument about gaming has merit.

References

Champion, E. 2008. Game-Based Historical Learning. In R.E. Ferdig (ed.), *Handbook of Research on Effective Electronic Gaming in Education*. New York: Information Science Reference.

——. 2009. Roles and Worlds in the Hybrid RPG Game of Oblivion. *International Journal of Role Playing*, 1, 37–52.

——. 2014. History and Heritage in Virtual Worlds. In M. Grimshaw (ed.), *The Oxford Handbook of Virtuality*. Oxford: Oxford University Press.

Champion, E. and Dekker, A. 2011. Biofeedback and Virtual Environments. *International Journal of Architectural Computing*, 9, 377–396.

Dekker, A. and Champion, E. 2007. Please Biofeed the Zombies: Enhancing the Gameplay and Display of a Horror Game Using Biofeedback. In B. Akira (ed.), *DiGRA 2007: Situated Play Conference*, Tokyo. DiGRA, 550–558.

Chapter 1

Digital Humanities and the Limits of Text

Names are important and definitions are important; the mission and goals of digital humanities will see course numbers, grant applications, centres and careers rise or fail. So I can appreciate the reasons behind the burgeoning literature attempting to define digital humanities (Cohen et al., 2011; Terras et al., 2013). Digital humanities (DH) is a big business, at least in terms of grants, novelty, media releases and career promotion.

While many proponents of DH talk of it as a broad church or even as a tent, I tend to view it more as a campsite, where positions and prime spots are visibly or surreptitiously contested and fought over under the veneer of collegial agreement. In particular, some definitions of DH worry me. There has long been a debate on what exactly DH is, but in 2012 I was struck by Dave Parry's succinct bifurcation of DH. In his chapter 'The Digital Humanities or a Digital Humanism' in *Debates in the Digital Humanities* (Gold, 2012), Parry raises the controversial question as to whether DH would be best considered as the application of computing or an inquiry into how digital media has irrevocably changed the humanities (Parry, 2012).

More recently, I have moved away from taking an either/or position; I believe that DH at a fundamental level considers how to integrate computing with humanities and attempts to understand how both computing and humanities must change. It needs to do so in order to best meld two quite different approaches together. What does worry me here is a subtle suggestion running through some texts that DH are primarily or uniquely or best viewed as computing services and tools applied to the digitalization and processing of text or literature (Baldwin, 2013). For various significant reasons that will hopefully become abundantly clear, a perspective arguing that humanities is primarily or fundamentally text-based would be mistaken, and such a viewpoint would impact negatively on the development of both non-text-based and text-based DH.

I have four reasons to be concerned with any idea that DH is primarily text-based (and in particular not related to visualization). Some might argue that there is a clear separation between written language and images, that to be a humanist or a humanistic scholar (which are not the same thing), one has to have high levels of literacy, that non-text-based media is not part of DH, or that visualization cannot provide suitably scholarly arguments.

In my opinion, visualization projects are typically missing or downplayed. This concern might seem a little paranoid; clearly, there are presentations on visualizations at DH conferences. So here are some examples of what appears to me be a text bias. The index to the book *Debating The Digital Humanities: A Reader* lists a 'visual turn' on page 179. Yet turning to pages 178–179, you will find that Patrik Svensson's chapter actually decries the lack of reference to visual media projects or to multimedia in general (Svensson, 2013). As Svensson points out, the field of humanities computing has focused on the textual, but this does not mean that other projects were not developed. To quote from Hannah Gillow, who was critiquing Stephen Marce's article 'Literature is Not Data: Against Digital Humanities' (Gillow, 2013):

> The first problem with this article is the title itself. In the best interpretation possible, the title suggests that Digital Humanities is limited to text mining and textual studies. Worst case, it suggests that digital humanities' only purpose is reclassifying all literature as simply data.

> As we are well aware, both these statements are patently untrue. Digital Humanities encompasses an incredibly vast amount of categories, textual studies being only one of them.

While Marce would be well within his grounds to point out the frequent hype that purports to be DH, to lambast the entire movement through attacking straw men does seem to be a step too far. However, the problem is more insidious than the opinion of just one critic. The low regard in which visualization is held seems to be shared by some of the academic press. For example, according to Lev Manovich (2012), the 'Cambridge University Press Author Guide' suggests that authors avoid illustrations as they will detract from the main argument.[1]

You might counter that DH derives from the humanities computing field, which is itself heavily indebted to text-based research. After all, Susan Hockey wrote the following in her chapter 'The History of Humanities Computing' in one of the first definitive books on DH (Schreibman et al., 2004):

> Applications involving textual sources have taken center stage within the development of humanities computing as defined by its major publications and thus it is inevitable that this essay concentrates on this area. (Hockey, 2004, p. 4)

On first reading, this seems reasonable. Yet one of the major journals listed was known at the time as *Literary and Linguistic Computing*. Weren't there great advances in archaeological computing at the same time, which were not necessarily text-based? Yes there were, but they weren't published in that particular journal.

More subtly, various ontologies for directories of DH tools and methods in European projects (such as DARIAH and NeDiMAH) and in American or international projects (such as DiRT Bamboo, currently known as DiRT) are heavily influenced by the ontology of DH as developed at the University of Oxford. This

---

1   I have not found this passage myself; hopefully it has been removed.

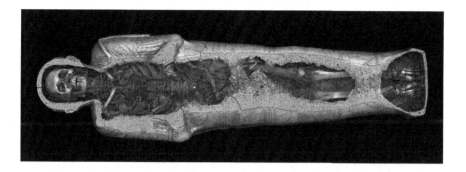

Figure 1.1   Digital Sarcophagus – Cat Scans of Pausiris Mummy
Source: Paul Bourke

in turn was based on the scholarly ontology devised by John Unsworth (2007). The University of Oxford definition of DH, at least on its webpage (undated), is text-based and desk-based. Its http://digital.humanities.ox.ac.uk/Support/whatarethedh.aspx page says that, amongst other new advantages, DH offers 'new desktop working environments' and 'new ways of representing data'.

Where is visualization as a research tool in its own right? Can't visualization actually create new research questions? Why must working environments be desktop-based? Must all humanists have a digital version of a horizontal writing surface? I would suggest that there are two main reasons for this: non-text-based humanities publish in other journals and present at other conferences; and many traditional humanities departments do not necessarily have access to or are even aware of the potential relevance of virtual reality and other non-desktop-based digital environments.

An example of visualization as research is the use of CAT scans to create a 3D model of a mummy without opening the sarcophagus, the Pausiris mummy projection created by Paul Bourke and Peter Morse for the Museum of New and Old Art (MONA), Hobart, Tasmania. There are two cabinets in the room. One cabinet contains the real Pausiris mummy (unopened) and the other the digital interpretation (Figure 1.1). Paul Bourke describes the museum exhibit on his website (Bourke, 2011):

> The digital representation reveals the interior of the mummy casket, slowly peeling away the casket and wrappings. One approaches the two display cabinets by walking on stepping stones, the room is flooded by black dyed water.

In many examples in archaeology, you can only see the artefact from visualization, be it the fall of light on a statue at solstice, the clap that creates the sound of a bird as acoustically reflected by Mayan temples, or the simulation itself; in many cases, we cannot see the object with the naked eye in the real world

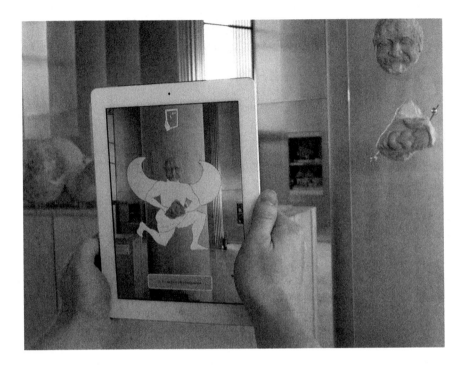

Figure 1.2   EU CHESS Project
Source: Fraunhofer IGD and the Acropolis Museum

– it has to be re-created or projected for us. Another example would be augmented reality, augmenting artefacts with knowledge that is no longer part of the physical object, such as the EU CHESS project, which will be discussed in Chapter 3.

A simple if cheeky test is to ask someone what the acronym 'VRE' stands for. If they say Virtual Research Environment (VRE), they are probably a European-based DH researcher; if they say Virtual Reality Environment, they are probably involved in a visualization-related field, but they don't have to be computer programmers (Das et al., 1993), they could be architects and designers or archaeologists (Acevedo et al., 2001; Slator et al., 2001), or they could be researchers in the area of tourism (Gurau, 2007) or educational design and psychology (Patera et al., 2008).

I have great respect for many of the DH projects at Oxford, and this approach to DH is an interesting one; those at Oxford did not create a DH centre, nor did they label certain people as 'Digital Humanists'. Instead, they provide support and facilities in DH for any academic with DH needs. And I agree with the below statement on their website:

> Doing digital humanities does not necessarily mean becoming a technology specialist, but it does entail gaining some idea of the relevant technologies and

exchanging expertise with technologists. Exchange is the key term: the digital humanities are most successful where there is a two-way collaboration between scholars and technologists, not where either side is merely at the service of the other.

DH revolves around not just what we can do with a million books, but also what the community can do with humanities; we require collaborative frameworks, tool-making systems and spaces (Factor, 2011; Kelly, 2014). We now have a near-instant audience (Elliott and Gilles, 2009) and even if technology can get in the way (Hitchock, 2012, American Academy of Arts and Sciences, n.d.), academics no longer have to wait years for people to read their books – academics and non-academics can now build infrastructure frameworks that allow others to build on and extend academic output. Social media has turned a comparatively one-way process of scholarly dissemination into an interactive circle. This is the revolution; we have moved beyond traditional research publications and beyond tools (that virtually make books and their successors) towards tools that allow people to make, share and collaborate on their own books (or whatever the media or even objects might be).

Considering that academia is supposedly concerned with the dissemination of knowledge, especially critical awareness of knowledge, communality, public accessibility and public visibility could easily be improved, even if Gibbs (2011) argued that public levels of complaints are very low. In the book *Digital Humanities in Practice* (Warwick et al., 2012) and on the related blog (Warwick, n.d.), Warwick, Terras and Nyhann have decried the lack of public dissemination of DH projects. In his 2010 blog post 'What is Digital Humanities' (2010), Matthew Kirschenbaum remarked:

> Whatever else it might be then, the digital humanities today is about a scholarship (and a pedagogy) that is publicly visible in ways to which we are generally unaccustomed, a scholarship and pedagogy that are bound up with infrastructure in ways that are deeper and more explicit than we are generally accustomed to, a scholarship and pedagogy that are collaborative and depend on networks of people and that live an active 24/7 life online. Isn't that something you want in your English department?

Digital humanities require more than the mere act of people coming together, they also require space that helps bring people and new ideas together. For example, Kelly noted (2014):

> Therefore, if we are going to do digital right in our departments, we need to create collaborative spaces where the *making* of digital history can happen.

Even if we manage to create the right sort of collaboration spaces, we also need to tackle the problem of literacy, digital literacy and digital fluency (Resnick, 2002).

Despite my rather utopian talk of a revolution in scholarly discourse, not all can read. A concern or predilection with text-based material is obstructing us from communicating with a wider audience. Multimedia, visualizations and sensory interfaces can communicate across a wider swathe of the world's population. And although literacy is increasing, technology is further creating a fundamental divide between those who can read and write and those who cannot. UNESCO (2014) reported:

> Over 84 per cent of the world's adults are now literate, according to the latest data from UNESCO's Institute for Statistics (UIS). This represents an eight percentage point increase since 1990, but it still leaves some 774 million adults who cannot read or write … Literacy also remains a persistent problem in developed countries. According to the Organisation for Economic Cooperation and Development (OECD), one in five young people in Europe had poor literacy skills in 2009, and some 160 million adults in OECD countries were functionally illiterate. This means that they do not have the skills needed to function in today's environments such as the ability to fill out forms, follow instructions, read a map, or help with their children with homework … 'This situation is exacerbated by the rise of new technologies and modern knowledge societies that make the ability to read and write all the more essential', said UNESCO Director-General Irina Bokova in her message for International Literacy Day.

Historically, the distinction between text and symbol has been blurred, from early European languages to Asian languages and as part of world history in general. For example, writing has been discovered in China that is 5,000 years old (Tang, 2013). Only this 'primitive writing … [lies] … somewhere between symbols and words'. This language exists, in other words, when five or six of the symbols are combined; they are no longer symbols, but words.

The alphabets for many modern languages were originally derived from images. Even today, language is geographically influenced, according to Mark et al. (1989, p. 4):

> Whereas human senses operate in very similar ways, regardless of culture or language, human *perception* (that is, the *mental interpretation* of sensory inputs) is influenced by language and interpretive image schemas (see Lakoff, 1987, and Johnson, 1988). The title of Leonard Talmy's (1983) seminal paper on this subject, 'How Language Structures Space', expresses this position very well … Depending on the situation, human languages may use gestalt reference frames, based on inherent properties of the ground or reference object, or canonical reference frames, based on the speakers' or listeners' viewpoint. There also are cross-linguistic and cross-cultural differences in reference frames; a good example is the common use of radial rather than Cartesian orientation systems by island-dwellers.

Even cave paintings were spatially planned – they were placed near resonant locations in the caves, and the density of the pictures appears to be 'proportional to the intensity of that spot's resonance' (Viegas, 2008; Brown, 2012): Cave paintings happened tens of thousands of years ago, so why are they still relevant? The answer is that they show the long-term association between image, space and meaning.

A contextual appreciation of Mayan 'writing' would necessitate understanding the essential link between image, glyph, building, space and audience. Their most sacred inscriptions were designed to showcase the noble and priestly class while hiding secret information from the public below. In a sense, the temples were both books and billboards, the layering of floor and paint (plaster) related to the spirituality of the city and ruler. Even books until the last few hundred years were heavily illustrated; audiences are even today not fully literate, and many find images much quicker and easier to understand than text. Are they to be shut out of the garden of the humanities?

So visualization is an extremely significant aspect of DH, and writers such as Burdick et al. (2012, p. 122) seem to agree with me:

> [C]ontemporary Digital Humanities marks a move beyond a privileging of the textual, emphasizing graphical methods of knowledge production and organization, design as an integral component of re-search, transmedia crisscrossings, and an expanded concept of the sensorium of humanistic knowledge. It is also characterized by an intensified focus on the building of transferrable tools, environments, and platforms for collaborative scholarly work and by an emphasis upon curation as a defining feature of scholarly practice ... The desktop environment – with its graphical user interface, real-time WYSIWYG tool-kit, and evolution from command lines to icons and window-based frames – not only vastly expanded the corpus of born-digital documents but also ushered in the gradual integration of audio, video, and graphics.

I agree that the World Wide Web in combination with the Internet – they are not actually the same thing – has forced us to look at documentation and the office in ever-new ways. One can argue over the importance of the World Wide Web in the integration of multimedia, but one cannot archive the Internet as a collection of text-only documents because then it is no longer the Internet.

While I have emphasized the visual contribution of DH, visualization can include other media, such as sound (Brown, 2012):

> Humanity's fascination with sound runs deep. In Utah's Horseshoe Canyon, ancient people drew artwork where echoes are loudest. Around the world, Stone Age artists typically painted in caverns with the greatest reverberation ... 'Such resonant spaces inspire singing', Lubman said. Paleolithic musicians may have used caves to amplify and focus music, just as choirs use vaulted churches today.

So if humanities are multimodal, then DH should be multimodal. Some of the most famous and far-reaching DH-related projects could not be considered text-based, for example, the Spatial History Project (http://humanexperience.stanford.edu/digital_humanities):

> The project brings together scholars working on projects at the intersection of geography and history using Geographic Information Systems (GIS) in their research. The overarching goal of the Spatial History Project is to create dynamic, interactive tools that can be used across the spectrum … to enable the creation of new knowledge and understanding of historical change in space and time and the possibilities for our present and future that may be found in the past.

Another example is the Pelagios project (http://pelagios-project.blogspot.co.uk/p/partners.html):

> Pelagios is a collective of projects connected by a shared vision of a world – most eloquently described in Tom Elliott's article 'Digital Geography and Classics' – in which the geography of the past is every bit as interconnected, interactive and interesting as the present. Each project represents a different perspective on our shared history, whether map, text or archaeological record, but as a group we believe passionately that the combination of all of our contributions is enormously more valuable than the sum of its parts.

And archaeologists are visual people. Their research explorations are often done with their visual imagination, even if this is not obvious in their publications. For example, according to the historian Robin Fleming (Graham, 2013):

> The field archeologists that I know all have this incredible visual imagination, and they can look at a site that's only from the ground down, excavate it out, and see what it looked like. Which is something historians just can't do. I have no visual imagination at all. So archeologists do those things, but they're not interested in looking – most of them, anyway – at the kind of range of archeological material being pulled out of the ground, against the background of the kinds of questions that drive historians, and writing a compelling story about the lived experience of people of the past.

In his blog post 'The Digital Humanities is About Breaking Stuff', Jason Stommel (2014) wrote that now we combine film and media: 'Our apparatuses for media-consumption juxtapose digital media, literature, and film: Now, we watch Ridley Scott's *Alien* in a window alongside Twitter and Facebook. Film no longer exists as a medium distinct from these other media.' I disagree, as would others; just as film cannot be reduced to mere text and 'we cannot mistakenly reduce a moving image work to its dialogue' (Mittel, 2012), we have not yet fully integrated these new types of media with film.

One distinction made between the humanities and DH is that the latter reveals process rather than just product (Stommel, 2014). Indeed, one of the great dangers to producing DH is the phenomenon coyly referred to as the 'managerial humanities' (Allington, 2013; Nowviskie, 2013) where administration rather than creation and evaluation is predominant. A manager of a DH centre said at the Digital Humanities Congress in Sheffield in 2013 that a digital humanist was someone writing a grant application or applying for a promotion. Now they need to talk to ministers, influence policy, develop social impact and quote numbers rather than users.

So who are the humanities for? In 2012, at the Digital Humanities: Now and Beyond symposium at Aalborg University in Denmark, John Naughton (Emeritus Professor of the Public Understanding of Technology at the Open University) said even though he was from the sciences and was not a humanist, he loved the poetry of T.S. Eliot. Why would a professor feel compelled to say that he was not a humanist? Does one need to be a Professor of Literature to be part of the humanities or to appreciate literature? There may well be many artists and writers who write in particular for the academics – and certainly Eliot, Joyce and others are not famous for accessibility – but there were many more who wrote directly of and to the general public, and many of them had little time for academics.

There is much discussion of what is or are the digital humanities, but no discussion of what is/are the humanities. Speaking after Professor Naughton, I suggested we should have at least a working definition of the humanities in order to have an understanding of the parameters of the DH. My suggestion was that the humanities should investigate the values and meanings that define culture and society.

This suggestion is based on the premise that critical thinking is essential to much of the humanities and seems to be backed up by the thinking of many famous humanities professors (Fitzpatrick, 2011), their faculties (Stanford University, n.d.) and learned societies (American Academy of Arts and Sciences, 2014). I mentioned in my brief talk referred to above that critical thinking does not always happen in science or in engineering, but what I should have mentioned is that it does not necessarily happen in the humanities either. Indeed, the humanities do not have an exclusive call on critical thinking, but my – perhaps contentious – call is that when scientists are utilizing critical thinking, they are likely to be employing aspects of the humanities (as an academic discipline).

This is why I regarded Leibniz, Pascale and Descartes as humanists; they were indeed scientists (and great ones), but their use of critical thinking as philosophers also marked them as part of the humanities. Less contentious, hopefully, is my claim that the humanities (as academic disciplines) should critically think through the values and meanings that define culture and society. When a scientist critically thinks through the issues and implications of science as it may or will impact on cultures and societies, they are thus not just critically thinking, they are also thinking as humanists.

Critical thinking is an ideal that animates many courses in the humanities (Johns Hopkins University, n.d.), but its impact and import is wider. Mark Kingwell (2012) succinctly articulated the wide-ranging significance of critical thinking:

> We say this a lot but don't do much about it. Here's what we need: courses in informal logic, so students can recognize fallacies in public discourse; in economic theory, since economists think they rule the world, and politicians believe them; and in computer programming, because you can't see the biases of the system unless you know how it was coded. The widespread view that technology is value-neutral, inevitable and always here to help needs to be exposed as the dangerous ideology it is.

Part of the confusion may be in thinking that the term 'humanities' refers to simply and exclusively those who study the humanities from within academic disciplines. It is a peculiar aspect of the English language that those who study the humanities are actually studying those who do not necessarily create, but who talk and write about those who create. Conrad Fiedler (1957), a nineteenth-century philosopher of art, would have been furious. He continually asserted, and I think with some justification, that many of the art historians and philosophers of art made so little headway in the understanding of art because they mistook categorization for the experience of art *as* art.

Who is a philosopher? An academic in a philosophy department or someone who writes books in their spare time? Before you answer this question with the former option, consider the sad story of the person who failed to get royal approval for their chosen career of astronomy and wrote books instead, after their tutoring job (Kant) or their school teaching job (mathematics teacher Hegel, and Wittgenstein, trained in engineering) or a person who paid the bills by being a watchmaker and never joined an academy (Spinoza). There may have been a Plato without a Socrates, but it is surely worth considering the possibility that Plato would have had far less impact if Socrates had only concentrated on his original profession of sculpture.

I once enrolled in a postgraduate philosophy course on Wittgenstein and we spent most of our time discussing people who argued about Wittgenstein's *Philosophical Investigations*, not the book itself. The academics in philosophy who argued about Wittgenstein may indeed be philosophers and may indeed be humanists (they are typically in the Faculty of Humanities), but I would be loath to include them as humanists and yet not include Kant, Hegel, Schopenhauer, Nietzsche (a philologist if we are to be technical), Leibniz, Pascale, Descartes and of course Wittgenstein (his passport said he was an architect).

In short, humanists do not have to be academics, and you do not have to be an academic to appreciate the humanities. Some people might even argue that academia can get in the way of appreciating the humanities, I recall a Professor of Architecture once commenting that architects don't get the time to appreciate architectural beauty as they are so often wondering how things were designed just so rather than sitting back and enjoying the space as an architectural experience in itself.

And where are the artists and designers? I am fully and often painfully aware of the battle between the faculties, between humanities and fine arts (and design) over who can use the arts for course titles, but even when we talk of DH encompassing the social sciences, or arts, there seems to be very little involvement from them.

As for other fields, even as recently as 21 March 2014 (the day before I wrote this passage), a keynote speaker to Digital Humanities Australia 2014 asked how many philosophers were in the room. Only one person put up their hand. Archivists and archaeologists from both hemispheres have often told me they feel removed from humanities meetings and infrastructures, for while there is increasing publication and presentation of visualization in DH conferences, it is typically visualization of text and word repetition.

Yet archives are not just text and the DH encompasses research projects that are collaborative and. Even the book itself is a material, embodied experience. The research of the University of Dundee's Poetry Beyond Text Project group is further evidence of the importance of image to the literature (University of Dundee, n.d.):

> The CRs [co-researchers] rated works in which they felt the text and image mutually enhanced one another more highly than works which they felt were 'fragmented' or disjunctive. For one CR, who gave both works 10 out of 10, the idea of how text and image worked together was pivotal to her discussion of each work and something that she explored in detail.

Literature itself is linked to both the image (Theibault, 2012) and to materiality (Rudy, 2011); the materiality of Icelandic sagas and runic inscriptions are considered by various scholars to be essential properties (Jesch, 2013). So my question to those who think that DH is primarily about text is to ask them what is left in the humanities if the arts and social sciences are excluded? You cannot comprehensively teach and research Freud without understanding his relation to Nietzsche, or understand Nietzsche's belief that he was a scientist and philologist without reviewing his research into the environmental physics of Helmholtz, or his background work in the etymology of ancient Greek architecture and performing arts. Even Immanuel Kant, in his attempt to understand aesthetic judgment and notions of the sublime, was compelled to give examples of sacred architecture (the Temple of Isis) and the decorative arts (for example, the Maori tattoo).

Literature is also inextricably linked to rhythm and movement. Politics and the brainwashing effect of nationalistic marches are related to an understanding of movement (Turner and Pöppel, 1988), and musical appreciation is heavily affected both by our mammalian heritage (Pankseppa and Bernatzky, 2002) and by the body in space (Sacks, 2007; Thomas, 2013). Music is not actually a completely removed, abstract experience after all. The importance of our body and our genetic heritage is not a recent phenomenon; Professor Iegor Reznikoff hypothesized the possibility that 'all of today's music could have resulted from an ingrained human memory of the acoustical properties of caves' (Viegas, 2008).

So, the humanities are not merely multimodal but are also embodied experiences. The objects in and on which the humanities are described, critiqued and preserved are more than just holders for text; they are essential artefacts, which give researchers essential clues in the interpretation of text and author. Material objects are not merely brute objects; they are symbolic as well. Archaeologists and anthropologists understand this. Consider ethnography and the cultural meaning of indigenous people – they too have a history, and even if it is not written in a conventional sense, it can also be inscribed, although it is often inscribed into the lived and symbolic world (McDonald and Veth, 2013).

If history is only that which has been written, then many cultures are excluded. Most worryingly, while the American public appear to be warming to the notion of the 'past', they are not warming to the word 'history' (Rosenzweig and Thelen, 2000). Neither the output of the public nor the output of the intellectual must be written down in order to be part our cultural memory. Even if Socrates' *Dialogues* (known today as a method or genre: Socratic dialogue) were not later written down by Plato, they would still be part of the humanities and of our cultural heritage.

Part of the complexity here arises from the notion of culture, which seems to function as both noun and verb, as a marker of 'primitive' societies, as popular culture or even as sophisticated 'high class' culture. If culture is the framework that interlinks external cognitive artefacts, it is also an escape, a direction, a path and a portal. So culture needs a context and it requires a constant questioning and redirecting.

As Kathleen Fitzpatrick (2011) remarked: 'In fact, the best scholarship is always creative, and the best production is always critically aware. The Digital Humanities seems another space within the academy where the divide between making and interpreting might be bridged in productive ways.' My one deviation from the sentiment behind the above quote is to point out that the humanities are not solely created, experienced, funded and understood within the professional and institutional 'academy' of the humanities. Such an understanding of the humanities would be historically, intellectually and culturally impoverished. Indeed, it may be logistically, ethically and commercially fatal (Nowviskie, 2013).

Even if you agree with me that the humanities are inherently a project of critical thinking and that the arts can be considered part of the humanities, you may not wish to support the idea that visualization can lead to scholarly arguments. And if this criticism is correct and if games are primarily visualizations, it may be hard for me to argue that games can be a critical enterprise. And yes, I could argue that some if not all games can be critiqued from a literary viewpoint, but then the multimodality of games does not proffer anything particularly interesting about games as a scholarly medium.

Visualization can be reflective and critical (Dörk et al., 2013):

> The notions of casual [21] and vernacular [26] visualizations highlight non-traditional uses and origins of information visualizations. In both cases, the

purpose of visualization is not so much to gain 'analytic insight', but rather to get a heightened recognition of an issue, awareness about an online community's shared resources, or even reflection about oneself.

According to Martyn Jessop (2008), digital visualization is more than just an illustration; it is also a scholarly methodology. Visualization is promoted at Stanford University's Digital Humanities workshops as both a tool and an argument (Robichaud and Blevins, 2011). Visualization workshops are becoming popular fixtures at DH workshops (Milner, 2014) and conferences (Weingart, 2013, 2014); some recent conference papers even promote the use of 'persuasive visualisations' (Hann, 2008). Archival organizations now offer tools to help humanities scholars to visualize new research questions: 'By replacing information with image, we can often see a different story hidden in the data' (Tocewicz, 2014). However, the challenge of adopting visualizations to the strategies of humanities is not always clear-cut, especially given that visualizations in the humanities tend to prefer to cover as many interpretations as possible (Sinclair et al., 2013).

On the other hand, Van den Braak et al. (2006) have indicated that some studies show that visualization tools have helped scholarly arguments. The Network for Digital Methods in the Arts and Humanities (NeDiMAH)'s specialist Information Visualization group, one of a number of European research infrastructure groups, has written on its website (http://www.nedimah.eu/workgroups/information-visualisation) that: 'Visualisation refers to techniques used to summarize, present and enact rich materials visually, and is becoming increasingly important as an integrated part of the research processes in the humanities.' Even at the government level, the relationship between visualization and story-telling is being promoted to enhance public communication (Lindquist, 2011):

> Story-telling enhances visualizations. There is widespread acknowledgement that even the best visualizations require parallel story-telling in order to draw out interesting facts and interesting issues. The audiences for visualizations are human: needing context, narrative, and often a guide to parse information.

Hence, visualization is an ally of story-telling, not a competitor. There should be no surprise that visualization is required for specialist areas such as spatial history, but how many historians and scholars from the wider group of humanities understand that visualization can itself be the research? In his essay 'What is Spatial History?' (2010), Richard White complained that colleagues from other fields do not understand the importance of map-making itself as research:

> [V]isualization and spatial history are not about producing illustrations or maps to communicate things that you have discovered by other means. *It is a means of doing research*; it generates questions that might otherwise go unasked, it reveals historical relations that might otherwise go unnoticed, and it undermines, or substantiates, stories upon which we build our own versions of the past.

Summary

I mentioned and then rejected four possible claims that the DH is primarily text-based, that non-text-based media is in general not part of the principle remit of DH, that there is a clear separation between written language and images, and that humanities is not related to visualization and that visualization cannot provide suitable scholarly arguments.

My response to these claims has been as follows: historically text has not lived in a hermetically sealed well all by itself; a world with literature but without the arts is intellectually and experientially impoverished, critical thinking and critical literacy extend beyond the reading and writing of text, and therefore visualization can make scholarly arguments. Utopia is still a few traffic lights down the road – there is still work to be done to show how DH, digital media and especially computer games are open to scholarly investigations and critical insights.

Computer gaming can touch on and investigate the wider spectrum of issues and research questions in the humanities that are relevant both to scholars and to the general public. That said, I am not convinced that the ideological aspects of computer games have been fully developed, and these issues need further clarification in order for us to grasp the value, promise and problematic natures of game-based learning applied to interactive history and digital heritage.

As Jerome McGann (2002) warned us:

> [T]he general field of humanities education and scholarship will not take the use of digital technology seriously until one demonstrates how its tools improve the ways we explore and explain aesthetic works – until, that is, they expand our interpretational procedures.

The above goal is the goal of the following chapters. To paraphrase the words of the 43rd President of the United States of America, George W. Bush, we have a job to do.

References

Acevedo, D., Vote, E., Laidlaw, D.H. and Joukowsky, M.S. 2001. Archaeological data visualization in VR: Analysis of lamp finds at the Great Temple of Petra, a case study. *Proceedings of the conference on Visualization '01*. IEEE Computer Society, 493–496.

Allington, D. 2013. The Managerial Humanities; or, Why the Digital Humanities Don't Exist. Available at: http://www.danielallington.net/2013/03/the-managerial-humanities-or-why-the-digital-humanities-dont-exist/–sthash.4iR0tyLo.UepsFJbr.dpbs.

American Academy of Arts and Sciences. 2014. Humanities Visualization. Available: at http://humviz.org.

Baldwin, S. 2013. The Idiocy of the Digital Literary (and What Does it Have to Do with Digital Humanities)? *Digital Humanities Quarterly*, 7. Available at: http://www.digitalhumanities.org/dhq/vol/7/1/000155/000155.html.

Bourke, P. 2011. Pausiris Mummy Exhibition, Digital installation by Paul Bourke and Peter Morse. Available at: http://paulbourke.net/exhibition/MONA.

Brown, A.S. 2012. From Caves to Stonehenge, Ancient Peoples Painted with Sound. *Inside Science*. Available at: http://www.insidescience.org/content/caves-stonehenge-ancient-peoples-painted-sound/571.

Burdick, A., Drucker, J., Lunenfeld, P., Presner, T. and Schnapp, J. 2012. A Short Guide to the Digital Humanities. In *Digital Humanities*. Cambridge, MA: MIT Press, 121–136.

Cohen, D.J., Frabetti, F., Buzzetti, D. and Rodriguez-Velasco, J.D. 2011. Defining the Digital Humanities. *Columbia University Academic Commons*. Available at: http://hdl.handle.net/10022/AC:P:14226.

Das, S., Engelmann, R., Hudson, R., Roy, T. and Siegel, L. 1993. Scientists in Wonderland: A Report on Visualization Applications in the CAVE Virtual Reality Environment. *IEEE 1993 Symposium on Research Frontiers in Virtual Reality*, October, 59–66.

Dörk, M., Collins, C., Feng, P. and Carpendale, S. 2013. Critical InfoVis: Exploring the Politics of Visualization. *CHI 2013 Extended Abstracts*, 27 April–2 May, Paris, ACM.

Elliott, T. and Gilles, S. 2009. Digital Geography and Classics. *dhq: Changing the Center of Gravity: Transforming Classical Studies through Cyberinfrastructure*, 3. Available at: http://digitalhumanities.org/dhq/vol/3/1/000031/000031.html.

Factor, R. 2011. If You Build it, They Will Come – Introduction to Digital Humanities. *Introduction to Digital Humanities (English 389 at Emory University)*. Available at: http://www.briancroxall.net/dh/2011/09/07/if-you-build-it-they-will-come.

Fiedler, C. 1957. *On Judging Works of Visual Art*. Berkeley: University of California Press.

Fitzpatrick, K. 2011. The Humanities, Done Digitally. *Chronicle of Higher Education*. Available at: http://chronicle.com/article/The-Humanities-Done-Digitally/127382.

Gibbs 2011. Critical Discourse in Digital Humanities. *Journal of Digital Humanities*, 1. Available at: http://journalofdigitalhumanities.org/1-1/critical-discourse-in-digital-humanities-by-fred-gibbs.

Gillow, H. 2013. Digital Humanities is More than Text. *Digital Humanities*. Available at: http://digital-humanities.com/node/149.

Gold, M.K. (ed.) 2012. *Debates in the Digital Humanities*. Minneapolis: University of Minnesota Press.

Graham, R. 2013. MacArthur 'Genius' Robin Fleming on Using Archaeology to Write History – Boston College's First Honoree Wants Historians to Stop Being Afraid of Science. *Boston Globe*. Available at: http://www.bostonglobe.com/ideas/2013/10/06/macarthur-genius-robin-fleming-using-

archaeology-write-history/1WqSGQ4RuRdscHR6ZoV6VM/story.html?utm_
medium=referral&utm_source=t.co.

Gurau, C. 2007. Virtual Reality Applications in Tourism. In W. Pease, M. Rowe and
M. Cooper (eds), *Information and Communication Technologies in Support of
the Tourism Industry.* Hershey PA: IGI Global, 180–197.

Hann, R. 2008. Visualised Arguments; or How to Pierce the Persuasive
Visualization and Other Arguments. *EVA 2008 London Conference*, London.

Hitchcock, T. 2012. Place and the Politics of the Past. *historyonics*. Available at:
http://historyonics.blogspot.com.au/2012/07/place-and-politics-of-past.html.

Hockey, S. 2004. The History of Humanities Computing. In S. Schreibman, R.
Siemens and J. Unsworth (eds), *A Companion to Digital Humanities.* Oxford:
Blackwell, 3–19.

Jesch, J. 2013. Runes and Words: Runology in a Lexicographical Context (plenary
paper). *Futhark, International Journal of Runic Studies, Proceedings of the
Seventh International Symposium on Runes and Runic Inscriptions, 'Runes in
Context'*, 4, 77–100.

Jessop, M. 2008. Digital Visualization as a Scholarly Activity. *Literary and
Linguistic Computing*, 23, 283.

Johns Hopkins University. n.d. What is Critical Thinking? *Great Books at Hopkins*.
Available at: http://humctr.jhu.edu/undergraduate/great-books.

Kelly, T.M. 2014. History Spaces (II). *edwired*. Available at: http://edwired.
org/2014/01/02/history-spaces-ii.

Kingwell, M. 2012. Mark Kingwell's Seven Pathways to the Stars. *The Globe and
Mail*. Available at: http://www.theglobeandmail.com/news/national/time-to-
lead/mark-kingwells-seven-pathways-to-the-stars/article4610505.

Kirschenbaum, M.G. 2010. Digital Humanities. *Academic Room*. Available at:
http://www.academicroom.com/topics/what-is-digital-humanities.

Lindquist, E. 2011. Surveying the World Of Visualization – Background Paper.
School of Public Administration, University of Victoria, Canada. Available at:
https://crawford.anu.edu.au/public_policy_community/research/visualisation/
Visualisation_roundtable_2_Background_Paper.pdf.

Manovich, L. 2014 2012. The Meaning of Statistics and Digital Humanities.
Software Studies Initiative. Available at: http://lab.softwarestudies.
com/2012/11/the-meaning-of-statistics-and-digital.html.

Mark, D.M., Gould, M.D. and Nunes, J. 1989. Spatial Language and Geographic
Information Systems: Cross-linguistic Issues (El Lenguaje Espacial y Los
Sistemas de Información Geográficos: Temas Interlinguisticos). Conferencia
Latinoamericana sobre el Technologia de los Sistemas de Información
Geográficos (SIG), Venezuela.

McDonald, J. and Veth, P. 2013. The Archaeology of Memory: The Recursive
Relationship of Martu Rock Art and Place. *Anthropological Forum*, 23, 367–386.

McGann, J. 2002. Preface to Radiant Textuality: Literary Studies after the World
Wide Web. *Romantic Circles*. Available at: http://www.rc.umd.edu/praxis/
contemporary/mcgann/mcgann.

Milner, M. 2014. Visualization Workshop . McGill Digital Humanities. Available at: http://digihum.mcgill.ca/blog/2014/02/18/visualization-workshop.

Mittel, J. 2012. Caption Mining at the Crossroads of Digital Humanities and Media Studies. *Just TV*. Available at: http://justtv.wordpress.com/2012/11/30/caption-mining-at-the-crossroads-of-digital-humanities-media-studies.

Nowviskie, B. 2013. Towards a New Deal. *Asking for it*. Available at: http://nowviskie.org/2013/new-deal.

Pankseppa, J. and Bernatzky, G. 2002. Emotional Sounds and the Brain: The Neuro-affective Foundations of Musical Appreciation. *Behavioural Processes*, 60, 133–155.

Parry, D. 2012. The Digital Humanities or a Digital Humanism. In M.K. Gold (ed.), *Debates in the Digital Humanities*. Minneapolis: University of Minnesota Press, 429–437.

Patera, M., Draper, S. and Naef, M. 2008. Exploring Magic Cottage: A Virtual Reality Environment for Stimulating Children's Imaginative Writing. *Interactive Learning Environments*, 16, 245–263.

Resnick, M. 2002. *Rethinking Learning in the Digital Age. The Global Information Technology Report: Readiness for the Networked World*. Oxford: Oxford University Press.

Robichaud, A. and Blevins, C. 2011. Tooling Up for Digital Humanities. Stanford University. Available at: http://toolingup.stanford.edu/?page_id=1255.

Rosenzweig, R. and Thelen, D. 2000. *The Presence of the Past: Popular Uses of History in American Life*. New York: Columbia University Press.

Rudy, K.M. 2011. Kissing Images, Unfurling Rolls, Measuring Wounds, Sewing Badges and Carrying Talismans: Considering Some Harley Manuscripts through the Physical Rituals They Reveal. *Electronic British Library Journal*. Available at: http://www.bl.uk/eblj/2011articles/article5.html.

Sacks, O. 2007. *Musicophilia: Tales of Music and the Brain*. New York: Alfred A. Knopf.

Schreibman, S., Siemens, R. and Unsworth, J. (eds) 2004. *A Companion to Digital Humanities*. Oxford: Blackwell.

Sinclair, S., Ruecker, S. and Radzikowska, M. 2013. Information Visualization for Humanities Scholars. *Literary Studies in the Digital Age, An Evolving Anthology*. Available at: https://dlsanthology.commons.mla.org/information-visualization-for-humanities-scholars.

Slator, B.M., Clark, J.T., Landrum I.J., Bergstrom, A., Hawley, J., Johnston, E. and Fisher, S. 2001. Teaching with Immersive Virtual Archaeology. *Proceedings of the 7th International Conference on Virtual Systems and Multimedia (VSMM-2001)*. Berkeley, CA, October, 25–27.

Stanford University. n.d. Why are the Humanities Important? Available at: http://humanexperience.stanford.edu/why.

Stommel, J. 2014. The Emergence of the Digital Humanities. Available at: http://emergenceofdhbook.tumblr.com/post/59772273737/you-can-now-read-the-introduction-at-the.

Svensson, P. 2013. Humanities Computing as Digital Humanities. In M. Terras, J. Nyhan and E. Vanhoutte (eds), *Defining Digital Humanities: A Reader.* Farnham: Ashgate, 159–186.

Tang, D. 2013. China Discovers Some of the World's Oldest Writing. Available at: http://www.huffingtonpost.com/2013/07/10/china-oldest-writing_n_3574624. html.

Terras, M., Julianne, N. and Vanhoutte, E. (eds) 2013. *Defining Digital Humanities: A Reader*: Farnham: Ashgate.

Theibault, J. 2012. Visualizations and Historical Arguments. In J. Dougherty and K. Nawrotz (eds), *Writing History in the Digital Age.* Ann Arbor: University of Michigan Press.

Thomas, B. 2013. Oliver Sacks Shares Tales of Musical Hallucinations. *Scientific American: Mind Guest Blog.* Available at: http://blogs.scientificamerican. com/mind-guest-blog/2013/04/22/oliver-sacks-shares-tales-of-musical-hallucinations.

Tocewicz, T. 2014. Visualising Helps Make Sense of Data. *Research Information: Analysis and Opinion.* Available at : http://www.researchinformation.info/news/news_story.php?news_id=1547.

Turner, F. and Pöppel, E. 1988. Metered Poetry, the Brain, and Time. In L. Rentschler, B. Herzberger and D. Epstein (eds), *Beauty and the Brain.* Basel: Birkhäuser, 71–90.

Unesco. 2014. Literacy for All Remains an Elusive Goal, New UNESCO Data Shows. *United Nations Educational, Scientific and Cultural Organization.* Available at: http://www.unesco.org/new/en/media-services/single-view/news/literacy_for_all_remains_an_elusive_goal_new_unesco_data_shows/back/9597/ – .Uuh1O3lm5UO.

University of Dundee. n.d. Materiality. Available at: http://www.poetrybeyondtext.org/materiality.html.

University of Oxford. n.d. What are the Digital Humanities? Available at: http://digital.humanities.ox.ac.uk/Support/whatarethedh.aspx.

Unsworth, J. 2007. *Digital Humanities Centers Summit, NEH, Digital Humanities Centers as Cyberinfrastructure* . Washington, DC: Digital Humanities Centers Summit, National Endowment for the Humanities, Washington DC.

Van Den Braak, S.W., Van Oostendorp, H., Prakken, H. and Vreeswijk, G.A. 2006. A Critical Review of Argument Visualization Tools: Do Users Become Better Reasoners? Workshop Notes of the ECAI-2006 Workshop on Computational Models of Natural Argument (CMNA VI), 67–75.

Viegas, J. 2008. Music and Art Mixed in the Stone Age. *ABC Science: News in Science.* Available at: http://www.abc.net.au/science/articles/2008/07/03/2293114.htm.

Warwick, C. n.d. Chapter 1: Studying Users in Digital Humanities. *Digital Humanities in Practice: A UCLDH BOOK PROJECT.* Available at: http://blogs.ucl.ac.uk/dh-in-practice/chapter-1.

Warwick, C., Terras, M.M. and Nyhan, J. (eds) 2012. *Digital Humanities in Practice*. London: Facet Publishing, in association with UCL Centre for Digital Humanities.

Weingart, S. 2013. Submissions to Digital Humanities 2013. *The Scottbot Irregular*. Available at: http://www.scottbot.net/HIAL/?p=39588.

——. 2014. Submissions to Digital Humanities 2014. *The Scottbot Irregular*. Available at: http://www.scottbot.net/HIAL/?p=39588.

White, R. 2010. What is Spatial History? *Spatial History Project, Stanford University*. Available at: https://web.stanford.edu/group/spatialhistory/cgi-bin/site/pub.php?id=29.

Chapter 2

Game-based Learning and the Digital Humanities

In this chapter I will outline several important features of games that distinguish them from typical computer software. Unfortunately, many of these features are also not common in education, and the development of games for education promises great benefits, but these benefits have often been hard to measure or to replicate. In Chapter 1, I argued that the digital humanities is more than text, while here I will provide three examples that both indicate the difficulties of conveying heritage and history through games and digital environments, and feature attempts to incorporate more material and embodied experiences of text. I will also table some popular game genres that may be suitable for portraying digital heritage and interactive history.

Computer Games are Not Efficient Pieces of Software

Virtual environment designers have recently become very interested in computer games and why they have succeeded so well when conventional virtual environments have not. There has also been a boom in game design studies, to the extent that computer game design academics have agreed that the field requires more rigorous criticism and evaluation.

Surely the latest academic research is required to explain why people want to play computer games, as game technology is advancing all the time? I am not convinced. Could traditional human–computer interaction (HCI) help create more enjoyable virtual environments or games? No, I don't think this is necessarily true either. My reason for both my answers is due to a paper I read some years ago by Thomas Malone (1982). This paper, entitled 'Heuristics for Designing Enjoyable User Interfaces: Lessons from Computer Games', was written nearly a quarter of a century ago, yet it has only recently resurfaced in the papers and theses of current game researchers.

This paper was an attempt to understand why games are 'captivating' and how they can be 'used to make other user interfaces interesting and enjoyable to use'. In order to answer this question, Malone set up three empirical studies (but only describes two) and takes away 'motivational features' to see which features add the most to captivation. He asked eight groups of 10 students to play a computer game (called 'Darts') and then another game ('Hangman'), but with one of eight features missing. He recorded how long played each the game (completion time), their personal opinions (as to which game they preferred) and their gender. The results indicated that fantasy was more important than feedback (as long as it is appropriate to its audience). A preference for fantasy over performance feedback may surprise some, but it did not surprise me, for games are designed to appeal to the imagination rather than to get a job done.

I was particularly interested by this simple method of evaluation. When I wished to evaluate the user experience of virtual environments, I was faced with choosing people to compare two virtual environments against each other (subjective preference), or to compare the task performance of two different user groups in two different environments. With the first method, people typically lack experience in judging virtual environments against each other as it is such a new technology, while with the second method, I had to pray that that the testers' relevant demographic factors would be spread relatively evenly across the two groups.

In his second study, using a similar method, Malone found that explicit goals, scorekeeping, audio effects and randomness were particularly important. These two studies were then followed in the paper by his claim that *challenge, fantasy* and *curiosity* were the important ingredients that make games captivating and fun to use.

Malone explained that HCI traditionally seeks to improve software that is easy to learn and easy to master, but notes that the founder of Atari said that games are designed to be easy to learn but difficult to master. Malone argued that computer games are more like toys than other software applications, which in turn are more like tools. Unlike shopping webpages or software designed for office use, games have goals, but they do not have to have clear outcomes. However, they do incorporate challenge and fantasy, and stimulate curiosity.

Malone defined challenge as involving 'a goal whose outcome is uncertain', as there are often variable difficulty levels or multiple goals (potentially distributed over different levels). Fantasy incorporates emotionally appealing features or well-mapped cognitive metaphors. He considered curiosity to be an 'optimal level of information complexity'. It may incorporate randomness or contextual humour.

Malone was perceptive enough to realize that challenge is not merely about making things difficult, but also making these barriers tantalizing to solve. When I evaluated over 80 people and how they learn about the original inhabitants through exploring virtual reconstructions of archaeological sites, I asked the users if the environments were challenging without realizing this subtle distinction. The users were confused as to whether I meant challenging as in 'this is difficult, I am not sure I can or want to complete it', or 'this is really testing me but I really don't want to do anything else until I crack it'. This second meaning of challenging is an important feature of a successful game; it affords *hard fun*.

Gestalt theory seems to be behind Malone's concept of curiosity as a motivating feature of games: he suggested that users want to have 'well-formed knowledge structures'. Computer games deliberately suggest such knowledge, but present the 'knowledge structure' as incomplete, inconspicuous or unparsimonious (by this I think he means that games provide red herrings or an overflow of potential clues).

Fantasy is the concept that I am least convinced by, not because it is not an important part of computer games, but because I am not convinced that we can create a successful sense of fantasy merely through creating emotional triggers, connotations and metaphors directed towards specific audiences. The fantasy element of complex game-worlds is not so easily circumscribed by heuristics, just as Malone did not convincingly explain why the boys rather than girls enjoyed the digital fantasy of popping balloons, or how this trait could best be used in designing future games.

For example, two of the most popular computer games have been 'The Elder Scrolls IV: Oblivion' (a single-player medieval-style quest fantasy for game consoles and computers) and 'World of Warcraft' (an online multiplayer role-playing fantasy). The degree to which players can choose their character attributes allows them to undertake the game using a myriad of skills and strategies in order to solve a variety of challenges. They do not buy these games because the games are programmed to have conditions and triggers, and they do not play these games because the games are rule-based systems; they play them because the games challenge them to change the world and to explore how these character roles embody and express aspects of their own personality.

What is also striking about these games is how they can motivate people without explicitly showing them what lies ahead. These games are mysterious knowledge structures that loom out of the dark, closed portals surrounded by long-lost instructions, or meeting grounds of conflict and competition where players do not actually know what happens next, only that there is the possibility of eventual success.

More recent publications, such as a doctoral thesis by Federoff (2002), and other papers (Desurvire et al., 2004; Jørgensen, 2004; Shneiderman, 2004) have stressed the importance of Malone's paper in explaining the unique features of games, how they differ in the way they are experienced from other types of software, and how a new set of heuristics is needed to address these specific game features. Knickmeyer and Materas (2005) have described how the coding scheme of 'Façade', an interactive narrative game, was inspired by Malone's three categories.

While I teach games design, my research is on developing and improving virtual environments in which people can learn more about the real world, especially history, heritage, and and cultural perspectives, such as the intrinsic worth of individual viewpoints, character motivations, traditions, rituals, mythologies and communal beliefs. The more enjoyable these virtual environments are, the more likely it is that users will learn and be interested in learning.

Malone's paper has reminded me that my quest is to create more challenging environments (and challenge in the sense of a difficulty people wish to face, not wish to avoid). It has reinforced for me a subtle gap between games and other software in terms of the way in which HCI could or should be used. And it has reminded me that using the latest technology or quoting the latest research does not automatically mean that the essential questions are being addressed.

I suspect Malone's work has resurfaced for at least two important reasons. First, writers have been arguing over the defining features of games, as they are attempting to build a critical research area that can describe and prescribe how to design games and how to improve them. Second, Malone's way of evaluating games is component-based rather than essence-based, so may offer flexibility over theories defining games as 'games must have X'. In non-essentialist definitions, games may need to have certain features, but they do not need to have every single one of these features at the same time in order to be games. This may explain why games have so far been so hard to define in terms of essence.

Computer Games as Rule-based Formal Systems

Juul (2003) defined a game as 'a rule-based formal system with a variable and quantifiable outcome, where different outcomes are assigned different values, the player exerts effort in order to influence the outcome, the player feels attached to the outcome, and the consequences of the activity are optional and negotiable'.

Where is the *fun* in that? A definition of computer games as systems does not address why users find games enjoyable. Despite appearing in relatively recent publications, such an essentialist definition does not directly lead us to producing better games that users enjoy more. Malone's paper reminds us that games are not played *because* they are systems, so defining computer games in terms of rule-based systems does not shed any light on the user experience. If games are systems, they are *fun-generating* systems.

In addition, the huge recent popularity of online multiplayer worlds cannot be explained purely in terms of usefulness or usability. Many of these games are crying out for help from HCI specialists to design improved interfaces and do not necessarily create entirely new forms of narrative or cinematic innovation, and yet they are still commercial successes.

In his 2011 book *Half-Real* (2011, p. 1), Juul wrote that: 'In having fictional worlds, video games deviate from traditional non-electronic games that are mostly abstract, and this is part of the newness of video games. The interaction between game rules and game fiction is one of the most important features of video games.' I cannot say I am convinced – fantasy is a part of non-electronic games and has been for decades if not for centuries. What is so distinct about computer games? And is this fictional world so widespread in digital games as opposed to non-digital games? How much of a fictional world does 'Tetris' contain? Surely a live action role-playing (LARP) game contains more of a fictional world?

Examining the seven most famous theories of definitions of games and merging them in a classical theory of games (2011, pp. 30–36), Juul argues that a game is first a rule-based formal system; it has variable and quantifiable outcomes; where different outcomes are assigned different values; the player exerts effort in order to influence the outcome; the player feels emotionally attached to the outcome; and the consequences of the activity are optional and negotiable. I note here that the first four theories (from Huizinga, Caillois, Suits, Avedon and Sutton-Smith) are about games, while the last three (Crawford, Kelley, Salen and Zimmerman) are computer game designers.

However Juul seems to stress the universality and comprehensiveness of these six features to such an extent that he later rejects any 'boundary cases' which do not have all six features – for example: 'This game model is the basis upon which all games are constructed' (2011, p. 7). And then he writes that the 'German philosopher Wittgenstein' had used 'the concept of games for building his philosophy of language, and games were singled out as an exemplary case of something that could not be defined or narrowed down' (2011, p. 8). Wittgenstein was actually Austrian and his famous book *Philosophical Investigations* used games as an example of the fluid nature of language. Thus, calling games 'exemplary' might be strictly true, but a little misleading. The shifting meanings of the word 'game' did not build Wittgenstein's philosophy of language, but was merely an example.

More importantly, in the writings of Juul and other theorists, games in general are continually made out to be unique and incredibly significant, but their writings run the risk of over-emphasizing the importance and significance of computer games per se. Games are hugely important to culture and society, but the value and usefulness of computer games may vary wildly. Even animals learn through games. While games are a vital part of social learning for humans as well, we don't need to fanatically push the usefulness of computer games. It would be better to understand and apply games where they are most effective and most needed.

In the case of *Half-Real*, the emphasis on computer games as rule-based systems leads Juul to state that: 'It is also the well-structured character of games that have made them into a stable of artificial intelligence research' (2011, p. 8). Herein appears a contradiction – games are hard to define, apparently, but are also well structured? It might be logically consistent if games are rule-based systems, but isn't there more than that to games? Juul does quote Hughes that as each player may have a different experience, games are more than rules. For games include gameplay, exploration, challenge and reward. Some games afford emergence, while others are genuine sandbox worlds (open worlds); if they are 'well structured', this would surely constrain emergence and discovery. Juul himself raised this question in another paper (2002): 'How can something made from simple rules present challenges that extend beyond the rules?' So games *are* more than rules!

I view the definition of games as rule-based systems as being too simplistic. There are the operational rules that allow computers to compute, the imagined world rules of the designer, the code that is coded by the programmer, the apparent rules that the player perceives as to the fictional world of the game, and what actually takes place (the rules that are actually triggered and calculated). An example might be a glitch, a bug appears in the running of the computer game, the code is diverted or corrupted, the fictional world is misrepresented to the player, or the player's input appears to create emergent results, or the player believes the results of the glitch show new or previously unseen rules to this fictional game-world. In other worlds, the procedural code that runs the computer and the computer game may never be directly appreciated or even perceived by the player. So saying a game is a rule-based system is not saying how the game is perceived to be a game by the player.

Juul is also critical of the theory of Roger Caillois. For example, he notes that Ilinx (vertigo) 'is but a single example of the infinite number of different types of experiences that a game can give' (2002, p. 10). I have to disagree; I think Ilinx is a very important feature of games and is often missing from computer games. This will be of significance when we look at simulations of heritage and history in the following chapters. Part of Juul's criticism of Caillois is that Caillois (2001, pp. 8–9) says games are either rule-based or make-believe; Juul of course believes that games are both rules and fiction (hence the title of his book). My suspicion is that Caillois meant that one has to follow 'rules' in a game, and they are either cultural/mythical, according to local conventions or the rules have to be directly made up. I am not sure that Caillois stipulates that games cannot have both rules and a fictional world.

Games are Hard Fun

Like Malone, James Gee reiterates that games are 'hard fun', but also that games are successful because game designers also have to learn the hard way; success in game design is through trial and error, ensuring that the very design of the game helps people learn them in a challenging but enjoyable way. Their income depends on it. Gee said: 'If people cannot learn to play a company's games, the company goes broke. So game designers have no choice, they have to make games that are very good at getting themselves learned' (2007, p. 2).

The above seems obvious to me, but Gee also goes on to say something rather fascinating. He argues that games are good 'if you act like a game designer while you play the game' (2007, p. 8). Obviously I agree with Gee that thinking and talking about games is important – one should not read or play games uncritically – but I wonder if one has to think like a designer to enjoy a game. In my experience, if you design objects, events and spaces so that people have to think like you to have 'good experiences', then much of the richness and the variety of potential experiences have been lost.

A potential confusion in reading Gee's work is that he emphasizes the advantages possible with games as if they are inherent in all games. For example, he has written that 'good games are problem solving spaces that create deep learning' and that 'good video games are hard work and deep fun. So is good learning in other contexts' (2007, p. 10).

Does that mean that to be good, a video game has to be all of the below?:

1. Hard work.
2. Deep fun.
3. Provide 'good learning' for other contexts, i.e. transferrable knowledge.

'Tetris', 'Pac-Man' and 'Space Invaders' are often considered to be good games, but I am not convinced that they fulfil *all three* of the above criteria.

And yet it would seem that good games must *always* create 'deep learning' and if games are sometimes tools, then they must *always be* 'new tools for letting people understand from the inside out the worlds other people inhabit or worlds no one has seen yet' (Gee, 2007, p. 7).

If games were always new tools that generated deep learning and reflection, I would not have to write this book! Unfortunately, Gee seems to be conflating the apparent *potential* of computer games with the current *state* of computer games. Another writer, actually inspired by Gee, has been critiqued in a similar manner. The book reviewer Dennis J. Seese (2012) criticized the author Jeremiah McCall (2011) for preaching to the converted and for not fully explaining the criteria by which a simulation game should be incorporated into the classroom.

Returning to Gee, I believe he is on stronger ground when he investigates the power of games as simulations. Gee argued that 'mind is a simulator' (2007, p. 2) and that a game as a simulation will 'prepare them for action they need and want to take in order to accomplish their goals'. He also wrote that games act as: 'Action-and-goal-directed preparations for, and simulations of, embodied experience ... a) they distribute intelligence via the creation of smart tools and b) they allow for the creation of "cross-functional affiliation", particularly important form of collaboration in the modern world' (Gee, 2007, p. 150).

Kim Sterelny's (2004) description of 'external cognitive artefacts' sounds similar to Gee's talk of 'smart tools'. Gee's 'cross-functional affiliation' observation may also hold for massive multiplayer online games. However, the description of many games as affording 'smart tools' does not necessarily mean that all good games should have such affordances. Gee (2007) also claimed that good games allow for horizontal learning and vertical learning. Horizontal learning is an interesting concept; people can stay at certain levels, until they are comfortable with skills and knowledge, before they level up.

Game are More than Systemic Artificial Conflicts

The following definition of a game by Salen and Zimmerman (2003, p. 80) is probably the most famous game definition in contemporary game studies:

> A game is a system in which players engage in an artificial conflict, defined by rules, that results in a quantifiable outcome.

Salen and Zimmerman talk of a magic circle that separates (but not always clearly) the boundaries of a game from the real world, but games do not have to involve explicit conflict. And a conflict in the game does not have to stay 'artificial'. Simulated conflict could become real and actual. Does that mean that the game is no longer a game? Possibly.

Salen and Zimmerman's definition also discounts games that may never have a final outcome (such as cricket) and does not incorporate the importance of strategy. Rules do not encapsulate games; they may be necessary components, but there may be games entered where the rules on entry are *redefined* while playing.

Here is my working definition of a game (different to Salen and Zimmerman): *a game is a challenge that offers up the possibility of temporary or permanent tactical resolution without harmful outcomes to the real-world situation of the participant.*

Actually, my definition is also missing a vital component of games – engagement: *a game is an engaging challenge that offers up the possibility of temporary or permanent tactical resolution without harmful outcomes to the real-world situation of the participant.*

One could easily question my working definition. It may not appear to be exacting enough; it seems to treat all games as challenge when the challenge element is not necessarily of the same importance in all games, and it emphasizes tactics when not all games require changing tactics and strategies. My response would be that if the game does not offer strategic resolution, then it is no longer offering a full and rich game – it is almost a game-shell or a game-vehicle. The procedures are the same, but the gameplay is no longer enjoyable and engaging. That said, for many virtual heritage projects, the location and audience may be museum-specific, so the duration and complexity of the experience may have to be reduced.

Thus, Sid Meier's definition appeals to me: 'A game is a series of interesting choices.' The fuller quote is: 'According to Sid Meier, a [good] game is a series of interesting choices. In an interesting choice, no single option is clearly better than the other options, the options are not equally attractive, and the player must be able to make an informed choice' (Rollings, 2003, pp. 200–201).

However, this explanation has its critics. Juul (2011) says that by 'interesting choices', Meier meant mental challenges of high quality, which Juul rebuts by pointing out that not *all* games are mental challenges of high quality. However, is that what Meier meant? I personally think that the concepts of engagement, strategy and agency are all succinctly referred to in Meier's statement. He was not, in my opinion, stating that a high-quality mental challenge is the necessary and sufficient attribute of games (Bateman, 2008). He was instead trying to suggest that non-interesting choices are the bane of good game design. One counter-argument might be that 'Snakes & Ladders' is a game, but does not offer choice (unless you count how a dice is thrown as constituting a choice).

Games: Advantages and Disadvantages

Marshall McLuhan once wrote that: 'Anyone who thinks there is a difference between education and entertainment doesn't know the first thing about either' (McLuhan, 1967). Recent reports have provided substantial evidence for the benefits of games (Oliver et al., 2011; Clark et al., 2014) and other publications have provided some evidence for the usefulness of games (Schrier, 2014) in both the classroom (Jameson, 2014; Lester et al., 2014) and the museum (Rowe et al., 2014).

Yet for all the literature on serious games and game-based learning, there are few explicit examples of transferable and useful skills learnt in serious games (Egenfeldt-Nielsen, 2007). Game-based learning still requires expertise in instructional design (Wouters and van Oostendorp, 2013) and increasing the motivation of learners beyond that achievable by conventional instructional media is not trivial (Wouters et al., 2013). Despite this, more and more people are beginning to see electronic games as a viable vehicle for learning (Dondlinger, 2007; Anderson et al., 2010).

Seymour Papert (1998) made some prescient observations in his article 'Does Easy Do it? Children, Games, and Learning', backed a decade later by James Gee (2007). Games are not fun because they are easy; they are fun because they are difficult to learn. Creating something that is easy is not making something engaging. In addition, Papert thinks that educational games that hide their true intention are misleading, if not immoral. Although I like the term 'games by stealth', I sympathize. Why hide the true nature of the games? What message do we send if learning must be disguised – can it never be undertaken voluntarily?

Further, games allow and in fact demand agency and effort from the player, and provide clear feedback and reward systems. Therefore, Papert encourages two things: conversation between the players and encouraging them to 'become game designers themselves'.

Finally, Papert responds to an angry instructional designer calling him out to name that games that help one learn and exactly what are these 'specific learning skills' that he talked about. He replied: 'The most important learning skills that I see children getting from games are those that support the empowering sense of taking charge of their own learning.' Yet this does not directly answer the question. My question to Papert is: where and when does this happen outside of games; when is this meta-skill or meta-confidence translated into non-game domains, such as the real world? I agree with Papert that this is the goal; I just see little proof of it in educational games.

Shavian Monsters

'Shavian monsters' is an expression borrowed from Papert that is in turn borrowed from George Bernard Shaw. Papert wrote that:

> Most of what goes under the name 'edutainment' reminds me of George Bernard Shaw's response to a famous beauty who speculated on the marvelous child they could have together: 'With your brains and my looks …' He retorted, 'But what if the child had my looks and your brains?' (1998)

So the Shavian monsters are those games that combine the worst of both worlds (that is, entertainment and education). Meetings in 'Second Life' likewise remind me of Shavian monsters. You sit down (so you cannot wander around) and you

Figure 2.1   A Meeting in 'Second Life'

cannot easily follow who is talking and you don't know where people are looking or what they think of the dialogue (unless they are responding next). 'Second Life' meetings seem to have all the boring attributes of real-world meetings and none of the affordances of human contact that help me keep track of the conversation and the responses of those attending (Figure 2.1).

Epistemic Games

The first chapter in the edited book *The Design and Use of Simulation Games in Education* (Shelton and Wiley, 2007), entitled 'In Praise of Epistemology', argues for epistemic games, which the writer David Shaffer defines as 'a game that requires you to think about the world'. He uses a real-world classroom debating game to show how students can be engaged by history and can learn to develop better critical and communicational skills. He also makes the interesting observation that the skill of professional historians in knowing which sources are more accurate than others is not assimilated by the students, but the chapter does not clarify how computer games can pass on such knowledge. The assertion that the debating game could easily transfer to a computer game setting is also not proven. To take one example from Hubert Dreyfus' (2001) controversial book *On the Internet*, surely the spontaneity and physical presence of real-time debating combatants is not such an easy task to replicate via a computer?

While I have enjoyed Shaffer's writing, I still cannot see how the musings in the above chapter are directly and effectively translated into educational computer games and simulations. I would also take him to task for his use of the word 'epistemic': epistemology is the (philosophical) study of what constitutes beliefs and knowledge, but 'episteme' merely means a belief or piece of knowledge, so I would argue that 'epistemic' by itself does not equate to affording reflection on a purported belief system (which is the type of game I believe the author wishes to promote). Epistemic is too specialized a word; I suspect the required term is somewhat closer to 'thought-provoking'.

Gamification

One of the most lucid descriptions of gamification is in a workshop call for papers by the Art & Civic Media Lab of Leuphana University (Fuchs, 2013). Explained as the use of game-based rules structures and interfaces by corporations 'to manage and control brand-communities and to create value', this definition reveals both the attraction of gamification to business and the derision it has received from many game designers and academics (Bogost, 2011; Deterding et al., 2011; Fuchs, 2014).

Gamification can be viewed as the addition to websites and learning environments of quantifiable actions that can be ranked and processed (and information stored), with immediate and vastly exaggerated feedback, and graphically designed in the idiom of well-known computer game genres. Task performance can be graphically rewarded and socially shared, and proponents have argued that gamification can provide deeper, richer and more engaging learning (Betts et al., 2013; Schoech et al., 2013; Hamari et al., 2014).

Although gamification might be of benefit for websites and repetitive work-based interfaces, some of the media promoting gamification should be treated with caution. For example, a blog article in *eCampus news* suggests that gamification ('the use of game design elements in non-game contexts') is a proven success story. While this may be true, the article cites a reference provided by a game-based learning company, the very sort of company that stands to make money from gamification (Stansbury, 2013).

The article also outlines three important elements of gamification: progression (incremental feedback and rewards); investment (achievements and social rewards); and 'cascading information' (various streaming and increasing-in-complexity rewards and opportunities). The definition is not highly revealing. To filter information is the mark of well-thought-out software, providing social recognition is an aspect of social media, and feedback on performance is a feature of games and instructional media in general. These features may be good guidelines for designing engaging software and websites, but they are not the fundamental features of games per se.

Most definitions that we considered in Chapter 1 would hold that a game is in essence an activity that:

1. has some goal in mind, the player works to achieve;
2. has systematic or emergent rules; and
3. is considered a form of play or competition.

The first feature does not seem to be a required aspect in gamification, but the other two features are relevant. While these criteria describe 'skill and drill' types of games, many of today's digital games are far more complex, providing an interactive narrative in which the player must test hypotheses, synthesize knowledge, and respond to the unexpected (Dondlinger, 2007).

Games don't have to explicitly provide the rules; part of the challenge might be to find them and predict what will happen next according to the player's understanding of what the rules are. One issue, though (especially if we are going to avoid the traditional game's clear reward and feedback system), is how the player will understand the historical appropriateness of their actions and performance, and whether their understanding is 'on the right track', understanding the priorities, the possibilities, the dead ends, the goals and how to complete them. What would 'achievement' mean to the player?

Procedural Rhetoric

While Michael Mateas has spoken of procedural literacy, and before him Janet Murray said that one feature of digital games was that they are procedural, Ian Bogost is probably most famously associated with this phrase. Bogost defined procedural rhetoric as 'a practice of using processes persuasively'. In *Persuasive Games* (2007, p. 8), he used the example of the book *Guns, Germs, and Steel* and declared 'Such an approach to history goes far beyond the relation between contemporaneous events, asking us to consider the systems that produce those events.' I mention this here not only as a historical example, but also to wonder if this is an important sub-criterion in procedural design. Should the player be led to 'consider the system that produces those events' as well?

Gonzalo Frasca, a collaborator and colleague of Bogost, had a similar phrase, simulation rhetoric ('simulations can express messages in ways that narrative simply cannot, and vice versa'). Frasca's chapter (2003) has a powerful message: understand simulation rhetoric as soon as you can, because advergames will definitely explore and exploit simulation rhetoric with or without you. I should however note that in his later book *Unit Operations*, Bogost defines simulation differently: 'A simulation is the gap between the rule-based representation of a source system and a user's subjectivity' (2008, p. 107).

While procedural rhetoric combines a humanities discipline with something that is obviously a key component of games, and even though it appears to have special importance for serious games, I still have reservations. Bogost himself raises the first potential flaw: he admits that for many people, rhetoric has a negative connotation. In the book *Arguing Well*, John Shand declared that: 'Logic must be sharply distinguished from what might generally be called rhetoric ... rhetoric is not committed to using good arguments' (2002, p. 23). On the other hand, Aiken and Talisse (2014) argue that we should not just argue from reason – we should also know how to engage with others when we argue.

I am not convinced that the rules of the game are the rules of the designer or even the rules of the player. The negotiations, changes and misunderstandings by the player as to what the rules are exactly are in my opinion important and creative parts of games and, by extension, computer games. While it might be reasonable to think that if the essence of the game is rules, it is another thing entirely to not even contemplate the possibility that a rule-based system could be random, changing or open to change by the player. Mary Flanagan's book *Critical Play* (2013) looks at critical gameplay as wilful subversion of the rules and she provides avant-garde art as exemplars (see also her earlier paper: Flanagan, 2010).

There have been other criticisms of the theory of procedural rhetoric. In the *Game Studies* article 'Against Procedurality' (2011), Miguel Sicart wrote: 'Proceduralists claim that players, by reconstructing the meaning embedded in the rules, are persuaded by virtue of the games' procedural nature.' Sicart argued that meaning is more than just the learning of rules through play; the value of gameplay becomes subservient, and if rules are all that matters, why should the designers have to explain them?

This leads me to another question. Computers follow procedure and designers design procedures (and please note that Bogost carefully explains that procedural rhetoric is not referring directly to programming). So how does or how can the player know that the system of rules that they may have a mental model of is the system of rules intended by the designer or the system of rules followed by the computer? And just because computers work by computation, by processing, does that mean that the definition, the essence and the ideal of gameplay is to follow and comprehend this system of rules? To enjoy stage magic, must we know where the hidden trapdoors are?

I have another concern here (depending on whether we are supposed to question the system of rules). Adherence at the altar of 'procedural rhetoric', whether intended by Bogost or not, can lead to people thinking that the designer's idea of the game rules are what matters. If so, we will have debates invoking the 'Intentional Fallacy' and the 'death of the Author' will be resurrected, only this time the debates will be over computer games, not literature. For rhetoric involves the art of persuading, not necessarily the art of opening up games as vehicles of critical discourse.

There has also been some criticism of Bogost's other (but related) book, *Unit Operations*. For example, Alex Wade wrote that the 'description of ancient videogames Pong and Combat as games with "tennislike attributes" … stretches the membrane of the operation of units beyond perspicuity and into the realm of fiction' (2007, p. 183). I am not so concerned with individual errors or stretched analogies in the books, but I am perplexed as to how unit operations and procedural rhetoric can be or should be employed, although other critics (such as Short, 2008) might disagree, suggesting it is unclear but potentially still very useful. While Bogost seems to be saying that we have to understand procedural rhetoric, other critics and game designers do not seem sure as to how they can implement these theoretical notions. In an otherwise complementary review of *Unit Operations*, Zach Whalen (2006) wrote that 'I'm eager to try my own hand at unit analysis, but I'm not sure how to proceed'.

When I consider the application of procedural rhetoric to interactive history and to virtual heritage, I am also perplexed as to where and how I could usefully leverage these theories. I am not interested in seeing unit operations in literature and I am not interested in borrowing from principles of advergames; perhaps the field of serious games, heritage and history is still so new that we need a far simpler applied and easily verifiable theory?

Are We Designing for Digital Natives?

I have not yet considered the audience, and they are no doubt a changing phenomenon. For example, the term 'digital natives' has been bandied about over the last 10 or 15 years. Are recent generations so technologically advanced that education has to be completely rewritten to accommodate them? Must games be used everywhere to connect with the new generation's 'digital native' minds? According to investigations that seem thorough and genuinely investigative (Bennett et al., 2008; Jones and Shao, 2011), it appears that the answer is no. For example, Bennett et al. (2008, p. 775) wrote in their abstract:

> The idea that a new generation of students is entering the education system has excited recent attention among educators and education commentators. Termed 'digital natives' or the 'Net generation', these young people are said to have been immersed in technology all their lives, imbuing them with sophisticated technical skills and learning preferences for which traditional education is unprepared. Grand claims are being made about the nature of this generational change and about the urgent necessity for educational reform in response. A sense of impending crisis pervades this debate. However, the actual situation is far from clear ... We argue that rather than being empirically and theoretically informed, the debate can be likened to an academic form of a 'moral panic'. We propose that a more measured and disinterested approach is now required to investigate 'digital natives' and their implications for education.

Jones and Shao (2011) are even more direct; they state that there is no such clear generational divide, ICT skills vary widely and students are not automatically experts or even frequent users of 'Blogs, Wikis and 3D Virtual Worlds'. I agree and would add that digital literacy is not the same as digital fluency. In the more specific area of games (and game design), I have met and taught many students who do not play games or follow game design; some of them were enrolled in my game design class and initially said they did not play games because they did not like them (and yet they still managed to pass).

What is digital fluency? Resnick (2002) argues that digital fluency is knowing how to construct things of significance with these tools. Belshaw (2012) suggested eight digital literacy concepts: *cultural* (what is the context of experience?); *cognitive* (how is the mind expanded?); *constructive* (what is new in such construction?); *communicative* (how is communication enhanced?); *confident* (how is failure addressed constructively?); *creative* (how can we move beyond the canon?); *critical* (how are conventions critically addressed?); and *civic* (how is a civil society developed?).

Digital literacy is much more complex than was initially trumpeted, and digital fluency is particularly important in game design and critical gameplay. How would we conceptualize digital fluency as regards interactive history and virtual heritage game-based interaction? Could we honestly claim that the general public have acquired it? Could we even claim that designers of these projects have created the learning platforms by which such digital fluency is possible?

Game-based Learning and Simulated Culture

The above theories have been well cited and explored for understanding games and game design. In the latter case, they have also been used for the study of game-based learning (Serious Games, etc.). However they have not been widely used for games employed for either interactive history or for digital heritage. As Flanagan wrote: 'Whatever their message, serious games are amongst the most challenging games to design' (2013, p. 249).

In the following three case studies, I will provide examples of problems I uncovered in designing components of virtual worlds for cultural exchange and game-based interaction (or virtual environments more generally) for heritage and history-based content. These problems need fixing, but the above theories are either inadequate to deal with the problems directly or perhaps we need a new and topic-specific theory.

I would also argue that the current types of interaction available in games are not particularly suited to studying heritage and history. Table 2.1 below is a tabulation of the more famous game series that have interaction modes and aims that may be of some relevance to our design intentions.

Table 2.1   Games and Interaction

Type of game	Closest examples in available games
Tourist game: aim to enjoy life of site from a safe and comfortable distance.	The relatively new travel game genre, like 'A Quiet Weekend in Capri' (2004), could be considered as puzzle games as they have a game mode and a sightseeing mode.
Puzzle Games: puzzle detection games aim to find what happened by examining material remains, material changes, epigraphy, etc. while minimizing damage to local artefacts. On the other hand, puzzle escape games aim to complete tasks using local affordances and artefacts.	Archaeologist learning about a past culture, for example, ArcDig. Perhaps murder mysteries or interactive fiction comes closest. The information is prescriptive, but the way in which information is synthesized is like creative detective work. The 'Qin. Tomb of the Middle Kingdom' game (1995, 1997) required the player to escape the Forbidden City by solving puzzles. 'Myst' (1993–2005) is probably the most famous. Or a 3D adventure game, such as the 'Tomb Raider' series (1996–ongoing) reflects a similar goal: reach objective by 'reading' site without personal health being adversely damaged.

Table 2.1   *Continued*

Type of game	Closest examples in available games
Resource management games: aim to understand the beliefs, roles and relationships of inhabitants and their surroundings (ideally without damaging local customs).	'Civilization' (1991–ongoing), 'Age of Empires' (1991–ongoing), 'Tribal Trouble' (2005–ongoing), 'Pharaoh' (1999) and the 'Caesar' series (1992–2006).
Historical strategic battle games: avoid being killed, take over territory, military strategies learnt.	The 'Total War' Series (2000–ongoing), 'StarCraft' (1998).
Historical combat games (need to get close to opponent).	The 'Assassin's Creed' series (2007–ongoing) is primarily a combat game with extraneous dialogue relating to historical information and some military-style missions.
Historical shooter games (could add to combat games).	'L.A. Noire' (2011) (although you have to investigate before shooting) is a realistic re-creation of late 1940s Los Angeles, using aerial photographs.
Role-playing games.	Games like the 'Elder Scrolls' series (1994–ongoing) allow players to take on their own character and profession (with related attributes), and to choose suitable quests. Often has a medieval and mystical or mythological setting (for example, Lord of the Rings).
Control games: aim to control or overcome inhabitants and other creatures.	'Shadow of the Colossus' (2005–2011), 'Darwinia' (2005) and 'Black & White I and II' (2001–2006).
Social mashup games: aim to create interesting encounters between semi-controlled characters.	'The Sims' series (2000–2011) and also 'Spore', although it is also a very unusual form of resource game/simulation.
Games that allow classroom role-playing of history through in-game camera capture (machinima).	The 'Unreal Tournament' series and the 'Unreal' game engine (1999–ongoing) allow mods (current mod editor: UDK). Other mod-making games include 'The Sims IV' (2014), 'The Movies' (2005), 'Second Life' (2003–ongoing, while not really a game, does produce machinima), 'Source Filmmaker' (2012, but not actually a game per se) and the 'Crysis' series (2007–ongoing).

The above table is not a hard-and-fast classification; I am merely trying to understand how the interaction relates to learning and the learning mechanics that arise from the game mechanics. You might notice I do not list have the 'Warcraft' series (1997–ongoing) in the above table; it seems to be used as a real-time

Figure 2.2 **'Tribal Trouble' – A Hybrid Strategy-Combat-Resource Game**
Source: Oddlabs

strategy game, or as a role-playing game, or even as something else, depending on the version and the audience. The online 'World of Warcraft' versions can also be used for machinima (as can at least some versions of Warcraft).

Games like 'Tribal Trouble' are interesting; they are not historical, only mock historical, but their mechanics could quite easily be used to explore the relationship between technological progress and environmental destruction (Figure 2.2). Because of the paucity of suitable game-style interaction, I have generally tried to create my own environments from scratch. The below is a selection of some experiences that may help future designers of heritage and history-based simulations.

Case Study 1: Language-based Worlds

In 2004 or so, I was asked by a research group at the University of Melbourne to help them script and evaluate language learning between Japanese students learning English and Australian students learning Japanese. The technology was 'Adobe Atmosphere', a 3D multiplayer forerunner (in a sense) to 'Second Life'. It was called the *Virtual Babel* project.

The tracking scripts I used were nothing out of the ordinary. However, in the 'Adobe Atmosphere' world I was designing, I noticed a bug. An avatar can visit your world and you see him/her in your virtual world and he/she sees you in his/ hers, but he/she doesn't see your world; only the avatars are shared. How could this be useful? You could use this bug to teach different linguistic concepts. When the other describes an object in their world, it appears in your world.

According to the linguist James Gee (2007, p. 2), games 'show that language has its true home in action, the world, and dialogue, not in dictionaries and text alone ... [They] show that collaboration and participation with others is essential to engaged thinking and learning'. Gee also believes that books are manuals to worlds that children cannot visit unless they play them.

My above idea might help language departments see the value of 3D (we certainly had trouble convincing them of the value of 3D in 2003), but the next step is of course for participants to share building across the shared worlds and see if by their conversation, they can affect each other's avatars or worlds. Perhaps an effective way of learning each other's language is to create language puzzles and traps for each other in these virtual worlds. The students will try to work out what is hardest to remember or use correctly, and will require the correct usage for these words or phrases or concepts in order for the other student to progress.

A lingering problem is how to seamlessly evaluate meaningful interaction without disrupting participant engagement. How do we determine that learning takes *place* and is aided by 3D cues (or we might as well use video-conferencing software)? Finally – and this is probably the crux of the matter – how do we improve learning taking place across countries in an internationally shared space? Can we culturally personalize and display or share cultural artefacts and rituals without the end result appearing clumsy, cheesy or appropriated?

Case Study 2: Interactively Visiting a Mayan Temple City

In *Playing with the Past* (Champion, 2010), I explained the evaluation project featuring simulations and re-creations of temples on the Mayan site called Palenque. However, I did not explain why the site was chosen, the humanities-related content and how technology could have been better suited to the content.

For my doctoral project, I chose the Mayan city at Palenque in Chiapas, Mexico in order to evaluate how well online digital media can help re-create a sense of place, a feeling that the place was uniquely and specifically viewed and used for a particular purpose, by people with a specific outlook. Palenque (or Lakam Ha, which means Big Water in Mayan) is well documented as the site where the Mayan language was first decoded by archaeologists, and is set in a spectacular landscape. Although not as famous as say Tikal or Chichén-Itzá, Palenque is not overly large and can be explored in a day or less on foot.

Mayan culture has a vivid belief system (such as prayer based on bloodletting, ballgame-creation myth, extensive trade, deliberate cranial deformation and a belief in communication between rulers and ancestors via 'sky-snakes'). To separate Mayan buildings from their landscape and rituals is to barely scratch the surface of a complex and highly delicate ecosystem. A possible way to understand and appreciate the hidden portals, wells, road signs and constellation maps of the Mayans is to re-create their myths and archaeological remains in digital form.

For example, the Mayans believed in three levels of existence: the sky, the earth and the underworld. Rites involving smoke, sacrificial blood, and offerings of food and artefacts were to thank the gods for their continual existence. Some artefacts were seen as magical aids that could help the spirits of the ruling class travel through portals to the other planes of existence. Cenotes (wells) and rivers were also symbolic links to the underworld, and many items of worship have been found there. Buildings were of extreme importance to the Mayans; they were living sources of energy and offerings to them appeased the gods, whose support was necessary for the growth of maize, the primary crop (Taube, 1985; Schele and Mathews, 1998; Foster, 2002).

Mayans layered their buildings on top of each other in order to augment their 'spirit energy' and each of the four directions required specific offerings. These buildings were memory palaces that the priests kept perfectly preserved for hundreds of years. New layers of buildings were built on top of older ones, as the Mayans attempted to augment the sacred 'energy' of the ancestors whom the buildings commemorated. Each of the four directions had special significance, as did the cenotes, the extremely deep wells to which the Mayans threw offerings and which were sacred paths to the underworld and to hell. The buildings are generally well preserved and the mapping project created an extensive laser-mapped model of the mountainous landscape that sheltered the buildings (Barnhart, 1998; 1999), but the paint has faded away and many of the sculptures have been severely eroded, lost or placed in museums.

Palenque was most prominent during the middle of the Classical period of Mayan civilization (300–900 AD) and three of its temples hold three tablets to three different gods, as recorded in the Popol Vuh, a Mayan story of creation. Palenque was the site where archaeologists made a major advance in understanding the complex Mayan written language (Schele and Mathews, 1998; Foster, 2002). The condition of inscriptions and setting of Palenque with its mountainous backdrop, imposing temples and collection of tablets, tombs and rivers have made it a popular tourist destination. The early morning fog can be so strong that some archaeologists believe it was created to resemble the Mayan mythical origin of the current world, magical mountains that took form out of the primeval sea (Reilly III, 2003).

Mayan tombs also had pipes constructed that linked the dead ruler in his or her tomb to the living world above (Schele and Mathews, 1998). The Mayans believed that the rulers had magical umbilical cords that connected them to the gods in the sky, and constructed their buildings so that certain events – such as the equinox – were framed by the outline of specific buildings (Spero, 1991). For example, twice a year, the sky appears similar to the Mayan depiction of the 'Flowering Tree' that connects the sky, the earth, the gods (Schele and Villela, 2014) and their ancestors (when viewed east from the Temple of the Cross).

The three tablets of the major temples, plus the sarcophagus found in the tomb of Hanab Pakal the Great in the Temple of Inscriptions, stress the relationship of heavenly bodies to the ascension of Kings and to the importance of maize. As the Palenque rulers suffered a break in paternal lineage, their temples emphasized the rulers' right to lead by recording creation myths of the gods and linking them to divine properties of the rulers. As was the tradition with other Mayan cities, Palenque's buildings were consecrated with human sacrifice (usually war captives), the ball court commemorated both trade and sacrifice, and slaves were found in the burial chambers of the kings (Kremer and Uc, 1993; Grube, 1996).

There had been previous work undertaken in digital simulations of Mesoamerican temple cities. Central and South American architecture has also featured quite prominently in virtual reconstructions. The Aztec city of Tenochtitlán was used to showcase Virtual Reality Modeling Language (VRML) (Hartman and Wernecke, 1996), and there are VRML models of Tikal and Chichén-Itzá. I also discovered an online master's project that re-created schematic models of Palenque. The models could be spun around and, in the case of the Palace, could have their roofs and various layers of buildings removed to show how the Palace had been built up over time. There was also a project remodelling Palenque in the Unreal game engine. However, it was only partially completed and did not have an accurate landscape model.

I decided to re-create the city site complex because online models did not create a sense of place. There was no way of accurately gauging the apparent scale or the spatial relationships of the buildings or even their apparent mass. Online models tend to float in space and do not convey a sense of embodiment. Further, they do not show the rituals and practices and the ways in which social roles are regulated by the building in the landscape. In the case of Palenque, the specific religious symbolism of the rivers, the orientation of buildings (such as the observatory), and the sheer visual effect of the buildings nestled against the mountains was missing.

Archaeologists group Palenque into a series of building areas. Three of the most famous buildings areas are the Temple of Inscriptions (which also contains an underground tomb with a sarcophagus), the Palace (which is really a group of buildings constructed over 200 years over a common substructure) and the three temples of the Cross Precinct (the Temple of the Cross, the Foliated Cross and the Temple of the Sun, known to archaeologists as the Cross Group). I built three versions of the site due to the size of the models and the textures, and because the virtual environments had to be delivered via the Internet.

In the Palace environment and for the Temple of the Cross Group (three temples), I created dynamic lighting, added specific sculptures and created three Mayan avatars (two of whom were models of kings and their traditional costumes). These Mayans acted as hosts (Figure 2.3) and were scaled appropriately (Mayan males were seldom five feet tall). Such a scale was important; only Mayan-sized

Figure 2.3 **A Tourist Leaving a Conversation with King Pakal at the Palace**

people could easily get into some of the nooks and crannies of their buildings, while the steps in some buildings were deliberately oversized, presumably to unsettle and impress visiting dignitaries. In the Temple of Inscriptions, the visitors were asked to find the original trapdoor discovered by an archaeologist 50 years ago, which led down to a tomb below ground level. Inside was found Pakal, the great Lord of Palenque, his skeleton covered in cinnabar (radioactive red ash).

I also created four more imaginative 'worlds' based on the cultural perspectives of the ancient Mayans in Palenque. As part of the evaluation, participants were asked to rank the imaginative worlds against the archaeological worlds in terms of a range of presence criteria.

The evaluation details, survey, statistics and so forth have already been published (Champion et al., 2012), but here I will briefly mention some of the unexpected results. If I told the participants they were playing a game, their navigation and understanding of the interface improved, but they found the environment less 'authentic' than if I had told them that the environment was

Figure 2.4   Palenque in the Unreal Engine

an archaeological simulation. The experienced game-players finished the tasks much more quickly, but remembered fewer of the facts and had more difficulty extrapolating the knowledge gained to other sites.

Very few participants noticed the dynamic lighting or the height of the local avatars (which were considerably smaller). And they typically found the more interactive environments more engaging and more fun, but less authentic. I had not fully utilized the multiplayer capabilities of Adobe Atmosphere and I strongly suggest supporting teamwork to solve puzzles, perform tasks and explore might be more pleasing and might help participants reflect and recall more effectively. The challenge did not have to be uniform and homogeneous, they could be fragmented, filtered and impossible or near-impossible to be completed by individuals. The game had technical issues; it had to run inside Internet Explorer and had trouble handling large landscapes, complex avatars or too many scripts.

In 2005 I organized a student project where the model was ported to a much more powerful game engine (Figure 2.4). We built a special environment where the game was projected onto three walls and a ceiling, roughly 2.4 metres square. People could navigate with a 3D joystick; their task was to find the Mayan version of the underworld (Xibalba). A shaman stick allowed them to control lightning, and if they found the Ballcourt, the Ballcourt split open and they were sent to Xibalba (modelled on the description in the Mayan book *The Popol Vuh*). When people are surrounded by a large game space in three dimensions that is bigger than they are and when they interact by standing and moving (we used sensor pads), the scale of the place and the embodiment of the visitor begins to develop into an entirely new perspective. For ritual spaces have a certain scale and direction – they help organize society symbolically.

To overlay digital models with authentic sound and traditional mythology as a game-based narrative is to involve the visitor in a culturally specific perspective to that place. There are many problems in both developing and delivering this approach, such as the need to separate fact from fiction, the lack of suitable non-violent interaction methods and a tendency of people to associate actual reconstructed events with mere game-style cues. The Mayan belief system may in fact seem so fantastical to us that re-creating what they believed might be met with disbelief.

Re-creation itself is a dangerously compelling tool, and those who are ignorant of their technical sophistication or wary of their ability to deliver serious learning outcomes often meet the use of game engines with scorn. Yet the potential for alluding to a sense of place that no longer exists, or exists but is endangered with fragile local customs, is too important to discard without a moment's thought. Rather than take up digital media for the re-creation of past places and lament their technical restrictions, we could explore their constraints as cultural constraints, to help people see things as socially embedded inhabitants. We do not see place with the same eyes, nor should we. However, this case study of Palenque did not fully address how we can best evaluate cultural learning, how to convey a different type of cultural perspective and how to separate fact from fiction. The issue of how to afford engaging game-based interactivity without lessening the apparent authenticity of the artefacts or events is also not easily addressed.

Case Study 3: Taoism in Ancient China

The below section was taken from a paper presented at the VSMM 2012, Milan Conference. The paper was entitled 'Chinese Culture Approached through Touch: Chinese Cultural Heritage Learnt via Touch-Based Games', written with a past student, Li Wang, based on his master's project.

Can recent technology help bridge cultures through playful interaction appropriate to traditional tacit means of acquiring knowledge? In order to help answer this question, my master's student Li Wang designed four Adobe Flash-based game prototypes and evaluated them via a touch-screen PC. The goal was to offer non-Chinese participants a playful way of experiencing aspects of traditional Chinese culture. The four single-player games were based on the Four Arts of China (music, calligraphy, painting and the game of Go!). In the evaluation, Li Wang asked non-Chinese and Chinese participants to evaluate the games in terms of learning, fun and cultural authenticity.

While this form of tangible computing proved engaging, it raised technical issues of how to convey appropriately the interactive elements without the help of the evaluator, how to evaluate user satisfaction and how to integrate more thematic interfaces that involve the audience, not just the participant.

Figure 2.5   Journey to the West ('Neverwinter Nights' Level)

In his dissertation, Li Wang noted that in ancient China, to be a scholar or a master is to be an artist, measured by one's grasp of the 'Four Arts'. The Four Arts are Music ('Qin'), the Chinese traditional board game ('Qi'), Chinese traditional calligraphy ('Shu') and Chinese traditional brush painting ('Hua'). Understanding the Four Arts was considered a doorway or a method which helped people 'perceive the ultimate doctrine of the heavens', 'make themselves [be] enlightened', 'express their emotions/their understanding of the doctrine', and 'inspire others' so that their lives achieve peace and harmony (Dainian, 2002).

Communicating tacit and poetic rather than literal knowledge is a particular problem when attempting to communicate aspects of Daoism and traditional Chinese culture. The manuscripts that record and preach these traditional doctrines were written in Chinese with poetic and inspiring but elusive figurative language (Billington, 1990), which creates difficulties for modern translators.

According to Li Wang, multimedia can be employed (Wang, 2009), but the majority of multimedia projects designed for Chinese cultural learning have been limited to hyperlinks, simple animations or easy quizzes that merely convey factual knowledge rather than reveal the 'spirit' behind the cultural traditions. These factors inspired Li Wang's project: to design a game to help those who are interested in Chinese traditional culture, but who do not have the relevant background knowledge to understand its spirit and atmosphere.

Teaching and supervising game design when at the University of Queensland in 2005 and 2006 triggered my interest in these ideas. I asked a group of postgraduate students to re-create the Chinese literary epic 'Journey to the West' using a game engine. The students decided to create the game level using the free editor of 'NeverWinter Nights' (Figure 2.5), even though the game content was medieval and Western fantasy-based.

Two students were not ethnically Chinese and did not speak Mandarin or Cantonese; the other was mainland Mandarin-speaking Chinese. Together, all three re-created the narrative as closely as they could, but found various technical limitations to the game editor. Of more relevance to this book was their discovery of two major issues.

The issues were conveying literature in another medium and inaccurate shareholder knowledge. Although they re-translated the original epic, they found it very difficult to re-create the original action scenes and moments of discovery as game devices. In addition, they found that Chinese players, who were familiar with a distorted version of the original piece of literature, were not aware that their cultural knowledge was not accurate and they did not appreciate being told this.

The above experience suggested to me that attempting to re-create a linear narrative through game design is torturous and likely to end in failure. To increase cultural understanding, we could instead educate people through allowing them to simulate the procedural knowledge of rituals and symbol making via thematically similar interaction techniques (Veltman, 2006). There are interesting uses of technology that leverage tangible media (Holleis et al., 2006; Shen and Do, 2009). On the other hand, although there are some examples in Japan, novel and appropriate media for traditional Chinese culture is rare (Song et al., 2005; Tosa and Seigow Matsuoka, 2006; Shen and Do, 2009; Song et al., 2009). Are there new and innovate ways that *thematically* incorporate digital media with traditional cultural learning processes?

We were interested in whether participants enjoyed the games and found them educational or whether education would get in the way of 'fun'. We had also carried out an initial earlier test (also in Adobe Flash) with 12 other participants (Wang and Champion, 2011) and had found marked differences between the experiences of Chinese-speaking and non-Chinese-speaking participants. The style of the games was inspired by the famous Chinese TV advertising 'ink in water' effect. After the introduction movie had finished, in the next screen the participant could choose one of four games: calligraphy ('Shu'); a game similar to checkers ('Go!'); music ('Qin'); and painting ('Hua').

'Shu' refers to traditional Chinese calligraphy, which was regarded as an expression of a person's spirituality. In this game (Figure 2.6), the player must recognize and trace characters written in six different styles; these styles reveal the evolution of the Chinese writing system. To help the player, they first viewed a short animation on the development of Chinese character design, and its relation to Chinese philosophy. The challenge for the player was to accurately write a character from memory, with the right sequence of strokes. Pre-set hotpoints calculated the player's accuracy.

Figure 2.6   Calligraphy Game (Shu)

'Qi' refers to a board game also called 'Go!' in English, which in Chinese literally means and meant the 'surrounding game'. Originally, it was used to simulate the cosmos for divination purposes (Shotwell, 2003). Unlike the Western game of chess, 'Go!' only has two kinds of pieces, black and white, which represent the two primary aspects of the world: 'Yin' (negative) and 'Yang' (positive). The winner of the game needs to occupy more space on the playing board than their competitor (Figure 2.7).

'Qin' (or 'Guqin') is a seven-string Chinese music instrument, a type of zither invented 3,000 years ago in ancient China. Learning to play the Guqin is not only to practise art, it is also a science and philosophy. The theory of composing with Guqin is derived from the 'Taiji' (tai chi) and 'Wuxing' (five steps or five elements) which were considered the core doctrines of the traditional philosophy informing Chinese culture.

This game was not designed to teach specific Guqin playing skills or composing theories, but to develop a basic knowledge of traditional Chinese music and its connection with 'Wuxing' (Figure 2.8). Players received hints as to which tone would be played next, then the player needed to hit the appropriate string. If the string was hit at the correct time, a very short animation was triggered. If the player selected the wrong string, an ink splash would appear. After the game finished, the screen displayed a phrase related to the success rather than to a numerical score.

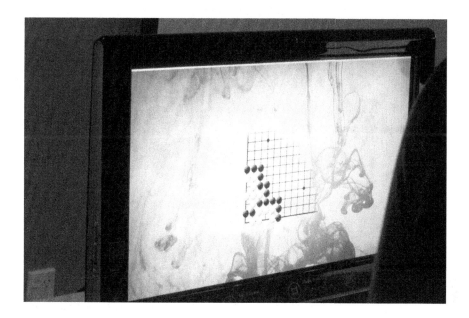

Figure 2.7   The Game of Go!

Figure 2.8   The Music Game (Qin)

Figure 2.9   Brush Painting (Hua)

'Hua' refers to Chinese traditional brush painting. Unlike Western painting, Chinese painting does not attempt to persuade through precise reproduction of real objects or real scenes; instead, it emphasizes personal expression. Ideally, the painting should reflect the author's emotional response to the scene. In this game (Figure 2.9), the player listened to a piece of music. The player needed to interpret the music by drawing in an appropriately empathic manner. If the player's expression matched the pitch of the music, pictures of ink painting would appear.

The single-participant test was conducted in a quiet environment, free from external distractions and supervised by one evaluator. The games ran on an HP touch-screen computer. After playing all four games, the participant was asked to complete a questionnaire and a rating form. The test typically took around 35–40 minutes. The design of the questionnaire was based on the following aspects: the general background of the participant; participants' feedback on the usability aspect of the games; their subjective response towards the games; and memory recall of the knowledge that has been presented in the games.

Twelve participants took the test and completed the evaluations. The results were divided into two groups: those with a Chinese cultural background (who spoke and read Chinese) and those with other cultural backgrounds. The ratings were based on four criteria: enjoyment of the gameplay; the usability of the game design; the graphic and the visual elements in the games; and the cultural authenticity of the games. The participants awarded points from '1' to '5' for each criterion ('1' for poor to '5' for excellent).

Li Wang also had a conversation with the participants after the test. The questions he asked about the test questionnaire were as follows:

Question 1: Would you like to play the games again?
Question 2: Do you think the games are more or less effective in helping you learn/understand traditional Chinese culture than other ways (such as books, lectures or video materials)?
Question 3: Do you think the games are more or less engaging than reading a book, having a lecture or watching a video on traditional Chinese culture?

The results indicated that the games can help people memorize features of traditional Chinese culture and that traditional Chinese culture can actually engage non-Chinese participants when aspects are conveyed through digital games. We also found marked differences in responses from Chinese-speaking and non-Chinese-speaking participants.

I would suggest changing future evaluations from *rating* games to *ranking* them. We also should test extrapolated knowledge rather than memory of simple facts. Game evaluations of this nature should develop a more comprehensive pre-test and post-test questionnaire, should more thoroughly examine how tacit knowledge could be learnt and evaluated, and should create a comparison test between touch-screen and non-touch-screen games.

The games can run on conventional screens with a mouse; they do not have to be touch-based, although the interaction appears to be 'smoother' on the touch-screen. In our formative appraisals we saw a marked improvement in engagement with the touch-screen, and hence we modified the games so they could run on a touch-screen, but further studies should more rigorously compare touch-interface versions with conventional (mouse-based) interfaces, and also deal with the touch-screen problem of hygiene. Designers might also like to consider a more three-dimensional interface in order to allow a further move away from text-based knowledge to tacit knowledge. This approach could involve sculptures, high-definition projection on rice paper or liquid media, with 3D audio effects and ambient movies that project on the background environment; the ambient movie could react to the player's physiological changes as detected by biosensors. However, much more research needs to be undertaken to examine how interactive digital media can convey tacit knowledge and how this tacit knowledge can be evaluated.

I had previously under-rated the element of touch and the larger screens. When people touch the screen and view others interacting with the screen, they themselves are also drawn into the spectacle. The change from brutal gamification as points and rewards has merit, and the issue of how to evaluate people who either have or do not have a specific cultural heritage is still raising some questions for me. However, we still need to improve on how textual and non-textual information is shared, and the games still require a human instructor; is this a necessary requirement for tacit cultural practices?

Summary

The major theories in game design that concentrate on serious games may all need to be re-examined and re-adjusted for interactive history and virtual heritage. For historical simulations, we may wish for players to understand the rules, and debate them, or learn how to extrapolate from them. For heritage, while we may wish for players to understand or to debate system rules, and we are probably going to stress the learning of local culturally constrained perspectives. In such a scenario, the fiction world–real world contrast parallels the contradictions between a world-view based on a local belief and the world-view of the outside belief system. Procedural rhetoric may also lose some of its appeal because the games/interactive environments are likely to be approached by a group, in a museum or similar institution, and so there would be reduced opportunities for continual repetition.

I have also briefly mentioned three case studies that attempted to address the spatially situated nature of text as it relates to cultural learning. The language-based virtual environments in 'Adobe Atmosphere' attempted to track social conversation, but future research also needs to examine how ostensive and non-ostensive vocabulary can be developed in virtual worlds to help social interaction between different social groups without conflating cultural differences. The two versions of the 'Palenque project' attempted to simulate a world heritage site where text and sculpture, ritualistic sports and public performances, kingly claims to power and spatially striated social status, and architectural design according to astronomical events were all incorporated into the design and inhabitation of the landscape. And the Taoist touch-screen games were an attempt to develop an awareness of an ancient cultural body of knowledge through touch-based tacit learning of calligraphy, Taoist chess, music and painting,

References

Aiken, S.F. and Talisse, R.B. 2014. *Why We Argue (and How We Should): A Guide to Political Disagreement.* New York: Routledge.

Anderson, E.F., Mcloughlin, L., Liarokapis, F., Peters, C., Petridis, P. and Freitas, S. 2010. Developing Serious Games for Cultural Heritage: A State-of-the-Art Review. *Virtual Reality*, 14, 255–275.

Barnhart, E.L. 1998. The Palenque Mapping Project, 1998 Field Season Report. *FAMSI*. Available at: http://www.famsi.org/reports/97024/index.html.

———. 1999. The Palenque Mapping Project, 1999 Field Season Report. FAMSI. Available at: http://www.famsi.org/reports/98063/index.html.

Bateman, C. 2008. A Game isn't a Series of Interesting Decisions. *Only a Game* [Online]. Available at: http://onlyagame.typepad.com/only_a_game/2008/07/a-game-isnt-a-series-of-interesting-decisions.html.

Belshaw, D. 2012. What is 'Digital Literacy'? A Pragmatic Investigation. PhD thesis, Durham University.

Bennett, S., Maton, K. and Kervin, L. 2008. The 'Digital Natives' Debate: A Critical Review of the Evidence. *British Journal of Educational Technology*, 39, 775–786.

Betts, B.W., Bal, J. and Betts, A.W. 2013. Gamification as a Tool for Increasing the Depth of Student Understanding Using a Collaborative e-learning Environment. *International Journal of Continuing Engineering Education and Life Long Learning*, 23, 213–228.

Billington, R. 1990. *East of Existentialism: The Tao of the West.* London: Unwin Hyman.

Bogost, I. 2007. *Persuasive Games: The Expressive Power of Videogames,* Cambridge, MA: MIT Press.

———. 2008. *Unit Operations: An Approach to Videogame Criticism.* Cambridge, MA: MIT Press.

———. 2011. Gamification Is Bullshit. *The Atlantic.* Available at: http://www.theatlantic.com/technology/archive/2011/08/gamification-is-bullshit/243338.

Caillois, R. 2001. *Man Play and Games.* Champaign, IL: University of Illinois Press.

Champion, E. 2010. *Playing with the Past.* London: Springer.

Champion, E., Bishop, I. and Dave, B. 2012. The Palenque Project: Evaluating Interaction in an Online Virtual Archaeology Site. *Virtual Reality*, 16, 121–139.

Clark, D., Tanner-Smith, E. and Killingsworth, S. 2014. Digital Games, Design and Learning: A Systematic Review and Meta-Analysis (Executive Summary). Menlo Park, California: SRI International.

Dainian, Z. 2002. *Key Concepts in Chinese Philosophy.* Beijing: Foreign Languages Press.

Desurvire, H., Caplan, M. and Toth, J.A. 2004. Using Heuristics to Evaluate the Playability of Games. *CHI'04 Extended Abstracts on Human Factors in Computing Systems.* ACM, 1509–1512.

Deterding, S., Sicart, M., Nacke, L., O'Hara, K. and Dixon, D. 2011. Gamification. Using Game-Design Elements in Non-gaming Contexts. *CHI'11 Extended Abstracts on Human Factors in Computing Systems.* ACM, 2425–2428.

Dondlinger, M.J. 2007. Educational Video Games Design: A Review of the Literature. *Journal of Applied Education Technology*, 4, 21–31.

Dreyfus, H.L. 2001. *On the Internet (Thinking in Action).* New York: Routledge.

Egenfeldt-Nielsen, S. 2007. Third Generation Educational Use of Computer Games. *Journal of Educational Multimedia and Hypermedia*, 16, 263–281.

Federoff, M.A. 2002. *Heuristics and Usability Guidelines for the Creation and Evaluation of Fun in Video Games.* Citeseer.

Flanagan, M. 2010. Creating Critical Play. In R. Catlow, M. Garrett and C. Morgana (eds), *Artists Rethinking Games.* Liverpool: Liverpool University Press, 49–53.

———. 2013. *Critical Play: Radical Game Design.* Cambridge, MA: MIT Press.

Foster, L.V. 2002. *Handbook to Life in the Ancient Maya World.* New York: Facts on File, Inc.

Frasca, G. 2003. Simulation versus Narrative. *The Video Game Theory Reader*, 221–235.

Fuchs, M. 2013. *CfP: Rethinking Gamification Workshop.* Germany: Art and Civic Media Lab at the Centre for Digital Cultures, Leuphana University Germany. Available at: http://projects.digital-cultures.net/gamification/2013/02/07/118.

———. 2014. Gamification as Twenty-First-Century Ideology. *Journal of Gaming & Virtual Worlds*, 6, 143–157.

Gee, J.P. 2007. *Good Video Games Plus Good Learning.* New York: Peter Lang.

Grube, N. 1996. Palenque in the Maya World. Eighth Palenque Round Table, 1993, San Francisco, Pre-Columbian Art Research Institute.

Hamari, J., Koivisto, J. and Sarsa, H. 2014. Does Gamification Work? – A Literature Review of Empirical Studies on Gamification. *The 2014 47th Hawaii International Conference on System Sciences (HICSS)*. IEEE, 3025–3034.

Hartman, J. and Wernecke, J. 1996. *The VRML 2.0 Handbook.* Boston, MA: Addison-Wesley Professional.

Holleis, P., Kranz, M., Winter, A. and Schmidt, A. 2006. Playing with the Real World. *Journal of Virtual Reality and Broadcasting*, 3.

Jameson, E. 2014. Research Roundup: Studies Support Game-based Learning. Available at: https://www.filamentgames.com/research-roundup-studies-support-game-based-learning.

Jones, C. and Shao, B. 2011. The Net Generation and Digital Natives: Implications for Higher Education. Higher Education Academy, York.

Jørgensen, A.H. 2004. Marrying HCI/Usability and Computer Games: A Preliminary Look. *Proceedings of the Third Nordic Conference on Human-Computer Interaction*. ACM, 393–396.

Juul, J. 2002. The Open and the Closed: Games of Emergence and Games of Progression. *Computer Games and Digital Cultures Conference Proceedings*. Tampere, Finland: Tampere University Press, 323–329.

———. 2003. The Game, the Player, the World: Looking for a Heart of Hameness. DIGRA Conference, 2003.

———. 2011. *Half-Real: Video Games between Real Rules and Fictional Worlds*, Cambridge, MA: MIT Press.

Knickmeyer, R.L. and Mateas, M. 2005. Preliminary Evaluation of the Interactive Drama Facade. *CHI'05 Extended Abstracts on Human Factors in Computing Systems*. ACM, 1549–1552.

Kremer, J. and Uc, F. 1996. The Ritual Suicide of Maya Rulers. In M.J. Macri and J. McHargue (eds), *Eighth Palenque Round Table, June 6–12, 1993, 1996, San Francisco*. San Francisco: Pre-Columbian Art Research Institute.

Lester, J.C., Spires, H.A., Nietfeld, J.L., Minogue, J., Mott, B.W. and Lobene, E.V. 2014. Designing Game-Based Learning Environments for Elementary Science Education: A Narrative-Centered Learning Perspective. *Information Sciences*, 264, 4–18.

Logan, R. 2012. Setting the Record Straight – McLuhan Misunderstood: Setting the Record Straight 2. *International Journal of McLuhan Studies*.

Available at: http://www.mcluhanstudies.com/index.php?option=com_conten
t&view=article&id=464:mcluhan-misunderstood-setting-the-record-straight-
robert-k-logan-university-of-toronto-slabocad&catid=98&Itemid=585&s-
howall=&limitstart=1.

McCall, J. 2011. *Gaming the Past: Using Video Games to Teach Secondary History*. London: Routledge.

Mcluhan, M. 1967. The New Education. *The Basilian Teacher*, 11, 66–73.

Oliver, M., Hall, J., Westwood, D., Ryder, A., Toro-Troconis, M., Childs, M., Chen, Y.-F., Frances, R., Heaney, R., Driver, P., Minocha, S., Hardy, C.L., Reeves, A.J., Marsh, T., Khan, K. and Noble, H. 2011. What Evidence Do We Have that Games, Simulations and Virtual Worlds Change Practice? In Oliver, M. (ed.). *What Evidence Do We Have that Games, Simulations and Virtual Worlds Change Practice?* London Knowledge Lab, Institute of Education, University of London.

Papert, S. 1998. Does Easy Do it? Children, Games, and Learning. *Game Developer, 'Soapbox' Section*, 88.

Reilly III, F.K. 2003. Enclosed Ritual Spaces and the Watery Underworld in Formative Period Architecture: New Observations on the Function of La Venta Complex A. In V. Fields (ed.), *Seventh Palenque Round Table, 1989*. San Francisco: Pre-Columbian Art Research Institute (PARI), 125–135.

Resnick, M. 2002. Rethinking Learning in the Digital Age. In G. Kirkman, P.K. Cornelius and J.D. Sachs (eds), *The Global Information Technology Report: Readiness for the Networked World*. Oxford: Oxford University Press, 32–37.

Rollings, A. 2003. *Andrew Rollings and Ernest Adams on Game Design*. Indianapolis: New Riders.

Rowe, J.P., Lobene, E.V., Mott, B.W. and Lester, J.C. Play in the Museum: Designing Game-Based Learning Environments for Informal Education Settings. *Proceedings of the 9th International Conference on Foundations of Digital Games*.

Salen, K. and Zimmerman, E. 2003. *Rules of Play: Game Design Fundamentals*. Cambridge, MA: MIT Press.

Schele, L. and Mathews, P. 1998. *The Code of Kings*. New York: Scribner.

Schele, L. and Villela, K.D. 2014. Creation, Cosmos, and the Imagery of Palenqué and Copan. In M.J. Macri and J. McHargue (eds), *Eighth Palenqué Round Table, June 6–12, 1993, 1996, San Francisco*. San Francisco: Pre-Columbian Art Research Institute.

Schoech, D., Boyas, J.F., Black, B.M. and Elias-Lambert, N. 2013. Gamification for Behavior Change: Lessons from Developing a Social, Multiuser, Web-Tablet Based Prevention Game for Youths. *Journal of Technology in Human Services*, 31, 197–217.

Schrier, K. (ed.) 2014. *Learning, Education and Games. Volume One: Curricular and Design Considerations*. Pittsburgh: ETC. Press.

Seese, D.J. 2012. Review of Gaming the Past: Using Video Games to Teach Secondary History by Jeremiah McCall. *Education Review*, 15, 1–7.

Shand, J. 2002. *Arguing Well.* London: Routledge.

Shelton, B.E. and Wiley, D.A. (eds) 2007. *The Design and Use of Simulation Games in Education.* Rotterdam: Sense Publishers.

Shen, Y.-T. and Do, E.Y.-L. 2009. Fun with Blow Painting!: Making Leaf Collages by Blowing at a Toy Windmill. *Seventh ACM Conference on Creativity and Cognition.* ACM Press.

Shneiderman, B. 2004. Designing for Fun: How Can We Design User Interfaces to Be More Fun? *Interactions,* 11, 48–50.

Short, E. 2008. The Unit is in the Eye of the Beholder. *Electronic Book Review.* Available at: http://www.electronicbookreview.com/thread/firstperson/ops.

Shotwell, P. 2003. *Go!: More than a Game.* North Claremont: Tuttle Publishing.

Sicart, M. 2011. Against Procedurality. *Game Studies: The International Journal of Computer Game Research,* 11. Available at: http://gamestudies.org/1103/articles/sicart_ap.

Song, M., Elias, T., Martinovic, I., Mueller-Wittig, W. and Chan, T.K.Y. 2005. Using the Chinese Calligraphy Brush as a Tangible User Interface Tool in Virtual Heritage Scenarios. *Computer Graphics,* 29, 41–48.

Song, M., Elias, T., Martinovic, I., Mueller-Wittig, W. and Chan, T.K.Y. 2009. Digital Heritage Application as an Edutainment Tool. *2004 ACM SIGGRAPH International Conference on Virtual Reality Continuum and its Applications in Industry.* ACM Press.

Spero, J.M. 1991. Beyond Rainstorms: The Kawak as an Ancestor, Warrior, and Patron of Witchcraft. In V. Fields (ed.), *Sixth Palenque Round Table, 1986.* Norman: University of Oklahoma Press.

Stansbury, M. 2013. Why You Should Care about Gamification in Higher Education. *eCampus News: Technology News for Today's Higher-Ed Leader.* Available at: http://www.ecampusnews.com/top-news/gamification-higher-education-028.

Sterelny, K. 2004. Externalism, Epistemic Artefacts and the Extended Mind. In R. Schantz (ed.), *Current Issues in Theoretical Philosophy, Volume 2: The Externalist Challenge.* Berlin: Walter de Gruyter, GmbH & Co.

Taube, K. 1985. The Classic Maya Maize God: A Reappraisal. In V.M. Fields (ed.), *Fifth Palenque Round Table, 1983.* San Francisco: Pre-Columbian Art Research Institute.

Tosa, N. and Seigow Matsuoka, S. 2006. ZENetic Computer: Exploring Japanese Culture. *Leonardo,* 39, 205–211.

Veltman, K.H. 2006. *Understanding New Media: Augmented Knowledge & Culture.* Calgary: University of Calgary Press.

Wade, A. 2007. Unit Operations: An Approach to Videogame Criticism – Ian Bogost. *Sociological Review,* 55, 181–184.

Wang, L. and Champion, E. 2011. A Pilot Study of Four Cultural Touch-screen Games. *Proceedings of the 12th Annual Conference of the New Zealand Chapter of the ACM Special Interest Group on Computer-Human Interaction.* Hamilton: ACM Press, 57–64.

Wang, S. 2009. The Roots of Chinese Philosophy and Culture – An Introduction to 'Xiang' and 'Xiang Thinking.' *Frontiers of Philosophy in China*, 4, 1–12.

Whalen, Z. 2006. Review of Bogost, Ian. Unit Operations: An Approach to Videogame Criticism. *Gameology*. Available at: http://www.gameology.org/node/1066.

Wouters, P., Van Nimwegen, C., Van Oostendorp, H. and Van Der Spek, E.D. 2013. A Meta-analysis of the Cognitive and Motivational Effects of Serious Games. *Journal of Educational Psychology*, 105, 249–265.

Wouters, P. and Van Oostendorp, H. 2013. A Meta-analytic Review of the Role of Instructional Support in Game-Based Learning. *Computers & Education*, 60, 412–425.

Chapter 3

Virtual Reality

This chapter focuses on intersections between virtual reality, games and digital humanities. Awareness of imminent technological and commercial innovations will allow us to develop long-term plans and collaborate internationally on projects, hopefully also encouraging developers and related companies to consider and work with these new markets in visualization research, interaction design and entertainment fields.

Mistaken Notions of Digital Reality as Limitless Space

Virtual environments are once again a favourite of science fiction and fantasy literature. Sprawling online worlds are portrayed, when in fact most academic virtual environments are typically designed for one constrained purpose and are far less hostile! Examples of the Hollywood-popular cannibalistic virtual 'worlds' are Neal Stephenson's *Metaverse* (1994) and William Gibson's *Cyberspace* (1995) or *The Matrix* film series.

Virtual environments in popular literature are often personified in terms of sensory overload (from the Neuromancer to the Matrix, they stem in effect from examples of the mathematical and dynamic sublime cited in Kant's eighteenth-century book on aesthetics). However, creating vast amounts of information requires vast amounts of processing power and there is no guarantee of the quality of content. Virtual reality as used in the above literature is interesting because it overwhelms with some sense of a mysterious and evil alien intelligence. The secretive government responsible for the dystopia in George Orwell's *Nineteen Eighty-Four* (Orwell, 1984) has been replaced with a mainframe computer, computer-generated karate kicks and designer leather trenchcoats as represented in the cinematic world of the Matrix.

The entertaining element, though, remains the same; Descartes' evil demon forcing the moviegoer to question whether their personal lived reality is actually a trick of the senses generated by some hostile (even demonic) force. The typical interest in virtual reality, at least from Hollywood, appears to be in depicting an evil agency rather than displaying ingenuity and creative fecundity of the virtual environment itself.

Perhaps the most impressive virtual environment is the holodeck (Holographic Environment Simulator) in the TV series *Star Trek* (Tulloch and Jenkins, 1995). The fictional computer generating the holograms that surround and respond to crew-members is truly innovative but currently impossible. The computer retrieves all past and present memories of the participants, creates realistic and apparently touchable characters, and, most impressively, generates engaging dramatic situations that totally immerse the participant. This consummate virtual reality is not merely due to 'realism', but engages and inspires people to react to thin air from situations based on their innermost fears desires and secrets. Freud would have been envious.

With future computers we could mix personalities, accumulate even more emotional baggage, or we could assimilate others' cultural perspectives, but as in the holodeck example, popular media expects the computer to do all the work. In these scenarios, reality is outside of us projected onto our retinas rather than augmenting our concepts. It was as far back as 1997 when Jane Murray published *Hamlet on the Holodeck: The Future of Narrative in Cyberspace*. This book forecast the computer as a future platform for interactive drama (Murray, 1997). The holodeck created convincing three-dimensional settings and characters, and the stories were generated from phobias, fears and triumphs in the visitor's subconscious. These virtual realities were seamless, dramatically compelling and authentic. So the technology of the holodeck was not its only virtue, it was also a story-making genius, a directorial mastermind and a psychotherapist par excellence.

I am not going to tell you that virtual environment technology or related content is anywhere near this stage of story-making genius. I will say, though, that recent technological developments have great promise, although the overall field of interaction design and the number of grounded case studies have failed to keep up. Will this new technology be of any use to digital humanities projects?

Virtual Reality Environments

Probably the most famous immersive virtual reality environment is the 'CAVE' (Cruz-Neira et al., 1992), a computer-assisted virtual environment where projectors are four, five or six of the walls of a room-sized cube (some people might think four walls are enough for immersion – I am not one of them). The projection can also be from behind the walls (rear projection) and people need to wear 3D stereo glasses to create a sense of spatial depth. Most importantly, the user is tracked, so the view changes as the user moves around. This allows objects to appear to float as 3D objects against a spatial background.

Thus, there are obvious advantages to the apparent spatial immersion. Disadvantages include having to afford expensive technology or, if using open-source equipment, typically sophisticated programming skills are required, plus considerable calibration and fine-tuning. A significant limitation is that the 'CAVE' works for one user only as only one person is tracked, and the projection is adjusted to look correct from their position (Czernuszenko et al., 1997).

However, there have been developments in this area, especially in terms of ease of use and affordability. The 'Crytek' and 'Unreal' game engines have been adopted to create 'CAVE'-like environments, 'CRYVE' (Nakevska et al., 2012)

**Figure 3.1   Virtual Egyptian Temple – Cylindrical Screen, HIVE, Curtin
University**

and 'CAVEUT' (Jacobson et al., 2005). So any games or game mods that run
inside the game engines can be projected onto surround walls. Paul Bourke at
the University of Western Australia has also given detailed instructions on how
to project 'UNITY' and 'Blender' environments (Bourke, 2003, 2008, 2009)
onto domes, from one-person semi-hemispherical 'iDomes' to large planetarium
domes. Although they still have sweet spots, domes can convey a sense of spatial
immersion without requiring stereo projectors and glasses. The sweet spot is also
larger than for a traditional 'CAVE'. Bourke's method also makes use of an easily
purchased curved mirror (like the ones used in shops) and some clever warping
code so that the image is warped correctly to fit on the surface geometry of the
projection surface.

The co-inventor of 'CAVEUT', Jeffrey Jacobson, has ported his models to
'UNITY', a real-time rendering engine for games, to provide archaeological
models to the wider community. Projects include the game 'Gates of Horus', which
is based on the 'Virtual Egyptian Temple' (Jacobson, 2014). The 'Gates of Horus'
is demonstrated in Figure 3.1, where Jacobson presented elements of the model
in Curtin University's HIVE facility. Other projects on the http://planetjeff.net
website include 'Pompeii' and 'The Egyptian Oracle'. In the 'Oracle' project,

Figure 3.2   The CryVE, TU Eindhoven University
Source: Marija Nakevska

students who study classical languages can perform caves using these game environments, and a puppeteer narrates and interacts in real time with the student performers in front of an audience.

The 'CryVE' (Figure 3.2) is another implementation of a game engine that can be run as a CAVE (Juarez et al., 2010). The authors have detailed the workflow that creates this set-up and made the information freely available (Nakevska et al., 2012).

This game engine is one of the most powerful game engines available: it can create realistic effects, vast landscapes and will allow you to edit the game environment in real time (while the computer is rendering it). The 'CryEngine Software Development Kit' can be freely downloaded for non-commercial use (http://www.crydev.net); it uses 'LUA' for scripting.

The Quality of Desktop Game-worlds

Games are becoming the dominant creation tools for virtual environment design, even if the movement started at least 14 years ago (DeLeon and Berry Jr., 2000). Most of the major game engines can create levels for consoles as well as for desktop PCs; many can also export 3D content for tablets and smartphones. A desktop computer with dedicated graphics is still probably the optimal solution for graphics processing, and now these home computers can rival the supercomputing visualization centres of just a decade ago. For example, this Iron Age virtual environment (Figure 3.3) was developed by Daniel Westergren, of Sweden (http://www.westergrenart.com), with help from local archaeologists. The Iron Age project

Figure 3.3   Iron Age Village in the CryEngine
Source: Daniel Westergren

was developed using the latest 'CryEngine' and was considered good enough by the 'Crytek' game company to be included in its 'best of CryEngine free SDK' trailer presented at the world-famous Game Developers Conference (GDC) in 2014.

Peer-around Space/Walk-around Space

Unmakeable Love (Figure 3.4) is a retelling of a Beckett play with a twist (Kenderdine and Shaw, 2010). The display is in essence six walls that you can walk around, but the illusive magic is such that as you walk around, the walls you are led by your senses to believe that there are actually 3D people inhabiting the inside of the display as a 3D space. The forerunner, 'VROOM' (at the Museum of Victoria in partnership with Swinburne University and others), aimed to create this illusion, but lacked suitable content. The play *Unmakeable Love* features (computer-generated) humans who appear to live inside the display. Spectators could light 'into' the space, which illuminates spectators on the other side of the display, reinforcing the illusion of a 3D display, a real place. This is not your typical display, but it gives a strong indication of the future and reminds us of how vital it is to match the technology with the content.

Head-mounted Displays and Head Tracking

Head-mounted displays are threatening to create a revolution (Dingman, 2014). While 'Google Glass' seems to be losing its hype factor (Scoble, 2014), other

Figure 3.4   *Unmakeable Love*
Source: Sarah Kenderdine

displays, particularly head-mounted displays, are promising to improve the spatial immersion of home entertainment. The 'Oculus Rift', as a head-mounted display, projects an image for your left eye and another for your right so that the brain can synthesize the two images into an apparently 3D environment. It was initially revolutionary because it was relatively comfortable and affordable.

While the original 'Oculus Rift' had substandard resolution and latency (Carmack, n.d.), the second version promises to be a major step forward in both aspects. Dingman (2014) reports that the second Devkit version tracks your head moving and leaning, while delivering higher-definition graphics (900-by-1080-pixel screens for both eyes) than its predecessor, while Parkin (2014) says the first commercial version will be 1920x1080 pixels. Dedicated hackers have also created virtual hands so that you can interact without conscious thinking in this virtual world, or you can use your hands to create three-dimensional designs in the air.

I am personally not so keen on head-mounted displays, as when we take up head tracking, we lose social connectedness with others. However, Philip Rosendale, the creator of 'Second Life', has worn an 'Oculus Rift' to see the brain activity of his wife (wearing an EEG cap); he can see which parts of her brain are affected when someone tickles her, for instance (Miller, 2014). He wants to

Figure 3.5   EU CHESS Project
Source: Fraunhofer IGD and the Acropolis Museum

Figure 3.6   The APA Game (The Reusable Game), Bologna
Source: Antonella Guidazzoli, CINECA

develop applications to create visualizations of players' brains and behaviours to evoke greater feelings of empathy when family and friends have been separated by the tyranny of distance.

'InstantAR' (http://instantar.org) is markerless augmented reality software used in the EU CHESS (Cultural Heritage Experiences through Socio-personal Interaction and Storytelling) project (Keil et al., 2013). The EU project was created for 'enriching the museum visit through personalized interactive storytelling experiences'. The software can be installed on normal smartphones to create games, videos and interactive images (Figure 3.5). The software can tell stories, provide information or recolour objects using techniques such as hotpoints or overlaid information automatically retrieved and placed according to computer vision. My understanding is that the project authors will release the framework to the wider community so that others can develop their own interactive stories.

Reusable Game Framework

One of the developments I am most excited about is the concept of creating a game framework for cultural heritage and then open-sourcing all the examples, assets and scripts. The Italian research consortium CINECA is doing exactly this with its 'APA Reusable game' project (Figure 3.6). It has used 'Blender' to create 3D digital simulations of the city of Bologna through various eras and has created virtual environments (using 'OpenSceneGraph' and Xbox Kinect camera tracking) and films shown on Italian television, and is now developing a Third

Person adventure game set in the thirteenth century, using 'Blender', the free 3D modelling and animation software. The project and the components will be made available to the public through the city council website.

3D Models

There is still not a great deal of archaeological models on the web that are easy to access, Jeffrey Jacobson's website lists Egyptian and Roman models (Jacobson, 2014), but there are not many easily accessible academic directories for three-dimensional heritage objects on the web. There are projects looking at crowd-sourcing (University College London Institute of Archaeology, 2014) and CyArk is one recommended solution, using 'Google Earth' (http://archive.cyark.org/project-world), but how can heritage models develop critical mass, where can we download realistic and quality models where authorship and related information is traceable? How could we develop and promote these online resources? Should we stick to archaeology expert-reviewed models? Alternatively, is there a way of integrating crowd-sourcing methods without confusing model quality and quantity with archaeological accuracy?

Infrastructure Issues

I propose something rather controversial: the way in which virtual reality research has been funded and implemented may actually have held back virtual heritage research. Since its inception, virtual reality has required a huge amount of expense, skilled staff and ongoing maintenance. The difficulty in transferring and sharing content resulted in research centres turning into research silos, the open-source formats only solved part of the problems of transferring content, and developers were slow to develop robust interaction and arguably provided few non-technical examples, especially from a humanities point of view.

In terms of performance, game engines have been gaining on specialist virtual reality equipment for least a decade and have arguably surpassed many specialist virtual reality centres. Although games and game engines are typically proprietary software, they are more quickly updated and maintained, arguably more robust and, most importantly, have large and helpful online communities. One limitation to bear in mind is that not all commercial game engines allow developers enough access to create new environments from scratch and it may be extremely difficult to change the default genre and thematic interaction of a commercial game.

Games and game mods still have to tackle the issues of archiving and become better integrated into research networks and infrastructures. There also needs to be a change at the institutional level. Funding systems and related grant processes need to change so that projects carried out address their aims and deliver to an audience with tangible results that can be extrapolated, replicated and incorporated into wider frameworks. We can help these institutions by developing more comprehensive criteria for evaluating success and failure.

Figure 3.7   AvayaLive
Source: Joe Rigby

Future Directions

Virtual Worlds

Second life editing tools were not easy for beginners due to the cost of servers and the learning curve in building tools (Crellin et al., 2009; Hughes, 2012). There are, however, alternatives, such as 'OpenSimulator' (http://opensimulator.org) and 'Sloodle' (http://www.sloodle.org). 'Sloodle' is so named because it runs inside 'Moodle'. There is also 'Realxtend' (http://realxtend.org), which is based on 'Ogre 3D'. I understand that the environment and servers are free, but commercial hosting is available. Other free options include 'Open Wonderland' (http://openwonderland. org), which is a 'Java open source toolkit for creating collaborative 3D virtual worlds'. I should also mention that there is an open-source version of Windows XNA 4 Framework called 'MonoGame' (http://www.monogame.net).

For commercial solutions, there is ReactionGrid's 'Jibe' (http://reactiongrid. com), a 'multiuser 3D simulation and virtual world platform' based on 'Unity'. 'Unity' (http://unity3d.com) can of course run inside webpages, on tablets and on phones. As an alternative, and possibly for teleconferencing, 'AyavaLive' (http:// avayalive.com) runs 'Unreal Tournament'-based environments on the Internet; the image shown (Figure 3.7) is of a virtual art gallery using 'AyavaLive'.

What about a robust, accessible, cross-platform, interaction-rich and downloadable web format for 3D models on the Internet? For the archiving of models, 'X3D' (http://www.web3d.org/realtime-3d/x3d/what-x3d) may serve as a suitable royalty-free format. For interactive environments, I am still waiting for the next great format. Possibly the next format will be the eventual victor of the current battle between 'WebGL', the 'Unity' plug-in and 'Adobe Flash'.

Smaller and Faster Devices

Objects are getting smaller and more aware, thanks to more efficient and reliable motion-tracking sensors, microchips and of course the ever-decreasing-in-price high-resolution displays (Parkin, 2014). As technology and software become more portable, faster, cheaper and more flexible, there will be increasing synergy for related fields, such as transmedia, tourism, community decision making, geospatial industries and even health.

The future is also promising for many small things. 3D printing, hailed by some as a revolution (Jascemskas, 2014), could prove to be of great interest to the prototyping of virtual heritage models and artefacts (Flaherty, 2012). Cheap physical models would improve decision making and prototyping, and can be incorporated into mixed media installations. Low-cost projectors could create stage shows using these models, projecting onto or past them.

Another revolution could be in programming. Several organisations promote programming, from academic journals (such as the *International Journal of People-Oriented Programming*), to 3D simulation organizations such as 'Alice' (http://www.alice.org). The Alice organization teaches programming with 'Sims' characters. They are all working to make programming more accessible for the general public. *The Programming Historian* (http://programminghistorian.org), for example, is 'an online, open access, peer reviewed suite of about 30 tutorials that help humanists', including tutorials on *Python*, the programming language.

Hopefully, this will also lead to a greater update of cheap and portable hobbyist computing devices such as the 'Raspberry PI' (http://www.raspberrypi.org), a 'low cost, credit-card sized computer that plugs into a computer monitor or TV', There are also sensors like the 'Arduino' (http://www.arduino.cc). The 'Arduino' is an 'open-source electronics prototyping platform based on flexible, easy-to-use hardware and software' and it has inspired offspring software, such as the biofeedback 'Arduino' kit entitled 'Bitalino' (http://www.bitalino.com). And wearable computing has transformed the portable backpack computers of 10 years ago into computers that strap lightly onto our wrist; we can record our heartbeat and sleep patterns, and share this information with friends, perhaps leading to body 'peripherals' such as artificial nails and makeup (Hayes et al., 2014; Vega and Fuks, 2014).

Speaking of devices, as the market leaves behind desktop computers and moves more towards tablets and phones, the camera technology of these devices will dramatically increase. Touch-screen smartphones are the new interface, and augmented reality software, already widely available, if it finds new ways of engaging content, will be a huge draw. The consumer-accessible photogrammetry software ('123Catch', or 'Photoscan' or the free 'Meshlab'), cloud hosting and the far higher resolution of camera phones appearing in the near future will all greatly benefit the public uptake of photogrammetry (Blake, 2013).

There may also be new developments in game narrative, with various game designers promising that they are on the cusp of something new. For instance, Ken Levine, the creative behind 'BioShock', describes his idea of narrative 'Legos', breaking story elements down into their smallest parts, then recombining them to create multiple narratives generated by gameplay (Crecente, 2013). This sounds somewhat like Ian Bogost's *Unit Operations* theory.

Summary

In line with the observation that virtual reality technology is becoming more and more accessible as it merges into entertainment technology, I suggest that community-led design tools will also develop and spread, as will frameworks with shareable components that are not site-specific and not constrained to operating with proprietary technology. While museums and science centres will still have needs for expensive and specialist visualization equipment, they will need to discover and employ new forms of collaboration and interaction design to attract people away from their fast-advancing home-based entertainment systems.

Academics could help spread a component-based system by helping provide more examples and documentation to help the wider public. This does not mean that academic projects will solve these problems on their own. There should be more industry-led practical studies and projects in the wild. Conferences could include more hackathons and thatcamps and needs from community shareholders, and they could prioritise projects where results are verifiable and shareable.

References

Blake, B. 2013. ArchDoc 2013: Dawn of the New Photogrammetric Age. *Billboyheritagesurvey's Blog*. Available at: http://billboyheritagesurvey. wordpress.com/2013/12/26/archdoc-2013-dawn-of-the-new-photogrammetric-age.

Bourke, P. 2003. Sphemir: Dome Projection on a Budget, Also Known as MirrorDome. Available at: http://paulbourke.net/dome/mirrordome.

——. 2008. Using the Unity Game Engine in the iDome. Available at: http://paulbourke.net/dome/UnityiDome.

Bourke, P. 2009. Blender Games in the iDome. Available at: http://paulbourke.net/dome/BlenderiDome.

Carmack, J. n.d. John Carmack Delivers Some Home Truths on Latency. *Oculus Rift Blog*. Available at: http://oculusrift-blog.com/john-carmacks-message-of-latency/682.

Crecente, B. 2013. Ken Levine on His Secret Post-BioShock 'Thought Experiment'. *Polygon*. Available at: http://www.polygon.com/2013/10/9/4816828/ken-levines-next-big-thing-isnt-so-much-a-game-as-it-is-a-reinvention.

Crellin, J., Duke-Williams, E., Chandler, J. and Collinson, T. 2009. Virtual Worlds in Computing Education. *Computer Science Education*, 19, 315–334.

Cruz-Neira, C., Sandin, D.J., Defanti, T.A., Kenyon, R.V. and Hart, J.C. 1992. The CAVE: Audio Visual Experience Automatic Virtual Environment. *Communications of the ACM*, 35, 64–72.

Czernuszenko, M., Pape, D., Sandin, D., Defanti, T., Dawe, G.L. and Brown, M.D. 1997. The ImmersaDesk and Infinity Wall Projection-Based Virtual Reality Displays. *ACM SIGGRAPH Computer Graphics*, 31, 46–49.

Deleon, V. and Berry Jr., R. 2000. Bringing VR to the Desktop: Are You Game? *MultiMedia, IEEE*, 7, 68–72.

Dingman, H. 2014. To Oculus and Beyond: Peering into the Future of Virtual Reality at GDC 2014. *PCWorld: Gaming*. Available at: http://www.pcworld.com/article/2110427/to-oculus-and-beyond-peering-into-the-future-of-virtual-reality-at-gdc-2014.html.

Flaherty, J. 2012. Harvard's 3D-Printing Archaeologists Fix Ancient Artifacts. *Wired*. Available at: http://www.wired.com/2012/12/harvard-3d-printing-archaelogy.

Gibson, W. 1995. *Neuromancer*. New York: Ace.

Hayes, J., Bizony, P. and Edwads, C. 2014. New Utopias for Old? *Engineering & Technology*, 9, 30–34.

Hughes, I. 2012. Virtual Worlds, Augmented Reality, Blended Reality. *Computer Networks*, 56, 3879–3885.

Jacobson, J. 2014. *planetjeff*. Available at: http://planetjeff.net/html/pro_gates.html.

Jacobson, J., Le Rendard, M., Lugrin, J. and Cavazza, M. 2005. The CaveUT System: Immersive Entertainment Based on a Game Engine. *ACM SIGCHI International Conference on Advances in Computer Entertainment Technology (ACE 2005)*. Valencia, Spain: ACM Press.

Jascemskas, R. 2014. Will 2014 Usher the Start of a 3D Printing Revolution? *TechSpot*. Available at: http://www.techspot.com/news/56131-will-2014-usher-the-start-of-a-3d-printing-revolution.html.

Juarez, A., Schonenberg, W. and Bartneck, C. 2010. Implementing a Low-Cost CAVE System Using the CryEngine2. Available at: http://cryve.id.tue.nl/paper/paper.html.

Keil, J., Engelke, T. and Pujol, L. 2013. Interactive Adaptive Storytelling with AR at Acropolis Museum. In A.C. Addison, G. Guidi, L. De Luca and S. Pescarin (eds), *2013 Digital Heritage Congress*, Paris, Marseille, 56–57.

Kenderdine, S. and Shaw, J. 2010. Making UNMAKEABLELOVE: The Relocation of Theatre. In R.B. Vanderbeeken and C. Stalpaert (eds), *Theater Topics: Bastard or Playmate? Adapting Theatre, Mutating Media and Contemporary Performing Arts*. Amsterdam: Amsterdam University Press, 102–120.

Miller, J. 2014. Mind Reading Comes One Step Closer to Reality with the Glass Brain. *Co.CREATE*. Available at: http://www.fastcocreate.com/3027904/mind-reading-comes-one-step-closer-to-reality-with-the-glass-brain.

Murray, J.H. 1997. *Hamlet on the Holodeck: The Future of Narrative in Cyberspace*. New York: Simon & Schuster.

Nakevska, M., Juarez, A. and Hu, J. 2012. CryVE: Modding the CryEngine2 to Create a CAVE System. In E. Champion (ed.), *Game Mods: Design Theory and Criticism*. Pittsburgh: ETC. Press.

Orwell, G. 1984. *Nineteen Eighty-Four*. New York: Signet Classic.

Parkin, S. 2014. Virtual Reality Startups Look Back to the Future. Available at: http://www.technologyreview.com/news/525301/virtual-reality-startups-look-back-to-the-future.

Scoble, R. 2014. Why Google Glass is Doomed. *thenextweb*. Available at: http://thenextweb.com/robertscoble/2014/01/02/google-glass-doomed.

Stephenson, N. 1994. *Snow Crash*. Harmondsworth: Penguin.

Tulloch, J. and Jenkins, H. 1995. *Science Fiction Audiences: Watching Doctor Who and Star Trek*. London: Routledge.

University College London Institute of Archaeology. 2014. Crowd- and Community-Fuelled Archaeological Research. Available at: http://www.ucl.ac.uk/archaeology/research/directory/community-bevan.

Vega, K. and Fuks, H. 2014. Beauty Technology: Body Surface Computing. *Computer*, 47, 71–75.

Chapter 4
Game-based History and Historical Simulations

Academic History versus Public Memories

A very important resource for this book was the publication and website of the very impressive book *Presence of the Past*, which also helpfully placed online its survey and methodology (at http://chnm.gmu.edu/survey). Non-historians do not necessarily realize that just like science, methods and data in various aspects of history can be interrogated, verified and replicated. For example, in 'Appendix 1, How We Did the Survey' (available at: http://chnm.gmu.edu/survey/appendix. html), the authors noted:

> This extensive piloting and pretesting taught us two crucial lessons. First, we needed to ask broadly framed questions if we were to learn what people were thinking and doing. That meant, in turn, that we had to ask people about 'the past' and not just about 'history'. Our pilot survey showed that three quarters of those we interviewed thought of 'the past' and 'history' as different concepts, with most people defining the past in more inclusive terms and history as something more formal, analytical, official, or distant. As Melissa Keane, one of the Arizona graduate students, later observed, most people 'drew a clear line between "history" and their own lives. "History" was often remote "book learning" – Columbus, Abe Lincoln, Henry VIII, the Norman Conquest – the "boring stuff from school"'.

Co-author David Thelen reflected that 'it matters little whether "the past" consists of a 200-year-old narrative, an account from a textbook, a display at a museum, or a tale recounted by a family member over Thanksgiving dinner'. Yet, he noted that 'academic history differs from everyday history' and added:

> In historymaking practice, terms and even whole languages often get in the way of recognizing our more fundamental similarities. The very word 'history' was associated by many respondents with their most unpleasant experiences with the past. Indeed, 'forced regurgitation' or 'spitting back' of 'meaningless' and 'boring' facts and dates on exams in school were their most common associations with the word. To call something 'history' is to describe it as dead and irrelevant, completely useless. For professionals, however, 'history' is both alive and useful. The term is practically synonymous with our occupational identity, and we associate it with

rigorous discipline and the authoritative use of the past. The word that seemed to have more meaning to our survey respondents – 'experience' – is dismissed by many professionals as random, private, shallow, and even self-deceptive.

On the accompanying website, co-author Roy Rosenzweig (1998) wrote the following:

> A history grounded in the immediate and the experiential also runs the risk of neglecting important stories that are temporally or geographically distant ... Our respondents told us of beginning with the personal and the intimate, and historians too must begin with their immediate worlds – the places where they teach and talk about the past.

Today the problem is still unresolved; there is a huge gap between the public appreciation of the past, their past and the historian's precise field of history. Can games and simulations bridge the gap? To be honest, I am not sure; there are still many problems and few solutions.

In Tim Hitchcock's (2012) interesting post on how mapping technologies are helping to bring together different disciplines, a reader, Elissa, remarked on the differences between residents and scholars that still need to be overcome. Elissa wrote:

> The piece makes me think not only about the [sic] disconects between historians and geographers (more generally), but how residents of an area (be it a parish, or a neighborhood) describe and navigate it spatially. A sense of place that stems from once contemporary quotidian life. Historians have picked up some of this from literature; now's the time to broaden that perspective. (10 May 2013, 12:48)

And on 18 November 2011, Robin W. Ness tweeted the following perspicacious question (@rwness, 18 November 2011): 'What are the history skills we want the public to have and how do we make history popular?' It is a great question. I suggest that a starting point is to consider the distinction the American public appears to make between history and the past: is this symptomatic of other countries and can it be resolved? How can we bridge the gap between the knowledge that historians might think the public require and the knowledge that the public want to acquire? And what is this knowledge acquisition – is it data or can it include skills and subject-specific judgement?

Sheila Brennan (2011) has commented that although in the USA, history museums outnumber art museums, they have been much slower in adopting technology and disseminating historical knowledge, and the public does not have an opportunity to develop 'historical thinking skills':

> most [history] museums do not make that process visible to the public and by keeping it hidden, museums are inadvertently reinforcing that there is a master

narrative of history – that is not open to re-interpretation by the visitor. If visitors can see and learn to model historical thinking skills visible in one exhibition, for instance, perhaps they can learn how to piece together and source evidence to develop their own interpretations in other exhibits or even other venues.

In another blog post, Brennan remarked (2012) that some history museums are 'testing out games, but not always in ways that serve students well because they are not teaching them how to do history, such as Building Detroit. You make random choices about which crops to grow and you earn points, but don't know why'. At the time of writing, Building Detroit is still online (http://detroithistorical.org/ buildingdetroit) and it offers various ways to build the city over five generations, along with lessons and a timeline.

However, as Brennan commented, it is difficult to understand what one should be able to do in a historically regulated way. I have the vague idea that certain people planted things and the colony/city grew, but it seemed to me that I just have to do x when asked, and then the next stage just happened. The simulation appears to be step-based, not rule-based, and agency seems limited to responding, but how one responds is not important as long as one clicks within the frame. I would be very interested to know the knowledge and conceptual understanding that the public takes away from this simulation and is expected to take away from the simulation.

History as Simulations, Not as Games

There is something to be said for designing a historical simulation rather than trying to build a game that teaches history. However, there is a risk that gamified history can trivialize reward systems and can create a variety of game choices that do not reflect the options that were available to the actual historical characters. Still, at least some games are really simulations. In his Gamasutra article, Tynan Sylvester (2013) nominated 'SimCity', 'Dwarf Fortress', 'Tropico', 'The Sims' and 'Prison Architect' as being driven by the Simulation Dream.

The Simulation Dream is the idea of making a complex simulation of a story world, which creates fascinating emergent stories as powerful as those you might write yourself. The idea is bursting with potential. And it appears everywhere. Early in the development of 'BioShock', the game featured an ecological system as well. There were three parts to it. Splicers would hunt Gatherers, who were in turn guarded by Protectors. The player was supposed to interact with and manipulate this simulated ecology system in order to survive.

In the game 'BioShock', there was a Splicer-Gatherer ecology that the player was supposed to maintain. Unfortunately, the players went on shooting sprees, which destroyed the whole point of a simulated ecological system. The designers removed the simulated ecology component. I was also told that in 'Elder Scrolls IV: Oblivion', the NPCs (non-playing characters) were given substantial artificial intelligence, but they ran amok, killing each other apparently randomly. The AI had to be severely weakened for the game to be playable. In commercial computer games, the designer's idea of a complex AI or inspiring self-contained and functioning game-world often has to be reduced, removed or simplified so as not to interfere with the player's gameplay.

As was noted in Chapter 2, the computer program has a simulation that it runs, but there is also a mental model in the player's mind constructed while they are playing. Sylvester argued that this is done by 'observing, experimenting, and inferring during the play'. I had suggested in my doctoral thesis that people learn about culture from observation, action and conversation, and I modelled the same virtual environment with these three different interaction modes (Champion, 2006). I can see some parallels with Sylvester's ludic trinity, and it would not take too much effort to create a cross-over model leveraging these three modes of mental model-making.

Sylvester went further – he suggested allowing for opportunities where the Player Model sees and believes things that are not actually in the Game Model. If the Game Model was reality (it isn't, but imagine this as an analogy), then the Player Model could be filtered reality plus bias, mistaken perception and/or mythology and superstition. Sylvester called this perception of meaning, events or relationships that are not there *apophenia*.

I can see advantages for artificial intelligence: it would not have to be that intelligent, it could just appear to be so (reducing processing requirements). Leveraging this feature of humans (extrapolating to see things that aren't actually there) would not necessarily add any more complexity or resources to the design of the game.

It is, however, problematic in terms of history-based games and historical simulations. Do you want students, colleagues and the general public to believe that things happened or characters believed things for which there is actually no evidence?

That said, Sylvester offers four useful steps to encourage apophenia:

1. *Borrow archetypes from real life and fiction.*
2. *Allow players to project themselves into the game.*
3. *Create uncertain situations with human-relevant values in the balance.*
4. *Express or imply simple, pure, primal emotions.*

The first suggestion is used in many commercial games to create a familiar plot or backstory, but it also allows personalized understanding of specific details. The second suggestion is interesting and may be possible using projected and stereo display technology or by integrating physical artefacts into the gameplay. The third suggestion, ensuring human values are at stake, is, as Sylvester contends, a basic part of story-telling. However, it is more problematic for history-based games and historical simulations. The fourth is problematic for the same reason – do you want people to be carried away by emotion and empathy, and risk them being so driven by emotion that they are now blind to the point of the exercise or to seeing values in other viewpoints and perspectives?

The above were my objections, because Sylvester was talking about games in general and did not have to worry about history per se. However, he did mention that war games where most of the time is spent driving people to the frontlines would be accurate but hardly engaging. So, in a sense, a ludic simulation *cannot* fully and accurately depict many events and situations; people would be simply too bored to continue playing.

Sylvester ended the article with his theory of 'Story-Richness: The Percentage of Interactions in a Game that are Interesting to the Player'. He suggested that to maximize story richness, one should 'Choose the minimum representation that supports the kinds of stories you want to generate' and, in addition, 'Use hair complexity for cheap fictional flavor'. The first recommendation means choosing the simplest level of information that provides a sense of immersion in a certain world (don't try to simulate everything – evoke it). The second suggestion is to create mini-simulations that do not affect the overall simulation, but make it appear that secondary simulations have a life of their own (even though they don't add to the complexity of the overall game-world).

The comments below the article are also worth reading. One reader questioned whether one can feel attached to a world without spending considerable time in it, another argued that one should hide the mechanics of the world and the creation of apophenia away from the players (Sylvester disagreed), while the third suggested that the success of the apophenia phenomenon would depend on the personal preferences of the audience.

One thing we can agree on is that how the designer conceives the game is *not* how the player experiences it. Although we may talk of the Player Model ('The whole value of a game is in the mental model of itself it projects into the player's mind') and the Game Model ('Designers create the Game Model out of computer code'), games are simulations rather than models. Here I think Beat Schwendimann (2010) explains the distinction quite succinctly:

> A model is a product (physical or digital) that represents a system of interest. A model is similar to but simpler than the system it represents, while approximating most of the same salient features of the real system as close as possible. A good model is a judicious tradeoff between realism and simplicity. A key feature of a model is manipulability ...

> A simulation is the process of using a model to study the behavior and performance of an actual or theoretical system. In a simulation, models can be used to study existing or proposed characteristics of a system. The purpose of a simulation is to study the characteristics of a real-life or fictional system by manipulating variables that cannot be controlled in a real system ... While a model aims to be true to the system it represents, a simulation can use a model to explore states that would not be possible in the original system.

This distinction is not clear in McCall's (2013) book. I suggest that we aim to design simulations rather than models. If we design models, then they should clearly communicate how to obtain further knowledge and should not be hermetically sealed silos of emotion. For then they are not even models, they are showcases. If history is a continually changing, democratic and collaborative process, then so should be the associated model that attempts to communicate historical knowledge. And yes, history may not be at all democratic or collaborative, but then the model is not a model, it is an ideological monument.

What is the Story?

Game designer Thomas Grip (2010) wrote the following thoughtful passage:

> It is very common that you change a story like this depending on your audience. If the people listening do not seem impressed by the hero's strength, you add more details, more events, descriptions and dialog. Your goal when telling the story is not be give [sic] an exact replication of how the story was told to you. What you are trying to do is to copy the impact the story had on you and any change you can do in order to accomplish this is a valid one.

> The moment you do something like this, you have realized, although perhaps unconsciously, that the essence of the story its [sic] not the words that make it up. Instead, the story is about something on a higher level.

What does Grip mean? That stories work independently of fixed narrative – the story around the campfire works because of the setting, the skill and the audience. It is not the same story told the next day around another campfire, not if stories are defined by the exact words in the stories. This sounds correct to me, but it causes further problems for history-based games. If you wish the audience to see a deeper truth beyond the words (of, say, an historical text), what are you aiming for and how do you know whether the audience has understood the meaning that the designer attempted to convey? It may be possible to convey a sense of the archaeologist Tim Ingold's (1993) taskscape, but not all historical data is layered with a phenomenological understanding of a landscape, with differing interpretations, undefineables and amorphous truths.

The Relation of the Player to the World

A blog post on the Astronauts blogsite (Chmielarz, 2014) highlights a problem of virtual world creation. Playing in a digitally simulated virtual world can leaving the feeling that the virtual world's entire causal mechanics rotates around the player:

> Didn't you feel like an intruder in Dark Souls, ICO or Shadow of the Colossus – games that a lot of people consider the most immersive experiences of their lives? …

> Here's the rule I propose: The convincing, immersive game world needs to be
> indifferent to the player and the player needs to feel like an intruder.

We have discussed how games can be critiqued as text. There are also DH gamifying
tools (I hesitate to call them games) that are also designed to help students critique
through a type of 'playspace' (Drucker and Rockwell, 2003):

> IVANHOE is a pedagogical environment for interpreting textual and other cultural
> materials. It is designed to foster critical awareness of the methods and perspectives
> through which we understand and study humanities documents. An online
> collaborative playspace, IVANHOE exposes the indeterminacy of humanities
> texts to role-play and performative intervention by students at all levels.

As this book was written before 'Ivanhoe' was released, all I can point the reader
to is a call for beta-testing of the new 'Ivanhoe'. Kingsley wrote (2014): 'The
Ivanhoe Game is a pedagogical and critical tool which enables scholars or students
to generate discussion and criticism on a subject through role-play.' It will be
available as a Wordpress game; it seems to be similar to a discursive gamified
group blog, which is still interesting. It is apparently designed to allow 'Critical
back-and-forth game play among scholars interested in applying different
theoretical schools of thought to the same work'. Each scholar can elect to be
different historical figures (Freud, for example) or a type of critic, and 'the "moves"
might constitute asides written by these players in response to action in the play'.
According to the designers, students can elect to role-play editorial teams, or role-
play historical events, or take sides in a hypothetical trial.

Games for History

Though games are great learning environments, they are not so well suited to
expressing and explaining cultural significance, history and heritage. Good
examples are few and far between. Technology is also a barrier (fast-changing,
hard to find and maintain the right people), but determining what exactly the
learning content needs to be is problematic. How to determine that people have
effectively mastered the learning content and its implications is similarly difficult.
It can also be hard for programmers and interaction designers to succinctly extract
from academics exactly which historical principles are used, learnt and applied.

As to the game content, shareholder viewpoints and perspectives are often
missing or, when they are included, can be sanitized and simplified. The scholarly
cycle is incomplete, as the assets do not include paradata and the specific
background information and decisions that determined how to portray historical
situations. Multimedia assets are hermetically sealed and cannot be extracted from
the game. How could we link digital assets dynamically and contextually? How
can we involve the wider community (and also subject experts) so that the content
is continually verified and updated, while user feedback and personal memories
are incorporated?

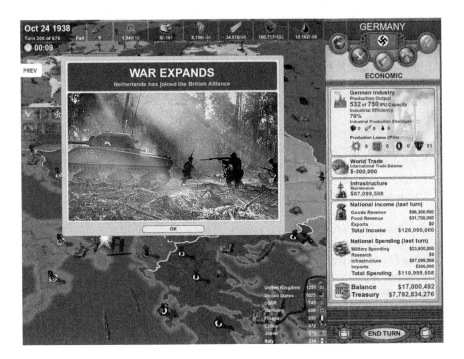

Figure 4.1   'Making History: The Calm & the Storm'
Source: Muzzy Lane Software

So how can we use games for history? At a very basic level, we can distinguish them as follows. Games can be used *discursively* to play and answer questions. The classroom can play them in a group or individually and then present their viewpoints on authenticity or character motivation to the class.

Second, games are *performative*, but they can also be performative in a more communal sense. Students could role-play game characters, with puppets, or as actors or as narrators, and could film their historical interpretations as machinima (film created by the in-game cameras).

Third, at least some games are *thesis-based kitset visualization machines*; they can help structure and procedurally test theories as to how cities and empires are formed. Players can mod cities and empires with events based on interpretative theories inside games that are moddable, or sandbox games. I don't have the space here to fully explore this type of game, but others have already done so. Many are using and testing the portrayal of history in games through their history class or in their research (Chapman, 2013; McCall, 2013), while at the other end of the spectrum the same games have endured some considerable criticism by practising historians.

For example, the famous historian Niall Ferguson wrote in the *New York Online* magazine (2006) that: 'Civilization and Empire Earth, to take perhaps the best-known examples, are not what the historian needs, since what they provide is such a crude caricature of the historical process.' I would hate to pick a polemical argument on this subject with Professor Ferguson, but I would add that games are certainly not the only type of media to crudely caricaturize the historical process. He did have some goods words to say about the computer game 'Making History: The Calm & the Storm' by Muzzy Lane Software, an American company specializing in strategy games and educational games. Ferguson went on to advise them for their 'Making History' series (http://muzzylane.com/project/ making_history).

A counter-example would be archaeological simulations such as Institute for Digital Intermedia Arts (IDIA)'s Stonehenge visualization for the History Channel. Journalist Gerry Dick (2013) relates that writer/director Darryl Rehr 'says it would have taken years to capture in real life all of the sun and moon alignments the producers wanted to explore', so they employed Ball State University's IDIA Lab to update its existing model with their own celestial alignment tool, using NASA sun and moon data. A major advantage was that IDIA did not have to rely on England's weather, and they were not forced to film the real-world site for many months using a huge number of cameras.

Fourth, games can be designed to include real or interpreted media, background images, cutscenes or panoramas. Thanks to the improved accessibility of camera tracking (think the Xbox Kinect or smartphone cameras, even if the latter are far less sophisticated than the Kinect), photogrammetry (as discussed in the last chapter), improved cross-platform coverage, and the increasing variety of design software to integrate external assets at runtime; a game can be a container or even a portal for various media assets. Game engines are far more flexible, with a wider range of asset creation and improved virtual cameras, and the ability (of graphic cards) to hold both three-dimensional and panoramic images and videos, not to mention the fact that panoramic movie cameras are rapidly becoming more financially viable to prosumers and households.

Augmented Reality (AR), such as the eduventure 1 and 2 projects (University of Koblenz-Landau, 2013) or the CHESS research project (Keil et al., 2013), are examples of developing applications for consumer smartphones that do not require markers in the physical environment and also allow interactive narratives and artistic sketch interpretations to be played back or overlayed over the original. Another example is Falaise Castle in Normandy, France, where William the Conqueror was born (De Sa Moreira and Lussan, 2013). The interior lacks historical artefacts, but Normandy Productions created an augmented reality experience (Figure 4.2), where murals, thrones and furnishings appear to visitors who are given a HistoPad ('digital tablets to travel back in time'). Visitors can also use a HistoCam (binoculars to see the past in Stereo3D) when they go outside, and children can also play a treasure hunt game.

Fifth, history can be learnt via game design when designing past artefacts, events or simulating rituals or customs. Games can be extended and made more collaborative by changing the peripherals (such as mouse and keyboard) to more

Figure 4.2 Falaise Castle in Normandy, France
Source: Normandy Productions

appropriate or imaginative peripherals. In a display I saw at the *Digital Heritage International Congress 2013* in Marseille, one company combined a virtual environment with a sandpit and a child's toy spade. Children could physically dig for artefacts and then, when they found the artefact, they could take it to a monitor (computer system) that recognized the radio-frequency identification (RFID) tag on the artefact and showed the relevant information or video on the computer screen.

At the same exhibition, an Icelandic new media company demonstrated its touch tables. Tokens with trackers allowed people to move the tokens across the top of the table, revealing the paths of actual reindeer, which at certain spots on the table would reveal camera footage from the reindeer's perspective (reindeer cam). The real reindeer had small cameras placed around their neck and they were tracked by GPS. Imagine these ideas with historical content – a tabletop display with movable markers could trigger GPS-recorded videos used by actors. Each video could portray historical perspectives from the point of view of the characters.

Ludic history can also be developed using virtual environments and virtual reality equipment. CryVE, a game environment using the Crytek engine, was developed at Eindhoven University. At publicVR (http://publicVR.org) CAVEUT (Unreal Tournament projecting 4–6 sides like a CAVE) was used. And commercial game engines like UNITY or QUEST 3D can work as virtual reality environments or as games on normal PCs. I explored the blurring of virtual reality and game engine technologies in the previous chapter, but here I would just like to say that the blurring between virtual reality and household games and related technologies also means that it is getting progressively easier to move historical content across to virtual environments.

Historical and Cultural Significance via Games

To evoke and communicate historical situations or heritage values, we must deepen understandings rather than simply memorizing facts (Bloom, 1956). I will explore this question in more detail in Chapter 5, but here we need to ask the following question: what is the cultural significance of what is represented and interacted with? We could, if you like, rephrase this and ask what is the social significance? And why is the content historically significant?

In Chapter 5 I will also examine in more detail my concept of *cultural presence*, a feeling in a virtual environment that people with a different cultural perspective occupy or have occupied that virtual environment as a 'place'. For historical simulations, this inhabitation-oriented concept may not be of immediate concern. A more appropriate question might be the following:

- Given your resources, what exactly do you want players to experience and retain in terms of historical understanding?
- Why and how will interactive environments (games, virtual reality, mixed reality) aid this experience and help participants reflect on the experience and the knowledge learnt? (At this stage, you may not have a clear idea on how the interactive media will achieve this, but it would definitely help if you have an idea about why the current media or state of the collection or archive or data is not fully engaging the audience.)
- How will you (and both the player and the audience) know when the audience understands the objectives and the results of their endeavours? Does this knowledge require a human trainer, narrator or evaluator? Or can the rewards, feedback and notification of goal status be conveyed by a computer?

Interaction over Changes in Time, Space or Viewpoint

In some historical games, you are not an inhabitant, but a god-like puppet master. How can a god or a character with extraordinary powers communicate and interact meaningfully with the games NPCs? And how do we interact with history over time? I have mentioned nine possible answers before (Champion, 2005) and I have discussed game-based historical learning (Champion, 2008), but I have not explained different game mechanics in any thorough way. These ideas (now numbering 10) do not just attempt to address variations in historical knowledge over time, but might also inspire some readers to reconsider the relationship of historical simulations to interactivity.

Ritual Knowledge

We could allow actors a myriad of actions, as long as their behaviour and actions achieved the right results, or their decisions were made at the right time and place (construct Stonehenge, invade Britain, take coffee beans from Arabia to Java, etc.). For example, no matter how they transport coffee beans, they have to select these coffee beans at the right time and take them to the right place.

Memetic Cause and Effect: Guns, Germs and Steel

A theory buzzing through the social sciences is memetics, certain 'killer' ideas that take on a life of their own, using people as carriers rather than as the progenitors. A meme is a popular self-serving cultural concept with no one owner, a cognitive equivalent to Dawkin's (2006) description of the 'selfish gene'. This sort of option could simulate the spread of ideas in a memetic way, independently of individual intention, but still socially inescapable and inexorable.

A meme is a popular self-serving cultural concept with no one owner. Actors have to choose the successful memetic idea, social force or artefact that changes the world in a significant way. Only if actors choose the correct object or idea can they advance through time and space. Each artefact may trigger other related events that also change history, so the actor can choose from a web of possible associations. If the actor chooses the wrong idea, they might have to endure a video of what happened before being told 'no, it never actually happened' – start again. A database could record the actor's choices against reality and against previous actors.

Counterfactual Histories

This method would allow virtual actors' interaction to change history with the result that actors find themselves in parallel possible worlds. This approach has been heavily used in science fiction (H.G. Wells' *The Time Machine, Black Adder, Bill and Ted's Excellent Adventure, Dr Who, Star Trek*, the Canadian film *Possible Worlds*, etc.). While fascinating from the 'what if' scenario point of view, it is not likely to be a worthwhile avenue for virtual heritage environments as players would concentrate on creating imaginative fictions rather than uncovering historical knowledge or different cultural perspectives.

Progress through Truth-finding

In the film *Groundhog Day*, the actor Bill Murray plays a weatherman caught in a time warp. No matter what he decides to do, he keeps waking up to the same morning. He eventually escapes the time warp by choosing a considerate and unselfish action for the first time in his life. In a similar fashion, a virtual heritage environment could allow actors to choose any action, but only one or a few would allow the historical plotline to move forward. And only the correct interactions would be recorded, although the number of times an actor chooses the wrong action could be counted.

Reversed Time Travel

All of the above options are chronological in a conventional sense: actors encounter problems, try to solve them and travel *forwards* through time as they do so in a forward motion. Yet the scientists' uncovering of the past (and hence the discovery of the content of virtual heritage environments) is looking *backwards* by thinking backwards. By uncovering fragments, scientists pierce together what happened before and after. So we have a conundrum: the player moves ahead in time, and their ability to change things increases. By contrast, the archaeologist imaginatively moves backwards in time, extrapolating what happened further and further into the past.

While there may be periods and places where we know more about the archaeological record in eras further removed from today, in many cases we know less and less about earlier eras. As such, gaming themes that allow players to increase their agency and ability to interact without this increased interaction competing with changing levels of historical knowledge over time are worth investigating further. Reversed time travel may allow for both increased interaction and decreasing historical knowledge and certainty to co-exist.

Virtual Worlds Augmented with Historical or Current Media

Using augmented reality, data mining or even just windows (and camera tracking), one could fill in the life and character of a virtual world with the assets of a real one. Perhaps players could fill in gaps in the virtual environment with photos, sound recordings, user-sourced web-based images or with external sensor data. Potentially other players or even a game master could fill in the gaps.

Role-playing without Affecting History

We could create ancillary characters that are not recorded in history and allow people to take on their roles. Given the ability to 'augment' history with their own personal interaction history (fictions), perhaps the interactions they have with historical figures (henceforth referred to as 'celebrities') could enhance or embellish the personality of the celebrities. If the AI deployed was highly sophisticated, the celebrity could remember past interactions and get bored with standard actions of the ancillary characters, forcing the non-celebrities to attempt ever less likely interactions.

Observe Character Development of NPCs

The main narrative follows historical events, but actors are given the opportunity to write down or otherwise record the emotional development and mental states of the main character celebrities. Actors might also have the option of recording in multimodal form any events they think are crucial turning points. While becoming the self-appointed scribes of history might be personally informative, actors are not likely to be highly engaged, as the interactivity is not varied and they do not contribute to the story. Perhaps the celebrities could punish scribes who are too inaccurate? The scribes' stories could be embedded into the virtual environment and be evaluated and commented on by other scribes.

Extrapolate Clues from NPC Dialogue

Players could observe and try to extrapolate motives or backstory from the NPCs when they speak (and where and to whom they speak). This information and contextual environmental clues could provide a backstory and hints as to what to do next.

Mimic NPCs (Reverse Cultural Turing Test)

In a virtual environment, actors could meet other actors who are actually locals of that site, academic authorities or computer-controlled characters, or even real actors that deliberately give misleading accounts of the area and of their own actions and beliefs. The goal could be to identify who are the locals, authorities and deceivers (agent-based or human actors), and what the truth actually is. I will talk about this idea further in Chapter 6.

Addressing the POV of the Original Inhabitants

The Point of View (POV) of the original inhabitants and actors in various historical eras is almost certainly lost to us. We may be able to gain an idea of personalities from Mesopotamian tax statements carved in stone (at least one archaeologist has told me that this is possible) and we may be able to gain a good idea of explorers from their diaries and records of their encounters either by the records of the explorers themselves or by the documentation of their associates. However, diaries, records, tax statements, paintings, photographs and artefacts will not give us a complete picture of how to behave in those settings and how people actually behaved, and the full range of their conscious and subconscious motives and desires.

At this point in time, the historical and psychological recreations and simulations of the *Star Trek* holodeck is not just unlikely, but a piece of fantasy. I have not even touched on the unlikelihood of creating engaging and moving historical simulations in 3D. Via interaction, users can learn the meanings and values of other perspectives (they can perceive alterity). Would the players need to interact as the original inhabitants did? At an exact level, no they would not. At a thematic level, I think it may be possible.

In the holodeck, computer-generated characters appear to be completely physical humans – one cannot tell the difference between real people and computer-generated and computer-driven avatars. For historical simulations, another problem would be how detailed, accurate and apparently intelligent NPCs would have to be. Would complete social behaviour be required? How could NPCs advance the story? At the risk of escaping this rather large challenge, I will speak more about roles and rituals in Chapter 6, while the use of drama, story and characters will be explored in Chapter 8. Here I will quickly suggest that conveying a feeling of a life for an NPC, and some response to the nearness and social adroitness (task performance or even understanding and response to local social mores) of the player's character may not be enough to create the semblance of a full living, self-standing world, but it may encourage the player to understand that there is a different type of life-world.

Awareness might seem to be less ambitious a step than full understanding, but it would still be an achievement. I think it would be a mistake to expect games and virtual environments to do all the heavy lifting. A more useful approach would be to see them as part of a media ecology: games, books, recordings and human experts are all part of understanding the past, and should be used appropriately, leveraging their relative strengths in concert rather than against each other. Gaps in knowledge, combative interpretations and socially divisive controversies can be used poetically and allegorically. If knowledge is not comprehensive and reliable, we should not try to plaster over the imperfections, especially if we have human-like characters as messengers of these differing viewpoints.

Summary

So should we be worried about the technological requirements or current limitations? I will rephrase this: can the limited and constraining nature of current technology help interaction become more meaningful, educational and enjoyable (Handron and Jacobson, 2010)? I suggest that a more positive (if less realistic) approach is to treat every problem as a research question pushed back to the player. Every gap, every problem is a challenge for the player or a question to be tested and addressed in the game, or a deliberate constraint to improve and not hinder the sensory experience, or to create a sense of challenge (but not unnecessary obstacle) to the player.

Here is a brief example. Thanks to a small grant in 2005 or 2006, I bought a relatively cheap head-mounted display (HMD). The HMD was designed to connect to commercial games, but when I moved my head, the view was updated very slowly (it felt like half a second passed between my moving my head and the view updating). The slow response – the latency – was frankly substandard, and typical games would be near unplayable, or at the very least uncomfortable. I reversed the problem by treating the slow update of the HMD as atmospheric and creepy, suitable for, say, a Minotaur game where the point would be to follow the sounds of a Minotaur in a dark and spooky maze in order to kill the half-man, half-bull monster. The latency problems would here add to the sense of suspense and fear felt by the player. Physical constraints can be 'killer' virtual features and can help immerse the player in mythical experiences; the technological constraints can become cultural affordances.

The following have not been fully tested and are my own opinions based on experience, but I currently believe that historical simulations should endeavour to achieve the following:

- Provide (at some stage of the experience) a framework in which the player (or perhaps participant is a better word) gains an overview of what has been documented, simulated or construed.
- Convey a sense of the historical context and the way in which it shaped the actions of the inhabitants.
- Affordances to help participants understand and explain the information in a way that suits them rather than the designer and to allow for different pathways, actions and goal selection.
- Encourage the participants to seek out more information for themselves beyond the historical simulation.

How can we find out how the original inhabitants and historical figures and associated secondary characters interacted? Each assortment of historical data and quasi-historical data will differ; there will not be an easy universal solution. However, any historical simulation should have some robust and consistent way to understand the level of engagement and knowledge and curiosity acquired by the simulation.

So I would suggest that a further step would be to incorporate a way in which the participant's engagement and acquired conceptual understanding (and/or acquired historical skills) can be ascertained without interrupting the participant's experience and without relying on evaluation that could be biased by the subconscious aims of the researcher or designer. In other words, the evaluator should not be the designer.

References

Bloom, B.S. 1956. *Taxonomy of Educational Objectives; Book 1 Cognitive Domain*. New York: Longman.

Brennan, S. 2011. History Museums are Not Art Museums. *Lot 49*, 22 November. Available at: http://www.lotfortynine.org/2011/11/history-museums-are-not-art-museums.

———. 2012. Getting to the Stuff: Digital Cultural Heritage Collections, Absence, and Memory. *Lot 49*, 29 November. Available at: http://www.lotfortynine.org/2012/11/getting-to-the-stuff-digital-cultural-heritage-collections-absence-and-memory.

Champion, E. 2005. Heritage Role Playing – History as an Interactive Digital Game. Interactive Environments 2005 Conference, Sydney, Australia.

———. 2006. Evaluating Cultural Learning in Virtual Environments. University of Melbourne.

———. 2008. Game-Based Historical Learning. In R.E. Ferdig (ed.) *Handbook of Research on Effective Electronic Gaming in Education.* New York: Information Science Reference.

Chapman, A. 2013. Is Sid Meier's Civilization History? *Rethinking History*, 17, 312–332.

Chmielarz, A. 5 March 2014. The Secret Of Immersive Game Worlds. *The Astronauts*. Available at: http://www.theastronauts.com/2014/03/secret-immersive-game-worlds.

Dawkins, R. 2006. *The Selfish Gene*. Oxford: Oxford University Press.

De Sa Moreira, M. B. and Lussan, M.E. 2013. Reenchant Historical Heritage. In S. Pescarin, A. Clay and L. De Luca (eds), *Digital Heritage International Congress 2013, October 2013 Marseille, France.* IEE Press, 58–59.

Dick, G. 2013. BSU Digital Simulation in National Spotlight. *Inside Indiana Business.* Available at: http://www.insideindianabusiness.com/newsitem.asp?ID=63067.

Drucker, J. and Rockwell, G. 2003. Introduction Reflections on the Ivanhoe Game. *TEXT Technology: The Journal of Computer Text Processing*, 2, vii–xviii.

Ferguson, N. 2006. How to Win a War. *New York News & Politics*. Available at: http://nymag.com/news/features/22787.

Grip, T. 2010. Story: What is it Really About? *In the Games of Madness: Official Blog of Frictional Games*. Available at: http://frictionalgames.blogspot.se/2010/10/story-what-is-it-really-about.html.

Handron, K. and Jacobson, J. 2010. Extending Physical Collections into the Virtual Space of a Digital Dome. Paper presented at the *11th International Symposium on Virtual Reality, Archaeology and Cultural Heritage (VAST)*, Paris, France.

Hitchcock, T. 2012. Place and the Politics of the Past *Historyonics*, 11 July. Available at: http://historyonics.blogspot.com.au/2012/07/place-and-politics-of-past.html.

Ingold, T. 1993. The Temporality of the Landscape. *World Archaeology*, 25, 152–174.

Keil, J., Pujol, L., Roussou, M., Engelke, T., Schmitt, M., Bockholt, U. and Eleftheratou, S. 2013. A Digital Look at Physical Museum Exhibits: Designing Personalized Stories with Handheld Augmented Reality in Museums. *Digital Heritage International Congress 2013, Marseille, France*. IEEE, 685–688.

Kingsley, S. 2014. Call for Ivanhoe Testers! *Scholars' Lab*. Available from: http://www.scholarslab.org/announcements/call-for-ivanhoe-testers.

Mccall, J. 2013. *Gaming the Past: Using Video Games to Teach Secondary History*. London: Routledge.

Rosenzweig, R. 1998. Afterthoughts: Everyone a Historian. Available at: http://chnm.gmu.edu/survey/afterroy.html.

Schwendimann, B. 2010. What is the Difference between a Simulation and a Model? [Updated]. *Proto-Knowledge*. Available at: http://proto-knowledge.blogspot.com.au/2010/12/what-is-difference-between-simulation.html.

Sylvester, T. 2013. The Simulation Dream. Available at: http://www.gamasutra.com/blogs/TynanSylvester/20130602/193462/The_Simulation_Dream.php.

University of Koblenz-Landau. 2013. Eduventure: Research Series on Game-Based Learning. Available at: http://www.eduventure.de.

Chapter 5
Virtual Heritage and Digital Culture

Applying virtual reality and virtual-world technology to historical knowledge and to cultural heritage content is generally called virtual heritage, but it has so far eluded clear and useful definitions and it has been even more difficult to evaluate. I have recently written about the history of virtual heritage and related general issues for the *Oxford Handbook of Virtuality* (Champion, 2014a) and I have also written about what culture means in a virtual heritage environment (Champion, 2005b), but I have not detailed the challenges and potential of games from a humanities perspective. For example, how can digital media complement rather than compete with the academic and public uses for history and heritage? What sort of realism and accuracy is required? How do we determine if interaction is meaningful and appropriate? How do we encourage collaboration beyond silo-creating computer screens? How do we incorporate ownership concerns? And in relation to evaluation, how do we make it meaningful?

With archaeologist Laia Pujol, I have written about six objectives when designing virtual worlds and game-based interaction for history and heritage (Tost and Champion, 2011). First, we should meticulously and comprehensively capture objects and processes of scientific, social or spiritual value. Second, we should present this information as accurately, authentically and engagingly as possible. Third, we should distribute the project in a sensitive, safe and durable manner to as wide and long-term an audience as possible. Fourth, we should provide an effective and inspirational learning environment that is appropriate to the content and to the audience. Fifth, we should allow the possibility to participate in its construction. Finally, we should attempt to carefully evaluate the project's effectiveness with regard to the above aims in order to improve both the project in particular and virtual heritage in general.

However, I have not explained the objectives in terms of game, and how to approach the issues critically through game design. While the potential of virtual reality technology applied to history and cultural heritage is rich and promising, teaching *and analysing* history through digitally simulated 'learning by doing' is an incredibly understudied research area. However, many issues can possibly be addressed by considerate game design: potential confusion between what is the past and what is history; the issue of realism when applied to the simulated portrayal of history and heritage; effective and meaningful interaction; how to maintain long-term usefulness; the ownership of cultural knowledge before, during and after it is digitally transmitted across the world; and how we can evaluate the successes and failures of this field.

What are We Recording?

We need to record all assets possible or virtual heritage. However, why do we need to record, measure and extract? What are the motivating reasons for virtual heritage?

Defining Virtual Heritage

Virtual heritage is considered by many to be a fusion of virtual reality technology with cultural heritage content (Addison, 2000; Addison et al., 2006; Roussou, 2002). Stone and Ojika (2000, p. 73) defined virtual heritage as follows:

> [It is] the use of computer-based interactive technologies to record, preserve, or recreate artifacts, sites and actors of historic, artistic, religious, and cultural significance and to deliver the results openly to a global audience in such a way as to provide formative educational experiences through electronic manipulations of time and space.

It is interesting that Stone and Ojika did not explicitly include virtual reality (sometimes abbreviated to VR). Although Professor Bob Stone is an expert in VR for simulations, training etc., like an increasing number of other researchers, he now investigates using and designing serious games for cultural heritage (Stone, 2009).

So while I agree with the broad sweep of the definition, I also need to extend the definition to cover intangible heritage, 'practices, representations, expressions, knowledge, skills – as well as the instruments, objects, artefacts and cultural spaces associated therewith – that communities, groups and, in some cases, individuals recognize as part of their cultural heritage' (UNESCO, 2003). There are also issues relating to the authenticity of the simulation and reproduction of knowledge, scholastic rigour and sensitivity to the needs of both the audience and to those of shareholders of the original and remaining content.

If we apply the above definition, then the more traditional aim of virtual heritage might be to visualize a culture through a digital depiction of its artefacts. Conventional virtual heritage is thus a 'visualization' or 're-creation' of culture. In virtual heritage projects, the aim is typically to 're-create' or 'reconstruct' the past through three-dimensional modelling, animation and panorama photographs. In some advanced cases, objects are laser-scanned, and accurate textures of what used to be there can be applied to the resulting digital models.

We also have to move beyond considering visualization as only covering the visual:

> Visualisation has been defined as 'to form a mental image of something incapable of being viewed or not at that moment visible' ... (Collins Dictionary) ... a tool

or method for interpreting image data fed into a computer and for generating images from complex multi-dimensional data sets. (McCormick et al., 1987)

While we might understand why people 20 or 30 years ago considered visualization be about the visual, surely virtual heritage today needs to be more inclusive? The 'London Charter' (Denard, 2009) defines computer-based visualization as: 'The process of representing information visually with the aid of computer technologies.' I suggest that we can extend the notion of visualization to include the non-visual (the haptic, auditory, olfactory and generally multi-sensory). It is a shame that we do not seem to have a more inclusive but also exacting meaning for the word 'visualization' in the English language. Visualization is also problematic as many scholars consider the visual to be an essential component of visualization (Kosara, 2007), but virtual heritage does not necessarily have to be visual.

It may seem that virtual heritage is *simply* the re-creation of what used to be there. Yet what used to be 'there' was more than a collection of objects. Those objects had particular meaning and relevance to the cultural perceptions of the land's traditional inhabitants. So reproducing the artefacts is not enough – we must convey the importance of that cultural heritage to the public. This is not easy. A culture may no longer exist and our understanding of it could be conflicted. Conversely, aspects of culture may be so ingrained that we do not normally notice or appreciate them. In other cases, the remains of a society or civilization may be currently inaccessible or scattered.

For example, according to the cultural geographer Yi-Fu Tuan (1998, p. 6), culture is that which is not seen: 'Seeing what is not there lies at the foundation of all human culture'. He has further defined culture as a shared form of escapism. Such a definition raises an interesting paradox for the visualization of past cultures. How do we *see* what is not there?

No doubt this situation is due to the many issues in the presentation of culture. The first issue is the definition of culture itself. The second is to understand how culture is transmitted. The third is how to transmit the local situated cultural knowledge to people from another culture. In the case of virtual heritage, a fourth also arises: exactly how could this specific cultural knowledge be transmitted digitally?

These considerations lead me to suggest an alternative definition: virtual heritage is the attempt to convey not just the appearance but also the meaning and significance of cultural artefacts and the associated social agency that designed and used them through the use of interactive and immersive digital media.

As technology and understanding progress, we may well have new ways of communicating culture in the near future. So, in order to address these issues, we need to record *beyond* what we will in the near future attempt to simulate. For our immediate purposes, for game design, we thus need to consider that the source materials are not necessarily part of the game. The game assets are a subset, and we need to choose a game engine and related technology where the basic model and related assets can be easily extracted, archived and ported to another platform if and when required.

Presenting Heritage and History

There is an important link between the capture of data and the display of data, and not just in terms of the level of detail required for the audience balanced against the capability of the machinery. Increasing computational power and an increasing ability to record and project a digital version of reality is a side-issue when the data to be simulated existed in the past. There can be an epistemological danger in virtually simulating data of the past; it implies by its apparent certainty a concrete reality (Eiteljorg, 1998), which we are in fact only extrapolating from unreliable sources, our imagination or the memory of others. We may also need to create personalization or cultural taboo filters for specifically sacred knowledge or for intellectual property. Will the reliability, contestability and comprehensiveness of the data be conveyed in the game or virtual environment? How will participants and players know that there is so much more not recorded or recorded but missing in the game or simulation?

History has traditionally been seen in the form of linear, written narratives, which may explain why knowledge custodians have resisted using digital media (Dreyfus, 2001; Wilmot, 1985). It seems to be a matter of common sense that the more realistic a virtual heritage environment, the more immersive and engaging the learning experience. Unfortunately, due to the technical restraints of real-time media, photo-realism almost invariably restricts interactivity. If a computer-generated environment struggles to convince people who have experienced state-of-the-art pre-rendered CGI films, then it will struggle even more to calculate and plausibly present photo-realism changing over time in response to meaningful user action. By concentrating on achieving photo-realism rather than on understanding the unique capabilities for digital media to enrich the user experience, I believe that the virtual heritage environment as a meaningful learning experience has suffered.

The issue is also a problem for the designer: many designers aim for levels of detail that are never noticed, or perhaps even considered important, by members of the general public. Audience requirements for a degree of realism may also vary between, say, an archaeologist and a member of the general public. 'Heritage always has been about people, but the challenge today is to make it relevant to a much wider section of people, and that emphasis will not necessarily be on the conservation of concrete objects' (Howard, 2003, p. 50). So while incredibly detailed conjectural models and environments may be required for experts, they may not need to be so scientifically accurate for the public, who may require far more supporting help, streamlined interaction or additional background knowledge.

As Shackley (2001) has noted, public expectation and the journey may be as important as the visit itself. If content designers view virtual heritage environments as stand-alone re-creations of objects, visitors may be short-changed in terms of the learning experience. They will not have the background contextual knowledge of the archaeologist, nor can they be relied upon to possess a well-trained deductive logic or a scientifically honed ability to create and test hypotheses.

In popular usage, there seems to be a conflation between the word 'virtual' (meaning to have the effect of the 'real' without actually having material or form) and 'virtual' when it acts as a synonym for the word 'digital'. Further, 'appears to be real' could actually mean 'An object looks like something that really exists' or 'I can believe that it exists'. Designers can use this conflation to persuade the viewer that high-resolution images imply a high degree of archaeological certainty when this is not the case (Eiteljorg, 1998).

An emphasis on exact visual representation and photo-realism is thus not *always* sought by archaeologists (Gillings and Goodrick, 1996; Kensek et al., 2002). More recently, virtual heritage and ICT specialists such as Roussou and Drettakis (2005) have also requested a more discursive simulation. Controversy (Kontogianni et al., 2013), multi-perspectivism (Ott and Pozzi, 2011), online public collaboration (Lercari et al., 2011) and varying levels of uncertainty (Zuk et al., 2005) are all factors that may need to be addressed in virtual heritage projects.

Cultural Significance

The overall argument I wish to develop in this chapter is that the fundamental point of virtual heritage is not to function primarily as a documented resource or archaeological tool, but to function as an experiential learning mechanism. Yet what is the learning mechanism for? My current and still vague answer is as follows: to learn about cultural information, more precisely, cultural significance. In an Australian context, the Burra Charter 2013 explains cultural significance in terms of place (Australia ICOMOS Incorporated, 2013):

> Places of cultural significance reflect the diversity of our communities, telling us about who we are and the past that has formed us and the Australian landscape. They are irreplaceable and precious ... Cultural significance means aesthetic, historic, scientific, social or spiritual value for past, present or future generations. Cultural significance is embodied in the place itself, its fabric, setting, use, associations, meanings, records, related places and related objects.

So how are UNESCO World Heritage Sites selected? They are selected (World Heritage Centre, 2014) in terms of their 'universal significance'. There are six cultural and four natural criteria (considered as a single list of ten criteria since 2005). The first six are:

> (i) to represent a masterpiece of human creative genius;

(ii) to exhibit an important interchange of human values, over a span of time or within a cultural area of the world, on developments in architecture or technology, monumental arts, town-planning or landscape design;

(iii) to bear a unique or at least exceptional testimony to a cultural tradition or to a civilization which is living or which has disappeared;

(iv) to be an outstanding example of a type of building, architectural or technological ensemble or landscape which illustrates (a) significant stage(s) in human history;

(v) to be an outstanding example of a traditional human settlement, land-use, or sea-use which is representative of a culture (or cultures), or human interaction with the environment especially when it has become vulnerable under the impact of irreversible change;

(vi) to be directly or tangibly associated with events or living traditions, with ideas, or with beliefs, with artistic and literary works of outstanding universal significance. (The Committee considers that this criterion should preferably be used in conjunction with other criteria).

For a World Heritage Site, at least, virtual heritage must explain why that site was chosen. Extrapolating, the purpose for virtual heritage is to present and communicate the cultural significance of a heritage site (or artefact), and leverage the technology to demonstrate this in ways that justified this technology. Thus, I believe that we need to understand the *cultural significance* of the heritage content, how it was valued and experienced by people in the past, and why it is of value to us today. Virtual heritage is a particular form of experiential learning of cultural significance of the past, the distant or the endangered. A successful virtual heritage project must therefore address issues of place and culture, which means it also has to tackle the challenges of meaningful context, required levels of realism and thematically accessible interaction.

Are we achieving this? I am not convinced. From reviewing conference proceedings, press articles and media releases over the last 14 years, I have come to the conclusion that we still do not have a clear shared understanding of what exactly is cultural information and how to provide for it or communicate it digitally. My suggestion to game and virtual environment designers is to improve our understanding of the design and evaluation of inhabitation, place and cultural presence.

Inhabited Place

The first design problem is determining which elements of a cultural place are missing from virtual environments. Merely creating a reconstruction of a cultural site does not mean that one is creating a platform for understanding and transmitting locally specific cultural knowledge. We need to understand what distinguishes a cultural site from another site and also to understand the features of place as a site of cultural learning. What creates a sensation of place (as a cultural site) in a virtual environment in contradistinction to a sensation of a virtual environment as a collection of objects and spaces?

It has been suggested that virtual environment design could be improved by being better informed by architectural and planning theory. However, places are not just built environments, they are also lived in and inhabited by non-designers. The interaction of environment dwellers and visitors gives each place its final character. Design by a single mind will not cover the complexity and contradiction engendered by those that are affected by place and who modify place through inhabitation. Nor will mere visitation suffice: 'all people live in cultural worlds that are made and re-made through their everyday activities' (Agnew, 1999, p. 90).

The most accurate, realistic and powerful virtual heritage environments do not necessarily produce a corresponding increase in user enjoyment (Mosaker, 2001). Such research indicates that lack of engagement with cultural perspectives of the past may have been due to a lack of meaningful content rather than a lack of realism. Tuan wrote that place 'helps us forget our separateness and the world's indifference. More generally, culture makes this amnesia possible. Culture integrates us into the world through shared language and custom, behaviour and habits of thought' (Tuan, 1992, p. 44).

A sense of presence in virtual environments and real experiences is not just a consequence of being surrounded by a spatial setting, but also of being engaged in another place. A place is particular, unique, dynamic and memorably related to other places, peoples and events, and as it affords interpretation, it is hermeneutic (Hodder, 1995).

I suggest that the broad objectives of virtual heritage environments are to impart the significance of a place and its importance to local cultural values and perspectives. Shackley (2001, pp. 16–17) refers to Eliade's contention that 'when a territory is permanently settled by a group it is regarded as sacred ground'. Inhabitation seems an essential part of the differentiation between place per se and place with cultural meaning. This relates to the concept of *geopiety* (Shackley, 2001), a place held in special esteem by a group.

Unfortunately, the caretakers of a sacred site must wrestle with the issue of inviting non-believers to these sacred sites, who on the one hand should be welcomed and on the other hand cannot be guaranteed to act appropriately. Large crowds can destroy the very attraction they wish to see, the 'spirit of place' which is often generated not just by visitation, but also by anticipation, collection and reflection (Shackley, 2001; Falk and Dierking, 2004). Creating a virtual environment that floats free of any background information may suffice for subject experts who can extrapolate and deduce, but for the general public, a place gains its identity not just through existing, but also through existing in relation to other places.

Cultural Presence

The second design problem is how to create an appropriate feeling of immersion or of presence in a virtual environment; how we make the past come alive for people so that they feel they are transported (not teleported) 'there'. This has often been seen as a technical constraint to the rendering of realistic virtual scenes (due to the speed of the Internet or network connection, limited processing power or the computer's capacity to render a large number of objects on the screen in real time). However, culture is not just a thematically identifiable set of objects. Historically, culture may be a level of perfection (a person of culture), a stage of social development (a society with a developed culture), the collective works of art and intellect (the cultural output of a society) or the way of life of a people (their cultural traditions and social perspectives).

Jenks (1993) wrote that most definitions of culture include the notion of organized knowledge and the use of symbolic representation. In contrast to culture as an organization of knowledge via symbolic representation, Bourdieu (1984) wrote that culture is rule-based. For Crang, culture consists of 'sets of beliefs or values that give meaning to ways of life and produce (and are reproduced through) material and symbolic forms' (Crang, 1998, p. 22). Crang stated that landscape is a 'palimpsest', and that culture is spatially and temporally embedded. Anderson noted that culture was seen to refer to non-Western people and to elites as in 'high culture' (Anderson, 1997; Crang, 1998). Culture is not a re-creation of what is real, but a social projection of what is behind or above or ahead of reality, made material by a social framework shared by individuals. For example, Tuan said that culture was a form of escape from reality (Tuan, 1998). Culture allows to us to materialize and make manifest to ourselves and to others the ideas that explain our existence, and why we keep struggling against life's trials and adversities. To create an object is not necessarily cultural. To create an object that communicates a shareable meaning to another person independently of the creator's presence, and without knowledge of the creator's personal background and personal motivation, is a better test for an object of cultural meaning. Nor must culture always be in tangible form (Skeates, 2000; Smith, 1985).

Regardless of the speed, power or size of recorded and computer-generated data, a virtual heritage environment can only be completely successful if it communicates a lucid and convincing reason to the end user as to why the heritage site deserves the time and effort required for digital re-creation. I also suggest that designers should foster engagement not only through realism, but also through contextually appropriate interaction. Which factors help to immerse people spatially and thematically into a cultural learning experience?

Virtual environments have traditionally evaluated the user experience in terms of presence. Presence has been defined as being in a place that has some present (current) meaning to the viewer (Slater, 1999). Slater suggests a definition of cultural presence, a feeling in a virtual environment that people with a different cultural perspective occupy or have occupied that virtual environment as a 'place' (Champion, 2003). Such a definition suggests that cultural presence is not just a feeling of 'being there', but of being in a 'there and then', not the cultural rules of the 'here and now'.

A sense of a cultural presence, when one visits a real site, is inspired by the suggestion of social agency, the feeling that what one is visiting is an artefact, created and modified by conscious human intention. For example, when a tourist visits a cultural heritage site of a long-lost people, signs and audio-visual tapes prompt us to look at specific items and tell us about the cultural significance of that site to its now-deceased inhabitants. An archaeologist does not require a guidebook; they can interpret not only from the land, climate and physical remains but also from their imagination, experimentation, indicative logic and ability to piece clues together at many different levels.

Objects develop special meaning when they are developed with resources that are not immediately or easily available. While on the one hand, a rediscovered artefact is often considered a cultural find, on the other hand, it is not specifically a cultural object as seen by the creator's culture. One requires background or local knowledge to make this distinction. There are thus at least two levels of culture: those objects that are seen as deserving of special care and consideration by a culture, and those objects that belong to a culture. I wish to use the former sense, as we do not just want the general public to identify but also to understand (or at least appreciate) a culture different from that with which they are accustomed. Archaeologists have a far stronger idea of cultural presence despite being offered less immediate clues than the general public who view artefacts behind a glass cage at a museum.

For example, the archaeologist Gary Lock wrote (2009, pp. 75–76):

> is it possible to represent within computer programs the more subjective and qualitative understandings of what it means to be human ... We routinely move from pot shards to questions of social and economic relationships, but to what extent is such multi-scalarity enabled or hindered by computer technology?

Unlike an archaeologist visiting a real site, a visitor to a museum will typically not see the rest of the site or experience changing local conditions (climate, wind, the existing landscape, flora, or fauna and possible dangers). A visitor to a virtual heritage site may not experience progression between the place and its neighbours, or experience a full sense of physical embodiment (which helps with a sense of scale, orientation and wayfinding), and they may be distracted by the novelty of the technology used or the actions of other visitors.

Merely creating, sharing or using an artefact does not necessarily create cultural significance. Nor do we need to directly experience social transactions to experience culture. Being surrounded by other members of our society in either real or digitally mediated space may actually hinder our awareness of a specific cultural presence (Champion, 2005a).

For example, if we allowed participants to appear in avatar form as typical tourists and to chat about whatever they liked in an online world, this social presence of like-minded others might destroy the cultural immersion necessary to understand the virtual environment from a historical and locally constrained perspective. If we instead give them contextually appropriate goals rather than letting them wander around at will (i.e. as travellers or inhabitants rather than as tourists) and provide contextual constraints and affordances (just as some games do), this may actually increase their enjoyment and understanding.

Experiencing cultural presence is not the same as social presence, nor is it presence per se. Cultural behaviour is a subset of social behaviour (behaviour between two or more people), where behaviour is governed by or understood in terms of a cultural setting involving the constrained use of artefact. Culture expresses shared beliefs and ritualized habits of social agents towards each other and their environment via artefacts and language.

To understand the culture as an insider, they need to understand these special objects, not merely those objects that identify a culture. Shackley (2001, p. 24) wrote of real-world sacred site management issues: 'part of the challenge of managing visitors at sacred spaces lies in difficulties associated with an interface between the sacred and the profane'. Hence, culture in a virtual heritage environment requires the transmission of cultural significance to understand how people valued things. In order to improve the ability of virtual heritage environments to provide this function, we also need to evaluate the effectiveness of transmitting the significance of this cognitive value system.

For many archaeological simulations, this requires the understanding of the inter-relationship of people, artefacts, rituals and landscape. For example, Gary Lock is an archaeologist, but is one of many interested in taskscapes, phenomenological ways of describing a landscape from the inhabitants' point of view. To quote Lock again (2009):

> Here the focus is very much on humanizing the landscape: how can GIS be used to link people, landscapes and archaeological theory, how can GIS become central within constructing the narratives of past life that are expected within archaeological interpretations today?

Using Ingold's (1993, 2000) ideas of taskscape, that is, landscapes becoming meaningful through activities, daily routine and practice, it is possible to link people's activities with different qualities of visibility. Resources such as lithics, wild boars and deer can be mapped through their distributions and territories, and then the movement of hunters and gatherers to reach those resources can be modelled. Integral to this modelling are changing visual characteristics – for example, the areas where boars could be hunted as seen from near and far distances.

Do we also need to communicate the paradata, the processes, the ways in which knowledge of sites and artefacts have been recovered and interpreted? All

Figure 5.1   The Fort Ross Virtual Warehouse Project
Source: Nicola Lercari

the archaeologists I have spoken to and whose books I have read have answered yes to this question. The data needs to be conveyed as well as the methods and the methodology, understanding the reasons for what was discovered, interpreted and reassembled.

So while archaeologists can see the potential of games for engaging the public, 'a no brainer of mythical proportions', according to Ethan Wattrell (2010), they also require games and virtual environments. For these digital simulations 'provide the vital intellectual context of that information, exploring how and why archaeologists and Egyptologists reached the conclusions they did about a given site, individual, historic event, cultural practice, etc.'. Kate Meyers (2012) would also remind us that it is 'necessary for students to know how this highly contested knowledge is constructed'.

The archaeologist and academic Shawn Graham went further. He stressed (Graham, 2010): 'Let the students do it ... the learning in doing'. Other archaeology academics have also told me of the unexpected but delightful learning benefits they and their students discovered when trying to simulate archaeological environments inside game engines. For example, the Fort Ross historical game project in Unity (Figure 5.1) had input from historians, staff and students (Lercari et al., 2013).

Distribution

An outside observer may believe that widespread academic interest, coupled with recent advances in VR, specifically in virtual environment technology and evaluation, would lay the necessary foundations for designing a successful virtual heritage environment. Ironically (for a heritage-related field), these papers are not always archived or made freely accessible to the public, and seldom if ever contain direct links to the projects being discussed. As virtual heritage projects are often one-off projects, criticism may not help improve them. However, we can hold out hope for learning from recent developments in DH such as DHCommons and the Open Library of Humanities, as well as the planned co-hosting and collaboration of many of these conferences. A fully archived, publicly accessible archive with links between projects, tools, methods and publications would be a great step forward for the field.

Academic distribution requires a community, which in turn requires like-minded people. For example, when I initially presented a paper entitled 'Researchers As Infrastructure', at Sheffield (Champion, 2014b), the audience questions centred mostly around the issue of people, not equipment. Questions included 'Do humanities scholars need to learn how to program?' and 'How do we keep our programmers?'.

I would suggest this is also a problem in virtual heritage; skills become so specialized that when a few people leave, an entire project can stop or even disappear. We must reward our skilled IT staff, as their input needs to be recognized as research output or they may leave for higher-paying jobs in the commercial world. For example, I was told by a programmer and simulation designer that this issue (3D models and programming were not considered research outputs) was one of the motivating reasons to stress the usefulness of paradata in the creation of the 'London Charter' (Denard, 2009).

We need to invite people into community forum groups in order to help maintain and filter appropriate tools, methods, events, profiles, grants and jobs. A community of such keen and eager people can research issues, target relevant funding opportunities, develop scholarly groups, compete for competitive seed funds, and link to and represent institutional partners (archives, etc.). Such a community will need to get feedback from their users. For, as Rosenzweig and Thelen discovered, more historians should actually find out from the public how they view history, as they might be very surprised by the response (Rosenzweig and Thelen, 1998).

We also need people to help manage and filter research papers. In the sciences, many research revisit, validate experiments and modify scientific findings, but in virtual heritage we seem to just publish papers. I know that most people visit my site to download and cite papers, not to debate, improve what was written or extend what was tested. We also do not have a shared and agreed-upon citation system (which is at least something that researchers in the games research area have been working on) and, unlike the International Society for Presence Research

(ISPR) (http://ispr.info), we do not have a shared community website with update tools, resources for people new to the area, and key publications and projects.

Virtual heritage without an audience will not satisfy its own aims. Sheila Brennan (2012) succinctly wrote that: 'As one participant tweeted from the Museum Challenges conference held in Australia this week, "Collections are useless unless they are used". With some notable exceptions, I found that most history museums did not share much of their content, collections, or expertise online.'

Training and retaining people is a huge step, which is one of the reasons why I have been so impressed with the V-MUST network in Europe, whose members are funded to run courses and share people. However, people are only one component of a healthy digital scholarly ecosystem. There are, for example, many virtual heritage-related conferences, but many of the papers were not archived and or made available online until recently (and if they are in an electronic library, it is often behind a paywall). I know of no common library for the models they discuss or how to link the papers to the final models, simulations and exhibitions. I would also suggest that something like the 'London Charter' (http://www.londoncharter.org), although it could do with more international collaboration to extend its content, could possibly inspire a mutually agreed generic virtual heritage ontology so that projects and project assets can be more easily shared and verified.

There should be an integrated research community that hosts research data and research projects, provides critical commentary and integrates feedback from cultural shareholders. Thanks to many enthusiastic students, we have managed to create engaging and educational prototypes, but how do we add them to an overall infrastructure? Although engaging and educational, it is not immediately clear how many projects could be incorporated into a research infrastructure. How can we evaluate and analyse the overall field when many models are locked away or fall into oblivion or have never been reviewed?

Sheena Brennan (2012) writes:

> Susan Stewart argues in her book *On Longing* that the act of collecting is really one of forgetting. The process of creating a collection implies selection and the application of a personal criterion that is meant to stand in for something whole, but that it is completely de-contextualized, re-wrapped into a somewhat artificial package. We are always missing pieces that we can never recoup, rarely reunite, and never recover what is thrown away.

What is missing is an international, easily accessible archive that links models, systems and projects with articles and with related tools, which can be annotated, shared and dynamically updated. Ideally, notes and references and models with some level of detail should be extractable from the system. For example, the EU Project CARARE (http://www.carare.eu) was designed to create a shared format so that people would download a 3D model of a PDF. How the public would visit the European portal to download and use these 3D models *inside a PDF* with some level of engagement and understanding is lost on me.

A more sophisticated example (which is also intended to address some of the above issues) would be Elsevier's *Journal of Digital Applications in Archaeology and Cultural Heritage* (http://www.journals.elsevier.com/digital-applications-in-archaeology-and-cultural-heritage). A 3D model to the right of an online paper can be viewed, scaled and rotated, or the reader can select a 'Fly Through' option, although it is still a little clumsy. The articles are behind a paywall, but with some open access articles. Why PDF? This is a standard format, but has limited functionality, is much slower (and not highly robust) and, most importantly, does not offer full screen size. If organizations want to hold on to their intellectual property, would it not make sense to give the public access to lower-resolution meshes and textures?

This would seem to be a better option to me than to compress, reduce and limit the interactive and educational possibilities by inserting a small 3D model into a PDF or into a webpage pane that only covers a small percentage of the screen. I do not even consider the technology to be new. I had to create my Adobe Atmosphere 'worlds' to run inside Internet Explorer; the format could run inside a PDF at the turn of the twenty-first century, but almost none of the virtual world designers participating in the online Adobe Atmosphere Forum saw any value in this. It possibly has advantages for mechanical models, 3D CAD, etc., but not for exploring worlds.

If we are to follow the guidance of the 'London Charter', then we need to monitor how the projects are used and the benefits (and issues) that they bring to their owners and to their audiences. We have a duty to explain what we are trying to do to our audience. Researchers at the French DH research infrastructure TGIR HUMA-NUM (http://www.huma-num.fr) told me that they also kept a record of all digital projects and a summary of what benefits the digital component added to the project. Virtual heritage could use similar summaries to promote the field.

It is not a fait accompli that digital media is inherently preferable to other methods. When visiting the Ethnographic Collection at the National Museum of Science in Bergamo, Italy, I was impressed with the tools and materials they left in each room, with thematic ideas for children (and adults) to create their own artefacts. In the mask room you could create masks, while in other rooms you could solve puzzles by relying on your knowledge of historical events or the names of animals. Humanities work can be interactive and collaborative – it does not need to be digital. So if inventiveness and collaboration is not essential, why should we use digital media and why do we need to talk about DH?

Members of the American public, when asked to recount their memory of school history, 'most often use the words dull and irrelevant'; even *Journal of American History* subscribers found many of the journal articles to be 'narrow, overspecialized, and boring' (Rosenzweig and Thelen, 1998a), but the authors (Rosenzweig and Thelen, 1998b) recount that those surveyed liked history in museums (not history in schools) which involved 'inspiring direct engagement with the "real" stuff of the past and its self-evident relationship to the present'.

How could we distribute both models and the discussion around them more effectively?:

- If the major conferences and journals and prize ceremonies shared at least some information on how papers and projects are reviewed or could be more consistently reviewed, it would be of great help to scholars.
- Discussion on the major issues in evaluating virtual heritage.
- Provide exemplars: standard papers and projects that address some of the issues that many people keep returning to without realizing it has already been critiqued/tested.
- References to current evaluation methods and strategies in related societies (archaeology, the ISPR, VR society, etc.).
- Marshal the references together or a portal to list related resources.

For example, recently I was explaining to someone problems with Likert surveys discussed in journals to which he did not have access. Many virtual heritage papers are scattered over the Internet, are not publicly available or are stored behind academic paywalls, and in too many cases the reader cannot find the actual projects on which the papers are based.

Learning

Games are growing in popularity and there are many applications for cultural heritage which have harnessed game technology and techniques (Anderson, 2003; Anderson et al., 2010; Bellotti et al., 2009; Bellotti et al., 2013; Christiansen, 2013; Germanchis et al., 2007; Champion, 2012; Jacobson et al., 2009; Mikovec et al., 2009; Wei and Li, 2010).

The heritage projects may use a game engine (Bellotti et al., 2009) or be games in the fuller sense of the word (Chen et al., 2013; Jacobson et al., 2009) and some may employ augmented reality (Papagiannakis et al., 2005). Some of these virtual heritage/game projects are now hard to find, but there have been recent surveys on games appropriate to cultural heritage (Anderson et al., 2010; Girard et al., 2013; Mikovec et al., 2009). To counter the burgeoning interest in games, there have also been papers warning of game ideas applied to cultural heritage with disastrous results (Leader-Elliott, 2003).

Using powerful game engines may help us to prototype digital representations of virtual heritage environments in a medium that is accessible to a generation that is less appreciative of books, but these games carry 'genre baggage'. Even first-year archaeology students are keen to find out what they can destroy in these virtual environments that are designed to show them past artefacts in use. They are accustomed to games and may attempt to do the same destructive things in game-based historical environments. This problem of using a toy as a tool is something

I have previously described as the 'Indiana Jones dilemma' (Champion, 2004), where the popular media presentation of archaeology dramatically increases its popularity while diminishing the public understanding of what archaeologists actually do.

This dilemma worsens the more we have actual user-accessible interactive content to model, something not shared with traditional, fly-through and instructor-controlled virtual environments. The more interactive the content, the more visitors will want to manipulate or even sabotage it. In my own 2004 evaluations of archaeology students and visualization experts, I found that game genres are both a blessing and a curse. When told that a virtual environment is a game, participants of all ages and both genders seem much more at ease and aware of potential affordances. However, they tend to look for interaction and personalization while disregarding the actual content, and they conflate fact, conjecture and fiction when a discursive and contestable simulation may actually be the preferred option (Kensek et al., 2002).

Interaction

Interaction (whether digital or not) appears to be the missing magical element. Rosenzweig and Thelen also noted (1998a):

> While the history wars have often focused on content – what should be taught in classes or presented in exhibits – our respondents were more interested in talking about the experience and process of engaging the past. They preferred to make their own histories. When they confronted historical accounts constructed by others, they sought to examine them critically and connect them to their own experiences or those of people close to them. At the same time, they pointed out, historical presentations that did not give them credit for their critical abilities – commercialized histories on television or textbook-driven high school classes – failed to engage or influence them.

The first issue is how to create interaction that adds to the learning experience and does not detract from it.

In addition, many humanities scholars have an understandable tendency to equate information with text. As there are less intuitive affordances in virtual worlds, information overload can also be a problem for players in the more complex and powerful multiplayer games. Yet attempting to navigate through a spatial field, while reading flashing test, is a heavy cognitive load for the brain. Designers may also by default add text to an interactive experience because 'text = instructions' seems self-evident to them (Mitchell et al., 2000). Even virtual worlds are typically based on a text-chat box. Traditional communities like the Well, or a MUD, captured some notion of a place-based history, but they typically did so through text, not spatiality. Even today, the virtual communities that offer virtual landscaping and house design may also remember vandalism by visitors, but the actual social history of the visitors and inhabitants is still textual, and social interaction is typically outside of the spatial environment, via forum or email, rather than being a materially embedded part of it.

It could be counter-argued that computer games featuring history and heritage can be used and interacted with in a meaningful way by teachers and students (which is the argument of McCall (2011)). While I mostly agree with this, it also depends on the interrelation of teacher and student (Grow, 1991; Sheldon and Biddle, 1998), and collaborative games in a modern social or institutional setting do not fully immerse the student in the *there* of virtual heritage environments. For example, Gaver et al. (2004, p. 888) wrote that the difference between ludic systems and typical computer systems is the following: 'If a system can easily be used to achieve practical tasks, this will distract from the possibilities it offers for more playful engagement.' This is a continual issue with learning environments in general.

Hein (1991) also argued that interactivity in exhibits creates more engagement by allowing users to apply the tool directly to their own life. Yet activity per se is not cultural; the visitors are not individually recognized and remembered. In 2007 Bharat Dave and I proposed a new categorization of virtual environments in response to an ACADIA 2001 paper by Kalay and Marx (2001) that described eight types of virtual places, but these notions were descriptive rather than prescriptive. In the 2007 chapter by myself and Bharat Dave, virtual environments are instead classified by their overall design goal: the first is visualization-based, the second is activity-based and the third covers 'inscriptive' (hermeneutic) environments.

The first type of virtual environment is visual (sometimes with sound). You can walk around, zoom in and out of objects (say buildings), and that is about it. Your orientation and view can be manipulated, but the environment is not really interactive, as it does not affect your actions and you cannot modify it. A three-dimensional fly-through of a building is one example. The advantage and disadvantage of this is that the environment is really a finished product; the inhabitants do not affect it and so the model manages to be definitive, immutable and appears consistent in appearance, which, however, is at odds with objects that change over time through fashion, fate or neglect.

As Meister (1998) notes in his discussion of temples, in order to understand the value of a building to the culture that builds and maintains it, we need to understand how people interact with it. For early virtual heritage projects (see, for example, the case studies in Barceló et al. (2000)), static computer models may prove suitable for education purposes when an archaeologist or local expert is a guide, yet the information and the discursive content becomes entrenched when viewed by a solitary audience.

Game designers may also be led to believe that games using historical characters, events or settings are readily adaptable and immediately appropriate to virtual heritage, but there are fundamental conceptual issues that are still to be addressed. To what extent is the past more or less important or retrievable than history and how is it attainable through interaction (as otherwise there is little point to using virtual environments)? One answer may be adopting virtual reality to represent the past or online digital worlds to represent the future, but it is still too easy to be taken in by the lure of technology and forget to concentrate on enhancing the user experience. For example, many have made the case for using game engines for virtual heritage projects (Stone, 2005; Lucey-Roper, 2006; Bottino and Martina, 2010).

Being much easier to upgrade, install and replace, the most popular form of virtual environment is now arguably the computer game (Trenholme and Smith, 2008). Current game consoles and desktop computers rival the supercomputers of just a decade ago in terms of power and performance. Games have context (user-based tasks), navigation reminders, inventories, records of interaction history (i.e. damage to the surroundings), social agency and levels of personalization. Games are a familiar medium to users (Petty, 2007; Cuenca López and Martín Cáceres, 2010) and, when in game mode, abstraction can be just as engaging to users as a sense of realism.

Games also form part of cultural learning and how to follow social rules, or learn about physical rules of the world, without risking personal injury (Miller, 1991; Petty, 2007). We socially learn (by stories and commands), we learn by observation (observing cause and effect, emulation and by imitation) and we learn by play (puzzles, toys and games). There are undoubtedly certain pedagogical techniques that virtual heritage environments can learn from game design. Yet, despite the rich detailing of environments, agents and artefacts, three-dimensional adventure games do not have a rich sense of cultural immersion. While this is not true for all games, the typical goal in adventure games is to collect artefacts in order to vanquish others. Social interaction is limited to violence, time spent on reflection is punished and we do not develop any feeling for the perspectives of the local inhabitants as their actions are typically 'fight or flight'.

Without a huge amount of time spent in a virtual environment, it is also doubtful that our cultural and social view of the environment will change very much. In order to think in another language and to be immediately accepted by others, we have to immerse ourselves in the actual context over a long period of time – long enough to learn from trial and error. So there are significant design challenges for virtual heritage environments, to portray accurate yet believable content, to provide appropriate yet meaningful interaction, and to link both content and interaction leading to significant and useful knowledge in an abridged time period.

We still have not truly grasped the native potential of interactive digital media as it may augment some form of experiencing of history, and that is why debate on the conceptual albeit thorny issues of the subject matter is still in its infancy. Perhaps there are specific needs or requirements of history that prevent us from relying on digital media and 'online worlds' experts? Is it perhaps not that the new tools are currently too cumbersome or unreliable, but instead that it is our conventional understanding of history and teaching history that needs to change? If we avoid teaching with digital media, how will the changing attention spans and learning patterns of new generations be addressed? To what extent is the past more or less important or retrievable than history and how is it attainable through interaction (as otherwise there is little point to using digital media)?

One answer may be to adopt game to represent the past or online digital worlds to represent the future, but it is often tempting to focus on the aesthetic quality of the game or concentrate on showcasing the new and improved features of the technology. While even archaeologists and technical experts have warned against an over-emphasis on technical developments, we still lack solid test cases that attempt to both build and test virtual heritage projects for the end user.

Meaningful Interaction is Meaningful Learning

In the following chapters, I will examine issues of rituals and role-playing, and violence, but I will make the controversial suggestion that there are not many developed examples of virtual heritage projects addressing these issues because such projects typically do not have advanced thematic interaction. And I am not alone in this view – Maria Roussou decried the current state of meaningful interaction and learning in virtual reality (2005, p. 94):

> To summarize, VR projects developed for museums or other, research-based educational VR studies have either not provided the analytical evidence to demonstrate learning or, where an educational impact was perceived, there is no explanation of how and why. And more importantly, the role of interactivity within learning has not been the focus of any of the evaluations carried out. Hence, the research question that emerges is how interactivity in a virtual learning environment can influence learning.

Whether cultural presence is transmitted via reading a palimpsest or by participating on a social stage, one must bear in mind that it can be perceived from the outside (etic cultural presence) or lived from the inside (emic cultural presence). Interaction is crucial in the creation of culture and, by extension, in the understanding of culture.

Games have the ability to synthesize narrative, conjecture, computer-generated objects, contextually constrained goals, real-time dynamic data and user-based feedback (Mateas and Stern, 2003). Through this interactive richness (rather than through a high-tech ability to reproduce elements of the real world), people can both learn and enjoy alterity (experience of the 'other'). In a virtual heritage environment, the more one can master local cultural behaviour, the more one can understand significant events from the local cultural perspective. Mastery of dialogue and artefact use, as viewed from a local cultural perspective, may lead to enhanced cultural immersion and may consequently lead to a heightened sense of engagement.

Is it useful, desirable or even possible to interact with digital reconstructions of different cultures in a meaningful way? Could interaction actually interfere with the learning process? According to Black (2001), research has suggested that children desire interaction and personalization in museum exhibits, but others have suggested that successful cases of 'edutainment' are far too rare (Papert, 1998).

If we do manage to create an engaging and believable virtual environment, will the novelty or entertainment value actually interfere with the cultural understanding gained by the users? Sceptics may argue that an attempt to make the experience engaging by looking at game design hinders the cultural learning experience, damages actual historical learning and creates a false sense of authenticity. It is also possible that attempting to create contextual affordances and constraints will put too heavy a cognitive load on the audience or require a high degree of skill and a large amount of time immersed in a virtual environment. In virtual heritage environments, this is particularly evident in the conflict between individual freedom to explore and the more pragmatic need to convey historical information. For example, we may create an entertaining game, yet, however entertaining that game may be, will it allow us to convey the varying levels of historical accuracy that archaeologists have sourced in order to reconstruct the past?

Do we have concrete examples of meaningful interaction in virtual heritage environments? According to the few existing user studies, so far this area is still too undeveloped (Mosaker, 2001; Roussou, 2005; Pujol Tost and Economou, 2006; Rodriguez-Echavarria et al., 2007). The ethnographic techniques used by researchers may be effective in recording activity, but they do not directly indicate the potential mental transformations of perspective that result from being subjectively immersed in a different type of cultural environment (Roberts-Smith et al., 2013). How can users learn via interaction the meanings and values of others – do we need to interact as the original inhabitants did? How can we find out how they interacted and, through the limited and constraining nature of current technology, ensure that interaction is meaningful, educational and enjoyable? How do we know when meaningful learning is reached?

Figure 5.2 is a picture of a VR project designed to involve students in Renaissance science and travel diaries (Carrozzino et al., 2013). The project was run by the Gunnerus Library of Trondheim, Norway, the Norwegian University of Science and Technology (Norway) and Scuola Superiore Sant'Anna (Italy). The collaborators in the project wished to explore ICT in museum education, particularly to see how historic manuscripts from the sixteenth and seventeenth centuries could convey knowledge through interactivity, without damaging the originals. They created an augmented 3D book, where objects appear to pop out of the page, an 'Information Landscape' and a VR display so that participants could view and share a digital simulation of the books. The relevant aspect to this discussion is that the project did not stop at digital displays; the participants perform experiments in the real world after visiting the digital environments. The collaborators in the MUBIL project are now examining gaming environments for the next stage of research.

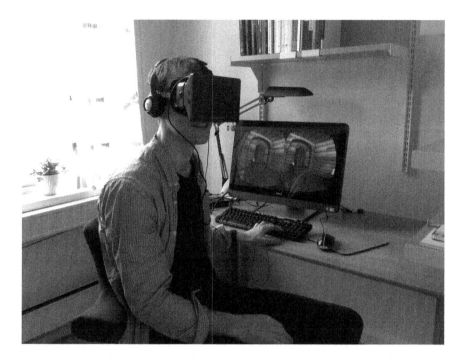

Figure 5.2   MUBIL, Gunnerus Library of Trondheim, Norway
Source: Alexandra Angeletaki

A very simple rule of thumb to uncover whether a game or virtual environment helps a meaningful learning experience is to ask, based on the data available, what do you want or expect the audience to learn? Which interaction method best achieves this? Does the resulting simulation add a new perspective that would be more difficult to design and deliver in other media? How can this new knowledge be used, communicated and transferred beyond the game? Does the knowledge also help uncover the process by which the original data was first interpreted or does it help the audience (students and teachers, the general public and scholars) to critique the ways in which this knowledge is typically presented and experienced?

Would a socially situated role help the audience understand how the place is inhabited and experienced? For example, a warrior might learn about weapon features, landscape advantages and disadvantages, a command system, wayfinding or the privileges of ranks. A thief might also learn about hiding places, but also about where people go and when, when they are on guard and where valuables are stored. A druid might learn about the cultivation of herbs, astronomy, medicine, etc. A merchant might need to learn about artefacts, the value of objects, certain ways of counting, the location of valuable items, barter methods, trade distances, dangers, foreign language and appropriate behaviour, optimal travel routes, etc.

The challenge is to match the knowledge to be provided with the interaction suitable to both the game and the audience.

In Chapter 2 I tabulated common interaction modes in commercial game franchises, and in this chapter I will extrapolate possible interaction modes as observation, detection, puzzle-solving, trade, combat, mimicry (attempting to imitate local behaviour), strategy, resource management, counter-factual history, role-playing, performance (performing with games and outside of games to an audience), social mash-up games and mind-control games (attempting to control inhabitants or opponents). These modes are not mutually exclusive; a game may feature several of these as game mechanics. To improve the meaningfulness of these games and simulations, I suggest we need to emphasize the situated uniqueness of the ways in which the simulated past was inhabited, and the ways in which that place had a special significance and cultural meaning to the original inhabitants.

Another interesting issue in game-based learning is in research into whether computer games can add to or will only detract from the student attention span. There is a school of thought in archaeology which disregards the learning capabilities of digital media, seeing visualization as purely a façade or even a distraction for the serious and scholarly pastime of reading and writing books (Parry, 2005). Yet if we avoid teaching with digital media, how will the changing attention spans and learning patterns of new generations be best addressed (Mehegan, 2007)?

There are many important, perhaps even critical problems in using computer game technology and conventions for virtual heritage environments. Some academics worry about the violence in many computer games or the time they take away from other pursuits (Yee, 2006). Others do not believe they test the appropriate cognitive skills. I am also concerned that game-style interaction is typically destructive and not conducive to developing either cultural awareness or an appreciation of the preservation of objects and the cultural values of others.

Yet cultural knowledge itself (as a 'cognitive map') is intimately concerned with ad hoc, procedural, vague yet constructionist-based knowledge acquisition (Renfrew and Zubrow, 1994), which is also a typical feature of game-based learning (Malone, 1982; Johnson, 2005). Further, the gaming media of today have succeeded in engaging current generations far more than the promises of traditional VR equipment or the first few versions of Virtual Reality Modeling Language (VRML). I believe that if we continually test and modify interactive digital media to both the content being portrayed and the requirements of the intended audience rather than treating the audience as akin to subject matter experts, then most of these issues can be solved.

Collaboration

Bonnie Smith stated that there has been confusion between history as meaning the past and history as being something produced by historians (Smith, 1995). Skeates (2000) has warned that in terms of heritage management, archaeologists need to reconsider their field as a communication medium and not just as a closed scientific discipline.

I suggest that archaeologists consider virtual environments and related digital media not as a rival to books or to conferences, but as a communication tool that can also gather feedback information from the general public and disseminate the processes and not just the findings of archaeological research. How can we learn (via digital interaction) about the meanings and values of others – do we need to interact as they once did? How can we find out how they interacted and through the limited and constraining nature of current technology help interaction be meaningful, educational and enjoyable?

Current types of learning about heritage and history in games seem to still be relatively limited in terms of interaction. In projects that I am involved with, I ask students to consider the meaningful space and interaction patterns that the expected users will work with. Peripherals taken from commercial games, visualization devices such as projections onto spherical mirrors, 3D joysticks and sensors all help to break down the traditional screen-based barrier between user and content, and create environments which appear bounded not just physically but also socially.

We continually explore both game genres and ways in which history and oral traditions are shared in order to attempt new genres that transcend typical aim-and-shoot game genres. This can be difficult for my students, as they have spent years learning how to play games and develop game genre patterns that help them quickly learn how to play new games. I am currently exploring new ways of creating interactive challenges and I believe that one way forward is AI that weeds out imposters (human users) who attempt to infiltrate a site by mimicking social roles, which I will discuss in Chapter 8.

Evaluation

Evaluating cultural learning is also problematic (Champion and Sekiguchi, 2005), so we have looked at using biosensors and brain scanning in tandem with traditional survey questionnaires to gain feedback on what does and does not work. Another option is to adapt digital exercise machines and build tracking devices into tangible interfaces that track individual user preferences and allow the experiences to be shared between individual users and a wider audience (Dourish, 2001).

Even if we decide on what we are evaluating, it is not clear how to evaluate. The ethnographic techniques used by researchers may be effective in recording activity, but they do not directly indicate the potential mental transformations of perspective that result from being subjectively immersed in a different type of cultural presence (Benford and Fraser, 2002).

Real-world tests will not necessarily be of help in assessing heritage reconstructions, unless the virtual experience is supposed to tally as accurately as possible with a given and accessible real-world experience of that culture. This is a problem if the real culture being simulated no longer exists in one place or at the current time, or if the cultural knowledge is fragmented or only circulated amongst experts and not amongst the general public.

This leads us to the thorny issue of how to evaluate such a concept. We could use questionnaires, we could test the ability of participants to extrapolate general cultural rules or other information and apply them to other heritage sites, and we could test whether participants could detect other players or non-playing characters that appeared to belong to or not belong to the resident culture. We could also test for engagement using questionnaires by recording physiological data or by testing the memory recall of the participants. A further option is to give users tasks to complete and then record their performance. A word of warning: this testing only records their technical proficiency and not necessarily their cultural understanding.

Applicable research requires continual evaluation via shared tools amongst a body of scholars who agree on suitable goals and methods. To achieve this ongoing research activity, the content to be examined must be clearly understood and capable of further analysis. Interaction in a virtual heritage environment requires suitable and appropriate context that communicates the meaning not just of objects but also between objects and their creators.

It is easier to quantify technical advances and to secure funding to do so, but the mission of virtual heritage is to communicate cultural knowledge rather than merely to show it. This may be why we currently have little evidence as to whether virtual heritage environments can afford useful and unique ways for augmenting and evoking awareness and understanding of distant places and foreign cultures.

Cultural meaning arises from situated interaction with a culturally significant setting. To disseminate this understanding, it is preferable to provide situations where the participant is not only immersed but is also given the opportunity to engage with culturally specific tasks, roles and challenges. Critical research needs to be undertaken on the specific abilities of digital media to aid engagement, understanding and awareness of other cultures. Education, funology and digital media are not extensively evaluated in combination, but they should be. Evaluation requires definitions, guidelines (heuristics) and dependent variables that can be tested. The results of this evaluation must then be effectively communicated to designers so that they in turn can effectively transmit cultural information digitally to a varied audience. Designers need to understand exactly what cultural information is and how to best communicate it digitally (Mulholland and Collins, 2002).

I would further add that the designer should deliberately evoke a sense of cultural presence. However, we do not have agreed definitions of cultural presence (I have defined it as a perceived encounter with digitally simulated cultural agency) and designers do not have clear ideas as to which factors most aid cultural presence, cultural learning, and both procedural and discursive archaeological knowledge.

In order to improve the transfer of cultural significance, I suggest that subject matter experts or domain experts, such as archaeologists and anthropologists, reconsider not only the technical but also the conceptual features of commercial and open-source computer games. Important features of games include the ability to learn through testing and exploring, the capacity to personalize, annotate and add content, and the ability of games to *challenge* people to complete tasks and try out new strategies, techniques and identities (Johnson, 2005; Boellstorff, 2006).

I would also ask subject matter experts to consider that their expertise may blind them to the immediate needs of the public. Subject matter experts may already know the facts, hypotheses and conjecture as to what was there, what was seen, what was believed, what was done and what was valued. However, the public needs to learn this, but also to develop the desire to learn this knowledge. They will not have the same incentive to read the background information necessary to judge the authenticity and appropriateness of virtual heritage projects. They need to experience and appreciate before they can judge.

Summary

There is a shortage of research integrating theory and practice on how best to augment or invoke the user experience of place via digital media. This is perhaps partly because meaningful interaction likewise requires suitable and engaging interactive context, while experimental testing requires set and clearly defined content.

The above chapter has listed six major issues. I have argued that the way in which data is captured and recorded does not always convey the processes, decisions and values inherent in the act itself. And how this information is to be presented raises issues of what is authentic and how to convey the accuracy or assumptions without losing or misleading the public. We also need to improve the accessibility of these projects to the public. This means that we need to consider the ways in which different audiences learn. If possible, we should invite the audience to debate, participate in and contribute to the ongoing project in order both to educate the public and to maintain the project, and to ensure both its usefulness and its longevity through improved methods of collaboration. However, how we evaluate these projects raises a myriad of interesting challenges.

Archaeological and architectural digital simulations have traditionally been concerned with the exact replication of facts rather than with understanding, for the latter raises the annoying dilemma of how to present scientific uncertainty. A computer model almost invariably implies certainty, which suggests to the viewer that it has faithfully and accurately replicated the 'facts'. Until recently, accurate digital simulations of historically uncertain or controversial findings were left unquestioned. Nonetheless, there are educational and scientific dangers in many current computer simulations that are based on apparent mimetic certainty and not on the cultural agency that informs understanding.

To clarify these issues, we could design and evaluate according to a simple classification of virtual heritage environments. The first type of environment surrounds and orientates us (spatial presence), the second directs us towards activities (allows us to do things) and the third identifies and embodies us or allows us to interpret the cultural perspective of others (is hermeneutic). Ideally, the third type of environment allows us to recognize, understand and become (it transforms our worldview), but it is hard to see how it can work in practice, especially if human experts or trained guides are not available.

There is also the option of classifying by game mechanics, by platform, by content or by audience. Unfortunately, the range of data, potential audience and supporting technology is dynamic, vast and highly content-specific. I have also briefly mentioned issues in the use of game engines and game genres; engagement versus learning and interaction versus historical accuracy are key concerns (Dondlinger, 2007).

For various reasons, evaluation of the learning inside virtual heritage environments has been relatively context-free and is not designed for user understanding of other cultures. Technology can overwhelm the content, especially when the knowledge driving the virtual simulation is incomplete, complex or contradictory, and the continual need for technology research funding can actually impede research of the content rather than develop it.

If virtual heritage has as its aim to educate and engage the general public on the culture of the original site, cultural artefacts, oral traditions and artworks, then the field needs to advance not only due to technology, but also in philosophical and creative ways, especially with regard to the issues of realism, interaction, evaluation and ownership.

References

Addison, A. 2000. Emerging Trends in Virtual Heritage. *MultiMedia, IEEE*, 7, 22–25.

Addison, A., Refsland, S. and Stone, R. 2006. Special Issue: Virtual Heritage Guest Editors' Introduction. *Presence: Teleoperators & Virtual Environments*, 15, iii–iv.

Agnew, J. 1999. Place and Politics in Post-war Italy. In K. Anderson and F. Gale (eds), *Cultural Geographies*. Melbourne: Addison Wesley.

Anderson, E.F., Mcloughlin, L., Liarokapis, F., Peters, C., Petridis, P. and Freitas, S. 2010. Developing Serious Games for Cultural Heritage: A State-of-the-Art Review. *Virtual Reality*, 14, 255–275.

Anderson, M. 2003. Computer Games & Archaeological Reconstruction: The Low Cost VR, Enter the Past. *CAA 2003 – Enter the Past + Workshop 8 – Archäologie und Computer Conference*, Vienna.

Anderson, M.L. 1997. Introduction. In K. Jones-Garmil (ed.), *The Wired Museum*. Washington DC: American Association of Museums, 11–34.

Australia Icomos Incorporated 2013. The Burra Charter, The Australia ICOMOS Charter for Places of Cultural Significance.

Barceló, J.A., Forte, M. and Sanders, D.H. (eds) 2000. *Virtual Reality in Archaeology Computer Applications and Quantitative Methods in Archaeology*. Oxford: Archaeopress.

Bellotti, F., Berta, R., De Gloria, A., D'ursi, A. and Fiore, V. 2013. A Serious Game Model for Cultural Heritage. *Journal on Computing and Cultural Heritage*, 5, 1–27.

Bellotti, F., Berta, R., De Gloria, A., Panizza, G. and Primavera, L. 2009. Designing Cultural Heritage Contents for Serious Virtual Worlds. *15th International Conference on Virtual Systems and Multimedia, VSMM'09*, 9–12 September, 227–231.

Benford, S. and Fraser, M.E.A. 2002. Staging and Evaluating Public Performances as an Approach to CVE Research. *Proceedings of the 4th International Conference on Collaborative Virtual Environments*. Bonn: ACM Press.

Black, G. 2001. Whats, Whys and Whos of Concept Design. In S. Drummond and Y. Ian (eds), *Quality Issues in Heritage Visitor Attractions*. Oxford: Butterworth Heinemann, 100–120.

Boellstorff, T. 2006. A Ludicrous Discipline? Ethnography and Game Studies. *Games and Culture*, 1, 29–35.

Bottino, A. and Martina, A. 2010. The Role of Computer Games Industry and Open Source Philosophy in the Creation of Affordable Virtual Heritage Solutions. In M.J. Er (ed.), *New Trends in Technologies: Devices, Computer, Communication and Industrial Systems*. Online: InTech.

Bourdieu, P. 1984. *Distinction: A Social Critique of the Judgement of Taste*. Cambridge, MA: Harvard University Press.

Brennan, S. 2012. Getting to the Stuff: Digital Cultural Heritage Collections, Absence, and Memory. *Lot 49*. Available at: http://www.lotfortynine. org/2012/11/getting-to-the-stuff-digital-cultural-heritage-collections-absence-and-memory.

Carrozzino, M., Evangelista, C., Bergamasco, M., Belli, M. and Angeletaki, A. 2013. Information Landscapes for the Communication of Ancient Manuscripts Heritage. In A.C. Addison, L. De Luca, G. Guidi and S. Pescarin (eds), *Digital Heritage International Congress (DigitalHeritage)*, 28 October–1 November, Marseile, 257–262.

Champion, E. 2003. Online Exploration of Mayan Culture. In H. Thwaites (ed.), *VSMM 2003 Conference*. Montreal: IOS Press, 364–373.

——. 2004. Indiana Jones and the Joystick of Doom: Understanding the Past via Computer Games. *Traffic*, 47–65.

——. 2005a. Cultural Presence. In S. Dasgupta (ed.), *Encyclopedia of Virtual Communities and Technologies*. George Washington University, Hershey, PA: Idea Group.

——. 2005b. What is Culture in A Virtual Heritage Environment? *Proceedings Cultural Heritage and New Technologies-Workshop 10 Archaeology and Computer*. Workshop 10 Archaeology and Computer, Vienna, Austria.

——. (ed.) 2012. *Game Mods: Design, Theory and Criticism*. Pittsburgh: ETC. Press.

——. 2014a. History and Heritage in Virtual Worlds. In M. Grimshaw (ed.), *The Oxford Handbook of Virtuality*. Oxford: Oxford University Press, 269–283.

——. 2014b. Researchers as Infrastructure. In C. Mills, M. Pidd and E. Ward (eds), *Digital Humanities Congress 2012 Proceedings*. Humanities Research Instiute, University of Sheffield.

Champion, E. and Dave, B. 2007. Dialing up the Past. In F. Cameron and S. Kenderdine (eds), *Theorizing Digital Cultural Heritage: A Critical Discourse*. Cambridge, MA: MIT Press, 333–348.

Champion, E. and Sekiguchi, S. 2005. Suggestions for new features to support collaborative learning in virtual worlds. *C5: The Third International Conference on Creating, Connecting and Collaborating through Computing*, 28–29 January, Shiran Kaikan, Kyoto University, Japan. Published in *Third International Conference on Creating, Connecting and Collaborating through Computing*. IEEE Computer Society Press, 127–134.

Chen, S., Pan, Z., Zhang, M. and Shen, H. 2013. A Case Study of User Immersion-Based Systematic Design for Serious Heritage Games. *Multimedia Tools and Applications*, 62, 633–658.

Christiansen, P. 2013. Capricious Fate: Videogames as Tools for Moral Instruction. Available at: http://www.playthepast.org/?p=4221.

Crang, M. 1998. *Cultural Geography*. London: Routledge.

Cuenca López, J.M. and Martín Cáceres, M.J. 2010. Virtual Games in Social Science Education. *Computers & Education*, 55, 1336–1345.

Denard, H. 2009. The London Charter for the Computer-Based Visualisation of Cultural Heritage. London.

Dondlinger, M.J. 2007. Educational Video Games Design: A Review of the Literature. *Journal of Applied Education Technology*, 4, 21–31.

Dourish, P. 2001. *Where the Action is: The Foundations of Embodied Interaction*. Cambridge, MA: MIT Press.

Dreyfus, H.L. 2001. *On the Internet (Thinking in Action)*. New York: Routledge.

Eiteljorg, H. 1998. Photorealistic Visualizations May Be too Good. *CSA Newsletter,* XI.

Falk, J.H. and Dierking, L.D. 2004. *Learning from Museums: Visitor Experiences and the Making of Meaning*. Walnut Creek, CA, AltaMira Press.

Gaver, W.W., Bowers, J., Boucher, A., Gellerson, H., Pennington, S., Schmidt, A., Steed, A., Villars, N. and Walker, B. 2004. The Drift Table: Designing for Ludic Engagement. *CHI'04 Extended Abstracts on Human Factors in Computing Systems*. ACM, 885–900.

Germanchis, T., Cartwright, W. and Pettit, C. 2007. Virtual Queenscliff: A Computer Game Approach for Depicting Geography. In W. Cartwright, M.P. Peterson and G. Gartner (eds), *Multimedia Cartography*, 2nd edn. New York: Springer, 359–368.

Gillings, M. and Goodrick, G. 1996. Sensuous and Reflexive GIS: Exploring Visualisation and VRML. *Internet Archaeology*. Available at: http://intarch.ac.uk/journal/issue1.

Girard, C., Ecalle, J. and Magnan, A. 2013. Serious Games as New Educational Tools: How Effective are They? A Meta-analysis of Recent Studies. *Journal of Computer Assisted Learning*, 29, 207–219.

Graham, S. 2010. My Glorious Failure. *Play the Past.* Available at: http://www. playthepast.org/?p=352.

Grow, G.O. 1991. Teaching Learners to Be Self-directed. *Adult Education Quarterly*, 41, 125–149.

Hein, G.E. 1991. Constructivist Learning Theory. In the Museum and the Needs of People. *CECA (International Committee of Museum Educators) Conference.* Jerusalem.

Hodder, I. 1995. *Theory and Practice in Archaeology.* London: Routledge.

Howard, P. 2003. *Heritage: Management, Interpretation, Identity.* New York: Continuum.

——. 1993. The Temporality of the Landscape. *World Archaeology*, 25, 152–174.

Ingold, T. 2000. *The Perception of the Environment: Essays on Livelihood, Dwelling and Skill.* Abingdon: Psychology Press.

Jacobson, J., Handron, K. and Holden, L. 2009. Narrative and Content Combine in a Learning Game for Virtual Heritage. *Computer Applications in Archaeology.* Williamsburg, VA.

Jenks, C. 1993. *Culture.* London: Routledge.

Johnson, S. 2005. *Everything Bad is Good for You: How Popular Culture is Making Us Smarter.* London: Allen Lane.

Kalay, Y. and Marx, J. 2001. Architecture and the Internet: Designing Places in Cyberspace. In W. Jabi (ed.), *Proceedings of ACADIA 2001: Reinventing the Discourse.* ACADIA, 230–240.

Kensek, K., Dodd, L.S. and Cipolla, N. 2002. Fantastic Reconstructions or Reconstructions of the Fantastic? Tracking and Presenting Ambiguity, Alternatives, and Documentation in Virtual Worlds. In G. Proctor (ed.), *ACADIA 2002: Thresholds between Physical and Virtual Conference.* Pomona, CA: ACADIA, 293–306.

Kontogianni, G., Georgopoulos, A., Saraga, N., Alexandraki, E. and Tsogka, K. 2013. 3D Virtual Reconstruction of the Middle Stoa in the Athens Ancient Agora. *ISPRS-International Archives of the Photogrammetry, Remote Sensing and Spatial Information Sciences*, 1, 125–131.

Kosara, R. 2007. Visualization Criticism – The Missing Link between Information Visualization and Art. *11th International Conference on Information Visualisation (IV)*, 631–636.

Leader-Elliott, L. 2003. Community Heritage Interpretation Games: A Case Study from Angaston, South Australia. *International Journal of Heritage Studies*, 11, 161–171.

Lercari, N., Forte, M. and Onsurez, L. 2013. Multimodal Reconstruction of Landscape in Serious Games for Heritage: An Insight on the Creation of Fort Ross Virtual Warehouse Serious Game. In A.C. Addison, G. Guidi, L. De Luca and S. Pescarin (eds), *Digital Heritage International Congress*, October. Marseille: IEE Press, 231–238.

Lercari, N., Toffalori, E., Spigarolo, M. and Onsurez, L. 2011. Virtual Heritage in the Cloud: New Perspectives for the Virtual Museum of Bologna. *Proceedings*

of the 12th International Conference on Virtual Reality, Archaeology and
Cultural Heritage. Prato, Italy: Eurographics Association.

Lock, G. 2009. Archaeological Computing Then and Now: Theory and Practice,
Intentions and Tensions. *Archeologia e Calcolatori*, 75–84.

Lucey-Roper, M. 2006. Discover Babylon: Creating a Vivid User Experience
by Exploiting Features of Video Games and Uniting Museum and Library
Collections. In J. Trant and D. Bearman (eds), *Museums and the Web 2006:
Proceedings, 1 March 2006.* Toronto: Archives and Museum Informatics.

Malone, T.W. 1982. Heuristics for Designing Enjoyable User Interfaces: Lessons
from Computer Games. *Proceedings of the 1982 Conference on Human factors
in Computing Systems.* ACM, 63–68.

Mateas, M. and Stern, A. 2003. Façade: An Experiment in Building a Fully-
Realized Interactive Drama. *Game Developers Conference*, 4–8.

Mccall, J. 2011. *Gaming the Past: Using Video Games to Teach Secondary History.*
New York: Routledge.

McCormick, B., Defanti, T. and Brown, M. 1987. Visualization in Scientific
Computing. *Computer Graphics*, 21(6).

Mehegan, D. 2007. Young People Reading a Lot Less: Report Laments the Social
Costs. *The Boston Globe*, 19 November. Available at: http://www.boston.com/
news/nation/articles/2007/11/19/young_people_reading_a_lot_less

Meister, M.W. 1998. The Getty Project: Self-preservation and the Life of Temples.
ACSAA Symposium. Charleston, SC.

Meyers, K. 2012. Dealing with Multiple Narratives of Truth and Creating
Meaningful Play. *Playing the Past.* Available at: http://www.playthepast.org/?
s=dealing+with+multiple+narratives&x=0&y=0.

Mikovec, Z., Slavik, P. and Zara, J. 2009. Cultural Heritage, User Interfaces and
Serious Games at CTU Prague. Virtual Systems and Multimedia, 2009. *15th
International Conference on VSMM'09*, 9–12 September, 211–216.

Miller, G.L. 1991. *Approaches to Material Culture Research for Historical
Archaeologists: A Reader from Historical Archaeology.* Germantown, MD:
Society for Historical Archaeology.

Mitchell, W.L., Economou, D., Pettifer, S.R. and West, A.J. 2000. Choosing and
Using a Driving Problem for CVE Technology Development. *Proceedings
of the ACM Symposium on Virtual Reality Software and Technology.* ACM,
16–24.

Mosaker, L. 2001. Visualizing Historical Knowledge Using VR Technology.
Digital Creativity, 12, 15–26.

Mulholland, P. and Collins, T. 2002. Using Digital Narratives to Support the
Collaborative Learning and Exploration of Cultural Heritage. *Porceedings of
the 13th International Workshop onDatabase and Expert Systems Applications.*
IEEE, 527–531.

Ott, M. and Pozzi, F. 2011. Towards a New Era for Cultural Heritage Education:
Discussing the Role of ICT. *Computers in Human Behavior*, 27, 1365–1371.

Papagiannakis, G., Schertenleib, S., O'Kennedy, B., Areval-Poizat, M., Magnenat-Thalmann, N., Stoddart, A. and Thalmann, D. 2005. Mixing Virtual and Real Scenes in the Site of Ancient Pompeii. *Computer Animation and Virtual Worlds*, 16, 11–24.

Papert, S. 1998. Does Easy Do it? Children, Games, and Learning. *Game Developer, 'Soapbox' Section*, 88.

Parry, R. 2005. Digital Heritage and the Rise of Theory in Museum Computing. *Museum Management and Curatorship*, 20, 333–348.

Petty, A. 2007. Discovering Babylon: The Opportunities, Challenges and Irresistible Potential of Video Games as an Educational Medium. *SBL Forum*. Available at: http://sbl-site.org/Article.aspx?ArticleID=672.

Pujol Tost, L. and Economou, M. 2006. Evaluating the Social Context of ICT Applications in Museum Exhibitions. In D. Arnold, M. Ioannides, F. Niccolucci and K. Mania (eds), *VAST: International Symposium on Virtual Reality, Archaeology and Intelligent Cultural Heritage*. Crete: Eurographics, 219–228.

Renfrew, C. and Zubrow, E.B. 1994. *The Ancient Mind: Elements of Cognitive Archaeology*. Cambridge: Cambridge University Press.

Roberts-Smith, J., Ruecker, S., Gabriele, S., Rodriguez-Arenas, O., Ruecker, S., Sinclair, S., Desouza-Coelho, S., Kovacs, A. and So, D. 2013. Visualising Theatre Historiography: Judith Thompson's White Biting Dog (1984 and 2011) in the Simulated Environment for Theatre (SET). *Digital Studies/Le champ numérique*, 3.

Rodriguez-Echavarria, K., Morris, D., Moore, C., Arnold, D., Glauert, J. and Jennings, V. 2007. Developing Effective Interfaces for Cultural Heritage 3D Immersive Environments. In D. Arnold, F. Niccolucci and A. Chalmers (eds), *Proceedings of the 8th International Conference on Virtual Reality, Archaeology and Intelligent Cultural Heritage*. Brighton: Eurographics Association, 93–99.

Rosenzweig, R. 1998. Afterthoughts: Everyone a Historian. Available at: http://chnm.gmu.edu/survey/afterroy.html.

Rosenzweig, R. and Thelen, D. 1998a. Introduction: Scenes from a Survey. Available at: http://chnm.gmu.edu/survey/intro.html.

——. 1998b. *The Presence of the Past: Popular Uses of History in American Life*. New York: Columbia University Press.

Roussou, M. 2002. Virtual Heritage: From the Research Lab to the Broad Public. In F. Niccolucci (ed.), *Virtual Archaeology: Proceedings of the VAST 2000 Euroconference. Arezzo, Italy*. ACM Press, 93–100.

——. 2005. Can Interactivity in Virtual Environments Enable Conceptual Learning? *7th Virtual Reality International Conference (VRIC)*, First International VR-Learning Seminar, Laval, France, 57–64.

Roussou, M. and Drettakis, G. 2005. Can VR Be Useful and Usable in Real-World Contexts? Observations from the Application and Evaluation of VR in Realistic Usage Conditions. *HCI International 2005 Conference*, First International Conference on Virtual Reality, Las Vegas, Nevada. CD-ROM.

Shackley, M. 2001. *Managing Sacred Sites: Service Provision and Visitor Experience.* New York: Continuum.

Sheldon, K. and Biddle, B. 1998. Standards, Accountability, and School Reform: Perils and Pitfalls. *Teachers College Record*, 100, 164–180.

Skeates, R. 2000. *Debating the Archaeological Heritage.* London: Duckworth.

Slater, M. 1999. Measuring Presence: A Response to the Witmer and Singer Questionnaire. *Presence: Teleoperators and Virtual Environments*, 8, 560–566.

Smith, B. 1985. Art Objects and Historical Usage. In I. McBryde (ed.), *Who Owns the Past? Papers from the Annual Symposium of the Australian Academy of the Humanities.* Melbourne: Oxford University Press, 74–85.

Smith, B.G. 1995. Whose Truth, Whose History? *Journal of the History of Ideas*, 56, 661–668.

Stone, R. 2009. Serious Games: Virtual Reality's Second Coming? *Virtual Reality*, 13, 1–2.

Stone, R. and Ojika, T. 2000. Virtual Heritage: What Next? *Multimedia, IEEE*, 7, 73–74.

Stone, R.J. 2005. Serious Gaming – Virtual Reality's Saviour? *VSMM 2005 Conference.* Ename, Belgium, 773–786.

Tost, L.P. and Champion, E. 2011. Evaluating Presence in Cultural Heritage Projects. *International Journal of Heritage Studies*, 18, 83–102.

Trenholme, D. and Smith, S.P. 2008. Computer Game Engines for Developing First-Person Virtual Environments. *Virtual Reality*, 12, 181–187.

Tuan, Y.-F. 1992. Place and Culture Analeptic for Individuality and the World's Difference. In W. Franklin and M. Steiner (eds), *Mapping American Culture.* Iowa City: University of Iowa, 27–53.

——. 1998. *Escapism.* Baltimore: John Hopkins University Press.

UNESCO. 2003. *Convention for the Safeguarding of the Intangible Cultural Heritage.* Available at: http://unesdoc.unesco.org/images/0013/001325/132540e.pdf.

Wattrell, E. 2010. Project Diary Red Land/Black Land. *Playthepast*, 15 December.

Wei, T. and Li, Y. 2010. Design of Educational Game: A Literature Review. In Z. Pan, A. Cheok, W. Müller, X. Zhang and K. Wong (eds), *Transactions on Edutainment IV.* Berlin: Springer, 266–276.

Wilmot, E. 1985. The Dragon Principle. In L. McBryde (ed.), *Who Owns the Past? Papers from the Annual Symposium of the Australian Academy of the Humanities.* Melbourne: Oxford University Press, 41–48.

World Heritage Centre. 2014. *The Criteria for Selection.* UNESCO World Heritage Centre, United Nations. Available at: http://whc.unesco.org/en/criteria.

Yee, N. 2006. The Labor of Fun: How Video Games Blur the Boundaries of Work and Play. *Games and Culture*, 68–71.

Zuk, T., Carpendale, S. and Glanzman, W.D. 2005. Visualizing Temporal Uncertainty in 3D Virtual Reconstructions. *Proceedings of the 6th International conference on Virtual Reality, Archaeology and Intelligent Cultural Heritage.* Eurographics Association, 99–106.

Chapter 6
Worlds, Roles and Rituals

Huizinga once famously described games as being bounded by magic circles: they are 'temporary worlds within the ordinary world, dedicated to the performance of an act apart' (1955, p. 10). Single-player games are now powerful enough to convey the impression of shared worlds with social presence and social agency. Unfortunately, there are few clear definitions of 'world' as it applies to commercial computer games or as it could be used to help improve these games. In *Playing with the Past* (Champion, 2010), I explored a simple framework for defining virtual worlds. Here I will apply my earlier simple framework to 'Elder Scrolls IV: Oblivion' in terms of phenomenological, social and cultural aspects.

Even though it is a single-player game, several key features allow 'Oblivion' to be considered as a social world. Despite these promising features, 'Oblivion' fails as a rich cultural world. It can be further improved as a social world and perhaps even as a cultural world through various techniques. I will provide some ideas as to how future mods and games in the Elder Scrolls series could be improved, but despite graphics and interface/interaction improvements, 'Elder Scrolls V: Skyrim' and the related online multiplayer game 'Elder Scrolls Online' (http://elderscrollsonline.com/en-uk) do not seem to be using these ideas – or at least not yet.

Role-Playing and Cultural Learning

Role-playing is both an important part of cultural learning (Hallford and Hallford, 2001) and an important genre in computer games (Tychsen, 2006). Roles are intrinsically related to the notion of social worlds, yet the mechanics of this relationship are not clear in the academic literature. There are few grounded theories in computer game studies on how role-playing works in sustaining and augmenting a thematic world. There are few clear descriptions of what 'world' means in this context and how roles, worlds and rituals are interrelated. Further, distinctions between social and cultural dimensions of both roles and worlds are seldom elaborated upon.

For historical simulations and virtual heritage projects, the cultural and social dimensions of both real-world and virtual-world playing are important, and commercial computer role-playing games (CRPGs) *seem to* offer more opportunities to support deeper cultural aspects of role-playing. Can 'deeper' notions of culture be conveyed through a deeper understanding of worlds, roles and rituals? My second aim is to examine the relation of cultural identity to ownership and social purpose, and how role-playing can be more fully and richly rounded out by computer-simulated gameplay.

I note in passing that my framework is simpler than but congruent to Mark Wolf's (2014) criteria for imaginary worlds: completeness; consistency; immersion, absorption and saturation; world gestation (ellipsis, logic and extrapolation), which is similar to the concept of apophenia; 'catalysts of speculation' (deliberate gaps of knowledge to provoke discussion so that the 'secondary world' is a popular and ongoing source of conversation); and connections and borders between the primary (real) world and the secondary (imaginary) world.

Worlds Inside Computer Games

Can a single-player computer game evoke the sense of a social or cultural world? Critics have focused on multiplayer social worlds, not single-player hybrid CRPGs. However, as an example of a single-player CRPG, 'Elder Scrolls IV: Oblivion' has much to offer in the interrelationship of world and player, and it has further potential in the simulation and affordance of social interaction, communal identity and cultural learning.

Single-player games are now powerful enough to convey the impression of shared worlds with social presence and social agency. Unfortunately, there are few clear definitions of 'world' as it applies to commercial computer games or as it could be used to foster improvements in these games. This is particularly significant for role-playing games and, again, what 'role-playing' means is seldom clarified. If one aspect of 'world' is how it offers up opportunities to individuals, then if virtual 'worlds' are currently only designed with spatial and social affirmances in mind, the actual role-playing of CRPGs will be severely impacted.

Roles and Virtual Worlds

In the web article 'GNS and Other Matters of Roleplaying Theory', Ron Edwards (2010) wrote:

> When a person engages in role-playing, or prepares to do so, he or she relies on imagining and utilizing the following: Character, System, Setting, Situation, and Color. Character is a fictional person or entity. System is 'a means by which in-game events are determined to occur'. Setting is 'where the character is, in the broadest sense (including history as well as location)'. Situation is a problem or circumstance faced by the character and color means 'any details or illustrations or nuances that provide atmosphere'.

As the real world allows roles to be transfigured, expanded, overtaken or replaced, so should game worlds. Critics have mentioned that roles in role-playing games are typically mere affordances and that the games do not involve genuine role-playing (Tychsen, 2006). What then are the features and dimensions of real-world roles and role-playing? I suggest that social roles in our real world do more than distinguish individuals, provide individual purpose in life or divide up responsibilities according to capabilities and political acumen. While it is true that roles are purposeful and goal-based and that they create and demarcate social identities, they also have a component of cultural curation (preserving and transmitting elements of social mores and values), while allowing for evolution and personalization.

Apart perhaps from the term 'cultural curation' (which I will expand upon later), this may seem self-evident. I would argue against this, as I suggest that the cultural rather than merely social aspects of roles and role-playing have been downplayed, to the immersive and engaging detriment of CRPGs in general and to a potential use as cultural learning environments in particular. In game studies and virtual environment research, 'culture' and 'society' are two terms that have been used interchangeably, and the term 'world' has been used loosely, while one important if often hidden aspect of 'world' (to afford, structure and separate personal decision making) has been downplayed or neglected.

The term 'world' has been used as if it is self-explanatory in many recent papers and publications (Darken and Silbert, 1996; Okada et al., 2001; Celentano and Nodari, 2004; Ondrejka, 2006). Even in a book entitled *Designing Virtual Worlds*, Bartle (2003) avoids a detailed definition of what is a 'virtual world'. Klastrup (2002) also points out the difficulty in clearly defining the phrase, while Ondrejka (2006) appears to see a virtual world as being a persistent virtual environment, that is, elements affected by a user are remembered and kept even when the user exits the world. However, this also describes an online database.

In what sense these virtual environments move beyond 'cyberspace' towards 'place' is not clear (Johnson, 2005). A world in this context can mean it allows for different ways of doing things or perceiving things (virtual environments typically do not have many options for expressive interaction). Johnson (2005) and Steinkuehler (2006) have also argued that current massive multiplayer game environments are typically a mixture of vague and clear objectives; people immerse themselves not merely by spatially navigating from point A to point B, but also by exploring the environment as a shifting world of possibility.

Second, a game world could have worldliness in terms of its social aspects. In such a game, the player may be able to or be forced to choose between a range of self-identifying livelihoods and positions that make it possible to develop and maintain social skills and status (Herold, 2006). Or a player could be rewarded or punished depending on how well they interact with other players or imitate appropriate social behaviour.

Third, a game world may involve learning how to translate and disseminate, or even modify or create the language or material value systems of real or digitally simulated inhabitants. In this situation, the gameplay hinges on how well culturally appropriate information can be learnt and developed by the player or passed on to others. 'Worldliness' in this sense is to what extent the virtual environment or game can store, display and retrieve information on the encounters of people in places.

In a similar vein, Hocking (Ruberg, 2007) has suggested that people explore spatially, explore the game-system or use the game to explore their own identity, values or inner conflicts. The first sense is aesthetic and the third is perhaps phenomenological and more externally related than it may first appear. The issue here is the daily conflict between our experiential sense of selfhood and the demands and surprises of the wider world.

How does this tie in with role-playing? The three broad aspects of 'worlds' have corollaries in role-playing. In full role-play and in richly explorative worlds, the player experiences a varied and rich gamut of choices, meaningful decisions and complex consequences. Not only is there a possible selection of various roles, there is some degree of freedom in terms of how one interprets and performs that role. So a world made for role-playing should capture some of that freedom of choice, individuality and complex fate. An important part of role-play is role-selection, and a world rich in such affordances would allow a multitude of possible paths.

The second aspect of a world tailor-made for role-play is its ability to adopt, adapt, fuse or fight the social identity and position of various roles in relation to others. Roles are social and while they are designed by society to avoid conflict (where everyone knows their place), they somehow create more conflict. The vaguely shared understandings of roles often create dissent and sometimes lead to open conflict. Roles are continually socially defined and their parameters are continually re-interpreted, identified with or identified against. As such, the polemical tendencies of real-world RPGs that Tychsen et al. (2005) have considered a weakness I consider to be a strength, for the conflicts between players and the game master are remembered and reflected upon, not the roll of the die. And there is the potential for social conflict between my perceived role and my role (and fitness for that role) as perceived by others.

The third aspect of a world tailor-made for role-play is not so obvious and it is the impetus for my writing this chapter. I suggest that in role-play, not only are we negotiating our interpretation of the role against practical everyday issues, not only are we interpreting and communicating roles in terms of others around us, but as role-players we are also acting as curators of tradition, for role-playing allows society to carry forward its goals, values, structure and messages.

In fulfilling a role, we are given some responsibility in filling out that role, consolidating the important parts through habit and ritual, and ignoring accidental features. The way in which society is preserved and passed on is due in no small manner to the way in which roles are interpreted, inhabited and disseminated by the role 'keepers'. So, in a sense, role-play is curatorial; we choose which aspects of culture are worth keeping and the rest of the information we discard. In the next section I will give an example (using a currently popular CRPG) of why distinguishing between cultural and social aspects of virtual world design is important.

The Environmental Aspects of 'World'

In *Playing with the Past* (Champion, 2010), I discussed the notion of 'extern'. An extern has been defined as 'phenomena that arise independently of people, like sunlight and clouds, wild plants and animals, rocks and minerals, and landforms' (Schiffer and Miller, 1999). Externs are larger environment objects and processes, but they are not human-created. This is a useful term as interaction in a virtual environment seldom makes the distinction between that inherent in the environment and that triggered by a user.

Extern does not only have relevance to archaeology. The notion of extern can be both an aesthetic and a phenomenological issue. In terms of aesthetics, encountering externs in a virtual world may evoke a sense of awe and wonder. Such an effect could happen independently of people or events. The size, scale and inevitability of simulated externs as aspects of 'world' may cause us to stop and reflect on how the mundane small details of our lives can or should mesh with the world beyond. Ideally, a virtual world would contain moments where it can either transfix us through its aesthetic qualities or cause us to question and reflect on our existence and relation to the world.

The Social Aspects of 'World'

Society defines who we are, how we communicate and the values that we strive towards. In Wittgenstein's *Private Language Argument* (Wittgenstein, 1963), sometimes rephrased as the Robinson Crusoe example, he imagines a human born alone on a desert island. Could that person develop his or her own private language? If this person was abandoned at birth on a deserted island, without defined rules or human contact, he or she is unlikely to attempt self-expression through modification or collection of any artefacts left from the wreckage of past civilizations. So, society is necessary for culture to take place. Adherence to cultural rules is ultimately socially governed, for without social motivation, culture is merely a pile of objects.

It is the acceptance or condemnation of other people in a society that separates social behaviour from individual habits. Even on a desert island, a human who was once part of society would endeavour to live according to his or her social upbringing, perhaps because these behaviours are so fully ingrained or perhaps in case he or she hoped to be eventually rescued and reunited with human society. Humans seek social affirmation. Human culture stores, expresses and disseminates the values and identities that help mediate social behaviour even if other social agents are not currently present. Perhaps that is why – and here I am recalling the philosopher Georg Wilhelm Friedrich Hegel – we as a species have medals. Medals are artefacts that represent the recognition of others.

In games we have reward systems that reflect medals, awards and social respect, but in single-player computer games we typically cannot gain the social recognition of others. Deliberately or subconsciously moderating one's external behaviour in response to or in anticipation of the opinions or actions of others while in a computer game is a sign that it is functioning as a social world. However, without social recognition, a single-player game is less likely to bind the player to social rules or laws, as players do not have social affirmation or condemnation to guide their social behaviour. We could also argue that a single-player game is less likely to compel a rich, expansive and creative experiencing of cultural learning and behaviour, as there is no sentient audience to act as cultural arbiters.

I have written about this definition before, but it is worth repeating (Kroeber and Kluckhohn, 1952, p. 357):

> Culture consists of patterns, explicit and implicit, of and for behaviour acquired and transmitted by symbols, constituting the distinctive achievement of human groups, including their embodiment in artefacts; the essential core of culture consists of traditional (i.e. historically derived and selected) ideas and especially their attached values; culture systems may on the one hand be considered as products of action, on the other as conditioning elements of further action.

An important point in the above quote is that culture is not simply passive, but it is also a storehouse of values, aspirations and identities. Culture can be viewed as being a material embodiment of social structure, mediating the relation between the individual and the community, and expressing (as well as protecting) the sacred from the profane. Culture also provides instructions on how habits can become intrinsically meaningful and socially ordered through the practice of ritual (Dornan, 2007). Role-play is thus curatorial: we choose which aspects of culture are worth keeping and the rest of the information we discard.

In many papers, articles and blogs that focus on virtual environments and game worlds, I see a worrying conflation between the cultural and the social. In presence research, for example, an important thread is to understand social presence in virtual environments. However, much of the literature that has 'culture' in the title does not clearly distinguish cultural presence from social presence (Riva et al., 2002; Schroeder, 2002; Bartle, 2003; Riva et al., 2004; Rozak, 2006a; Rozak, 2006b). The archaeologist Laia Pujol and I have commented on this conflation (Pujol and Champion, 2012).

It is not clear whether we can say that social presence is a group of people aware of each other while in a virtual environment (or computer game), because the general and more specific meaning of a society is that people who belong to it have shared values, beliefs and/or identity. Even if social presence means the feeling that another sentient human being is in the same virtual environment and is capable of social interaction or at least capable of displaying social behaviour, this does not mean that social presence corresponds directly to cultural presence. An example would be people in an Internet-based chat room; they may well be experiencing human co-presence, but they will not be experiencing a strong sense or level of cultural presence.

People create culture, but it can exist in some form without the creators. So I suspect that we can gain a sense of cultural presence without experiencing explicit social presence. To quote Agnew (1999, p. 90): 'all people live in cultural worlds that are made and re-made through their everyday activities'. Even though we live in cultural worlds, this does not mean that we fully understand them. If a virtual environment or computer game contains a collection of artefacts that can be observed, interpreted or understood as a coherent materialization by intelligent beings of a shared social system, this may be considered passive cultural presence. We can see culture, but we either cannot participate in it or with it due to a lack of culturally constrained creative understanding or because the originators have long since passed away.

Crang argues that culture is a collection of 'sets of beliefs or values that give meaning to ways of life and produce (and are reproduced through) material and symbolic forms' (Crang, 1998, p. 57). Crang extended Sauer's early writings and remarked that landscape is a palimpsest, and proposes that culture is spatially and temporally embedded. Culture is both an intangible connection and rejection of perceived patterns over space and time. How cultures are spread over space and how cultures make sense of space are interdependent. A visitor perceives space as place, place 'perpetuates culture' (frames it, embeds it and erodes it) and thus influences the inhabitant.

If we view archaeology as a 'kind of spatial text that varies from reader to reader' (Tringham, 1994, p. 172), we can entertain the prospect that there may also be more than one group of originators. Their interactions could have left cultural traces of their 'micro-scale' (to paraphrase Ruth Tringham) life-worlds in the game environment. Any premise that visitors require other real people in the virtual environment in order to feel cultural presence is thus problematic. Cultural presence, albeit in a weakened form, is thus possible in the absence of social presence. This is important for designers who wish to convey a sense of cultural presence but do not have the technology to simulate believable and authentic non-playing characters (NPCs) and avatars as cultural agents.

While place modifies culture, culture is heavily affected by society – it is socially created, defined and managed. Culture is expressed via language, sounds and artefacts, physical objects that decay, and so culture is vaguely bounded, open to interpretation and liable to shift over time due to both the vagueness of its boundaries and the fragility of shared memories. To demarcate the boundaries of culture clearly and accurately is thus highly problematic.

Being able to observe a distinct cultural presence does not necessarily indicate that a great amount of cultural learning has taken place. In order to evaluate the effectiveness of cultural learning, there needs to be a measure of the cultural 'immersivity' of a virtual environment. For want of a better term, I suggest hermeneutic richness, the depth and vividness of a medium that allows for the interpretation of different cultural and social perspectives as judged from an emic or etic viewpoint.

Hermeneutic richness does not mean photo-realism or social presence. If cultural presence is a measure of how deeply a cultural force is perceived to imprint or ingrain itself on its surroundings, hermeneutic richness may be the depth of affordance that a virtual environment gives to the interpretation of a natively residing culture in that virtual environment. The ability of an artefact to convey a sense of that creator's agency is a reflection of its 'hermeneutic richness' (akin to the archaeological notion of the 'trace'). The perceived sense of that creator's agency through an artefact is itself cultural agency, for an artefact is itself a cipher – a mark of cultural agency.

In order to evoke cultural learning of a historical nature, this passive 'hermeneutic richness' is the elusive and intangible quality one should aspire towards. Hermeneutic richness also exists in two distinct ways. On the one hand, this type of virtual environment might act as a symbolically projected identity, dynamically customized by us as the visitor to reflect our social and individual values and outlook. On the other hand, a virtual environment might be hermeneutic when it affords meaningful interpretations of its shareholders (clients and subjects) to those that visit it.

For example, many fantasy role-playing games portray previous cultures or cultural beliefs, whether real or imaginary. The games may feature named characters, treasure, 3D objects, goals and so forth, but they often lack distinctly cultural places, and this is perhaps because there are no identifiers as to how to behave in another culture.

Role-playing Games as Virtual Worlds

It may appear that computer games do not afford a sense of cultural presence unless they are multiplayer environments that allow human players to create and leave artefacts that represent their cultural perspectives. The computer game 'Oblivion' has encouraged me to change some of my views on the paucity of inhabited social or cultural worlds, despite its single-player nature and some gameplay shortcomings. I count at least half-a-dozen features of lived-world creation not common to most computer games, but I have suggestions on how to also further improve them in order to create the illusion of 'Oblivion' becoming not just a social world, but also a cultural one.

Environmental Presence

Rozak has written on the careful balancing of procedural and hand-designed objects that form the 'Oblivion' landscape (Rozak, 2006a; Rozak, 2006b; Nareyek, 2007). In terms of how a physical sense of world is afforded, 'Oblivion' features animals ranging from butterflies to bears, sheep and deer that graze and move independently of the player, and plants that grow back seasonally after being picked by the player.

The flora also appears to have a geophysical relationship to the landscape. There are also attempts to symbolically convey colder, hotter or more humid microclimates. Rain, fog and changes between night and day are major aspects of the landscape, and are done so well that independent game designers have remarked that they have travelled the virtual landscape purely to watch sunsets (Ruberg, 2007).

Hocking is correct that 'Oblivion' affords a rich sense of 'self-motivated exploration' and that there is also the sense of physical immersion. One can drown, be burnt, frozen or electrocuted, due to extreme climates, bodies of water, hidden traps or the weapons of enemies (humans, demons, monsters and animals). There are several avatar animations to learn beyond the typical game mechanics of aiming and strafing, such as sitting, special movements with weapons, opening locks, and shifting between first- and third-person viewpoints (with the added vanity option of circling one's own avatar via a third-person camera). The skin, facial features, age, gender, body shape, race, profession, birth sign and other aspects of the avatar can be chosen and changed while in the first level of the game, but with one notable exception (being transformed into a vampire), these features are fixed after level 1.

Objects can be picked up and collected or stored (or even transferred to NPCs), and they weigh down the avatar in terms of speed. Heavier objects make noise when they move or fall down steep inclines or are accidentally knocked from tables, and the heavier the object picked up, the more likely it is that a player is spotted. NPCs can be bumped out of the way, but can also hear or see people in good conditions within a certain range. So the sensory and spatially explorative aspects of the game are powerful and rich, but 'Oblivion' seems to struggle with the second type of world, the social one – it lacks expressive agents (Mateas, 2003).

Social Presence

However, there are both resolvable and less resolvable social presence issues and limitations with 'Oblivion'. There are a few minor glitches. The monsters level up with players, the dialogue dialects do not appear related to the races or towns, and the same character can have different voices for different dialogues. Even so, there are major design areas where 'Oblivion' can be more engaging and enriched as a game world (if not as a game), namely, through player embodiment, object possession, social stigma, persuasive interaction and gossip.

The first striking social behaviour feature of 'Oblivion' is that of constricted and automatic gaze-directed physical co-presence. The player and inhabitants automatically have their gaze directed towards each other within a certain sight-range and their bodies twist (even when seated) to look at you. This is a form of alterity, otherness, but also awareness of this otherness.

In a genuine RPG, the player is more of a puppet master. Perhaps there could be an option allowing the player's avatar (the hero) to take on common player actions and decisions as default behaviour. The game could also allow the hero to become more self-directed when enchanted or tired, or become more self-directed when the situation is directly related to the quest, and the player has been single-minded in solving quests one by one rather than by skipping between them at various stages of completion.

Being more accustomed to online virtual environments that lack this automatic head following of other avatars, I initially found this technique conveyed a powerful sense of presence, but it begins to lose its impact with ongoing familiarization. In the current version, the default head movement seems to be a universally standard convention. If head movement and speed were tied to the excitement level of the NPC, this might better express individual character development and heighten the dramatic tension. The alacrity, speed of movement and range of movement could be related directly to the health of the player's avatar or to its stamina, or to how many enemies have recently attacked it. Conversely, actions such as fighting and spellcasting currently require deliberate action on the part of the player, which means that the player's avatar is really a three-dimensional placeholder.

I remarked above that the player's avatar, the hero (although anti-hero or villain can also be chosen), also has a default head swivel when NPCs walk past. This is useful to remind the player of other avatars in the area, but it could also be more expressively tied into the gameplay. As the hero can act slightly independently of the player (upon entering a room, the hero automatically glances at other people), why not, when the hero is enchanted or for some other situational or event-based reason, increase the auto-behaviour of the hero independently of the player's intentions? Perhaps unknown animations or skills of the hero could be triggered when passing near certain key objects, phobias or environmental conditions, or would this break immersion?

There are character attributes that help the hero to sneak past hostile NPCs, depending on what they are wearing, the size of any object being picked up and how dark it is. The detection factor is apparently directly related to how observant the NPCs individually are, but this factor could be enriched by also considering how much the hero is carrying and how reflective their armour is. Interestingly, the hero can increase their sneak skill, but only when NPCs are nearby, and the hero's sneak skill also increases with successful pick pocketing (Anonymous, 2006).

Sneaking is one of the most polished of the game mechanics in 'Oblivion', so I am only suggesting a slight modification. If the hero could create diversions and deflections while sneaking and if the music could gradually change (slow down or stop playing), this might also add to the sneaking experience. When people sneak in real life, their relative speed is so slow that everything in fast motion appears even quicker; perhaps game engines could also make use of this psychological phenomenon. As an aside, if moving quietly underwater, perhaps breathing could slow down if the swimmer moves very slowly.

The AI can also be modified, dramatizing the NPCs' spatially triggered and event-held adherence to perceived feelings of possession and privacy, and the ways in which they react in terms of physical action and facial expression to the hero, history and appearance. For example, when you (as the hero) enter a house, especially if you have picked the lock, the NPC may run towards you and tell you to leave. Unfortunately, the possessive behaviour of the NPCs seems hard-coded; so far as I can see, there are no interesting variants or hero-related variables to this behaviour, and NPCs do not seem worried about the hero making a mess or eating fruit or affecting other objects.

Although rooms have many artefacts that can be moved, picked up, pick-pocketed or stolen, the ways in which they are handled is not satisfactory. For example, a hero can enter a smithery or armourer's workshop and bump into everything, which then falls on the floor. Despite all the ensuing noise, the inhabitant (a trader, smith or armourer) appears to remain oblivious to this accidental or deliberate vandalism of their shop. The artefacts are usually just empty props (although carrying them can slow down the player's character or augment the character's attributes).

The player can also buy a house in many of the towns, but cannot lock it. Dynamic vandalism by the NPCs would, however, create an interesting dilemma for players who like to both hoard artefacts and to wander. The player can just drop objects and then return to them later. Nobody steals the player's possessions even though the towns and the Imperial City are full of thieves and beggars, and bandits roam the countryside.

In the guide to 'Oblivion' (Bethesda Softworks, 2006), the player is warned that unsheathing a weapon can draw a hostile social reception from the NPCs, but I only managed a few scowls from the guards – it did not seem to affect gameplay. Although NPCs automatically watch the hero walking past, the type of clothing or armour the hero chooses to wear (with one exception – Necromancer robes) does not draw attention (although 'Skyrim', the next version of the game, does feature NPCs telling any barely clothed avatar to dress properly). Hence, a hero in nothing but a loincloth can walk into a church with no comments from the local clergy.

If a hero exits from the sewers under the Imperial City or has not slept for many days, there are no adverse comments from the NPCs. Since 'Oblivion' has quests where environmental extremes such as frost and fire can affect the hero, and as one of the hero's character attributes is their charm, it seems remiss not to have a 'cleanliness to uncleanliness' feature. The appearance of the human player only draws distinctive NPC responses in extreme cases, such as when the player is wittingly or unwittingly turned into a vampire (many NPCs refuse to trade or converse if this happens). Conjuring also creates a few comments from NPCs, but does not seem to affect gameplay.

The NPCs may have information that would help a human player solve a quest, but they need to be charmed or bribed to feel friendly enough towards the player before they will divulge this information. Many players have criticized this feature for being clunky and breaking the player's immersion. Although the idea is good, the implementation (at least on the PC) is let down by the ugliness of the procedural facial animation and by the non-intuitiveness of the spinning 'bribe wheel' (this is my term and is not used by the game).

We don't see our own avatar, there is no body language and the psychological mapping of the interface is unnatural. Perhaps if there were interfaces allowing players to guess the timing of jokes via breath or pitch or stress on individual words, this would appear more realistic. The NPC's face could lean forward or backwards, or the sound of their breathing could change as we coaxed, bribed or joked with them. To gauge bribes on the appearance, race or professional class of the NPC, how close NPCs are to guards or the shabbiness of the area the NPC is currently in may also help to improve the believability. 'Oblivion' lacks emotionally expressive avatars; such avatars, according to Fabri et al. (2002) and Mateas (2003), augment social immersion.

The NPCs wander around on their own daily and weekly 'beats' (paths) (Fabri et al., 2002), but they also meet up and talk to each other. I emphasized talk to rather than talk with, as it becomes very clear to the player that this chatting shows itself to be monologues randomly set and rarely reveals meaningful information to the hero. Along with more appropriate tips on the loading screens, the gossip could be more dynamically adjusted to the progress and developing back story of the hero.

As the player has many options in developing their hero's attributes, the game could track the personalization tendencies of the player and offer helpful hints. For example, if the player tends to level up via agility rather than via luck, the NPCs could drop hints as to where agility-enhancing quests or artefacts are located. As 'Oblivion' is hampered by the NPCs having set voices, perhaps there could be NPC travelling bards who mimic both the information and the voices of people they have met, the NPCs could talk in their sleep or in a trance (i.e. while possessed by spirits), or the information could be written down as fading overlaid notes on top of books (although now we are approaching a notion of a cultural world).

Cultural Presence

'Oblivion' does not meet my requirements for a cultural world. Part of the blame may lie with the points system. Evolving from the traditional RPG game, the points system may make sense for such clear and measurable qualities such as strength or speed, but it starts to lose believability in terms of intelligence and personality and seems downright foolhardy in terms of varying races and cultures. For example, there are references to past histories (that could be told by or for any race), and while NPCs make references to racial or cultural characteristics, the differences between the races (or species) seem to be merely how many more points they tend to have in specific character attributes.

NPCs remember failure or success of individual quests, but the actions of the player do not really impact on the main world (apart from the main quest). Because there are no real cultural affinities to landscape or to artefacts, and as the races are found in the same towns and ruins, cultural differences primarily show up in character animations, scales and weaknesses to frost or fire. Despite being a fantasy similar in genre to, say, the epic *The Lord of the Rings* by Tolkien, 'Oblivion' does not open up the sense of a self-supporting cultural world. It does not make us believe that the races have a perceived cultural destiny, that knowledge is lost to them or that it is protected, or that they each speak dialects or idiolects or share symbols that are incomprehensible or alien to other cultures.

The other potential cultural aspect of 'Oblivion' is as an explored library. The many books found throughout the settlements and ruins are really for entertainment purposes only; although they occasionally provide tactical advice, they do not really expose the inner workings of different cultural values or ideals. As the game engine uses dynamic three-dimensional modelling and texturing as well as shader-generated screenshots, it would have been possible to create graphic overlays over the books that dynamically personalize them with the quests or physical appearance of the player's avatar.

I can, however, give one example of real-world-related cultural knowledge. One can learn how to pick flowers, plants and mushrooms in order to create potions with varying effects. Each type of plant will cease to exist if picked incorrectly (each plant differs in its 'picking spot', which is typically the stem, edge or centre). As specific plants are required for certain potions (which may in turn be required by specific quests), learning to identify the correct plants and how and where to collect them becomes an acquired skill. If there were social challenges where the hero was quizzed on which ingredients are which (say, in order to advance in the Mages guild), this could add to the depth of the game.

Unfortunately but understandably, 'Oblivion' already has so many options that it does not force the player to learn all the correct symbols; the player only needs to know how to access the menu. If there was an option to force the player to learn symbols in order to survive (a form of 'twitch knowledge'), this might add to the feeling that genuine skill and knowledge are developed by immersion in the game.

Early virtual environments and early virtual worlds were considered sterile and empty. 'The Elder Scrolls IV: Oblivion' is superior to its predecessor, 'The Elder Scrolls III: Morrowind', in fleshing out a simulated sensorial environment featuring both procedural and handmade texturing (Rozak, 2006b). This richness of place qualia is not only due to the detailed NPCs, buildings and artefacts, but also to the rich and dynamic environmental processes that occur independently of the player (such as climate, weather, flora and fauna). In the sense of a world as a meta-set of environmental externs, 'Oblivion' is very impressive.

Second, 'Oblivion' also appears to be a rich social world in terms of the way in which the NPCs appear to exist independently of the player and the player quests, through their daily rituals and a sense of property ownership, but also in terms of how they glance or look at the player. 'Oblivion' also features social conversation, sneaking, target maps, inspiration and repel features, automatic close-ups and the ability to pick up and move objects.

Yet 'Oblivion' is arguably weak on role-playing. If we could use Dornan's three criteria (Dornan, 2007) of a good role-playing game (narrative, social and ludic), 'Oblivion' fails on the social criteria. For example, the stories embedded inside books may further remind the player how much social creativity is not actually within the game, the roles and attributes one chooses seem rather arbitrary and independent of the external environment (but not combat situations), and the NPCs that the player deals with only in rare cases affect the player's social standing with others. In short, the actual role-playing is weak.

There are also more technical design flaws. The gossip is not meaningful, the mapping and observation is not subtle, and the bribe-style function is clumsy, but these issues can be resolved. I would further punish players for being careless, for knocking over objects or bumping into NPCs, or for dressing inappropriately.

Until these flaws and omissions are rectified, 'Oblivion' does not go far enough as a social world, let alone as a cultural one. And even if writers such as Rozak (2006a) conflate the cultural and the social, there are important reasons to distinguish between the two. However, its extensive modding ability does at least promise to extend the notion of a virtual world as interconnected socially controlled realms rather than as a static and ubiquitous virtual environment.

Improving Computer Role-playing Games

Books as Power

Fortunately, the next version of the game, 'Elder Scrolls V: Skyrim', does have some interesting new features. Like 'Oblivion', 'Skyrim' features books containing minor narratives to help gameplay. Librarians also play an important part in the meta-narratives and minor quests, as does a certain dragon archivist. These books can be stored or traded, but now they can also be modded via the game's 'Creation Kit'. The game can be modded and videos can be inserted as cutscenes, but the books can also feature new text and the text can be automatically read by new voices. Here are some ideas for using the new book modding tools in 'Skyrim'.

Books can become gameplay keys: when collected together, text from books adds to map information or provides more abilities or gateways to different places (portals). Books can also double as triggers: the designer or player could place books to trigger specific events.

Books could also be created from text fragments. The fragments might need to be found and placed together in the right sequence for the entire book to appear. It is also possible to import RSS feeds as images (PNGs). Books could be collected and used to train NPCs: by opening books to specific pages, certain events or other forms of knowledge could be communicated to the NPCs.

There could also be a version of the memetic drift idea that was discussed in Chapter 4. The player could be required to trade specific books in order to see a progression of ideas or counterfactual worlds. Perhaps trading specific books affects the NPCs or changes in the cultural dynamics.

Another idea might be that of an augmented story-teller. For example, the player is asked to find flowers and herbs and connections or metals or crafts, and to match these to descriptions that they read in books in the game. With some modifications, the game could add player-created screenshots and movies into the books to create alternative histories, individual travel guides or personal memory collections.

A more complicated idea would be that of author discovery. The player's task might be to find specific book authors. They might be required to match the written dialogue to the spoken language used by NPCs; the authors are hidden in the game as typical NPCs.

Improved Embodiment

'Oblivion' has a mild form of spatial detection – it is possible to be directly behind an NPC and attack repeatedly without being detected, but generally the NPCs find attackers from the direction they were attacked from and they can be bumped from observing special areas without them noticing who bumped them! However, 'Oblivion' lacks a social understanding in this spatial awareness. Social worlds often feature attempts at natural language processing (Perlin, 2005), which understands a player's keyboard-inputted questions and answers. Of course, this misses the tone and stressing of verbal dialogue, but a great deal of real-world social understanding is also acquired through viewing the gestural, facial and postural expressiveness and habits of other members of a community.

In designing a social world, a believable NPC should have some idea of how a human player's avatar feels inside the space, their intentional state and affinity to objects, and how they behave in the space according to their perceived role and social status. Creating a believable emotionally expressive actor (NPC) is difficult (Fabri et al., 2002; Perlin, 2005), but the problem also involves giving the NPC enough information about the player behind the hero character (Perlin, 2005).

If head tracking (via commercially available sensors attached to caps or similar), eye-gaze tracking (via a webcam or similar) and biofeedback data were fed directly into the NPC's AI, the NPC could make more player-related choices. Tracking head movement, gaze direction and perhaps postural changes could allow the NPC more ability to relate directly to the intentional and focused state of the player, and it could also help the ability of the player to mimic roles of NPCs in the game (see below for an elaboration of this point). Luckily, 'Skyrim' can be played with an Xbox Kinect and modifications could allow more subtle gestural actions.

Andrew Dekker and I have also connected biofeedback to games, as I will explain in Chapter 9. Using the 'Source' game engine of 'Half-Life 2' (Dekker and Champion, 2007), we fed galvanic skin response (GSR) from the player into the game to change the zombie spawning and shaders of a horror level mod in direct response to the 'excited' level of a player, which I talk more about in Chapter 9. Using biofeedback creates more problems. One major problem is how best to indicate to the player how their biofeedback affects gameplay. If done well, communicating this biofeedback via NPCs could increase the immersivity of the game and it could also enhance the apparent intelligence of the NPC.

However, this biofeedback should also be communicated indirectly back to the player through triggered or default behaviours of their avatar. Perhaps the avatar becomes jumpy when the player's GSR goes up; perhaps when the player's heartbeat or breathing slows down, their avatar does not visually scan so often. 'Oblivion' and 'Skyrim' allow the player to switch between first-person and third-person view, but biofeedback could automatically override this when the player becomes excited. When music suggests a nearby enemy, the field of view could automatically widen and the view could switch to first person.

Dynamic External Cognitive Artefacts

Sterelny traced the ancestors of the map (cave paintings) back over 30,000 years and in *Playing with the Past* (Champion, 2010), I have outlined his theory that cave paintings are 'specialised epistemic artefacts'. To Sterelny, maps are 'tools for thinking'. This means that maps are epistemic artefacts; they are items that structure our knowledge outside of our minds. They are not just external to us but are also portable, being designed to function as representational resources.

How could a game-based social world use this idea? Consider an 'Oblivion' floor map: it shows where the hero is located and where the quest object or person is (but the mapping system gets confused by different floors). Imagine an overlay of faint footsteps reminding the player where their hero character has looked on previous visits. Perhaps the translucency of floor areas and wall outlines become more opaque the more the player's character has used or approached them. Using biofeedback, maps of pre-visited areas could perhaps have overlay colours relating to the level of excitement the player experienced when last visiting the area.

We could also apply this strategy to artefacts. Boess (2008) has noted that role-playing in design education is greatly helped and augmented by the use of props, while Dornan (2007) has noted the lack of ritual in computer games. It is true that in 'Oblivion', weapons and other artefacts are damaged by continual use or are more effective against certain other artefacts, and their effectiveness is also modified by the skills of the player's avatar. Yet this is not role-playing – how well the player fills or innovates a role does not directly affect the artefacts.

If artefacts were so affected and their time in use, where and how they were used, and against or for certain types of roles were recorded, such an expressed process might help encourage more nuanced and compelling role-play. Consider a multiplayer game where the more-often used artefacts could also have more faded textures; popularity fades the objects in question or conversely makes them more prevalent. For significant quest objects, snapshots of previous encounters could be triggered when the hero picks up the object. With biofeedback, the popular or significant artefact or building could glow according to its popularity or impact on previous players. As for artefacts that are used for rituals, perhaps they could only

Figure 6.1   Oblivion Mod – Nefertari's Quest
Source: Elizabeth Goins

be employed effectively when external conditions are more peaceful (less active) and the hero's speed and gaze direction is slow and consistent.

I note in passing that 'Oblivion' has been used for archaeology and heritage mods. 'Oblivion: Nefertari' used the medieval setting but inserted an Egyptian chamber (Figure 6.1). Goins et al. (2013) have described how they modded the game 'Oblivion' to create the Egyptian simulation 'Nefertari's Quest'. The goal was on 'teaching players how to identify pigments with polarized light microscopy and instrumental analysis'. First, the player has to re-enact the ordeals of Nefertari, as revealed on the walls of the tomb, and then they must 'learn the rules of Senet in the museum library in order to open the tomb'.

Social Role-playing Mimicry

I will expand on this idea in Chapter 8 (and there I will call it a reverse Turing test), but the idea is not new (Champion, 2005). I mention it here as it has specific significance for CRPGs, even though it would require elaborate spatial awareness, hero expressivity and natural language processing. Essentially the idea is to convey cultural knowledge through an impostor-style game where the hero has to adopt, steal or change (via a spell) their appearance and try to infiltrate a local community through effectively imitating certain professions, races or individuals. Unfortunately, 'Oblivion' currently does not clearly and consistently distinguish between NPCs in terms of race, locality, profession or voice, and it would require more spatial awareness to allow for a rich role-playing experience.

Luckily, this may be possible in 'Skyrim', which can be played using an Xbox Kinect, and it can detect some speech commands. Using the Xbox Kinect or a similar interface, it may be possible to teach players a limited vocabulary in order to control the gameplay. For example, an Icelandic saga game could encourage players to learn how to pronounce and project sacred words in order to protect a monastic library from marauders. This type of learning could help not just the player's pronunciation but also improve memory recall and perhaps the appropriate use of words.

Multiplayer Staggered Quests

'Oblivion' is not multiplayer (Bethesda Softworks, 2006) and Bethesda Softworks has stated it will remain that way (Onyett, 2006), but there is a community mod currently allowing two players (and in future up to eight players) to visit the same game world (Paulsen, 2006). There will be a multiplayer online version, but at the time of writing it has not been released. I have not seen the feature list of the new version, but perhaps there could be added staggered quests to increase the sense of a lived-in world with characters that have full social agency. Fans of the game have designed voluntary role-playing activities, so there does appear to be interest in more social role-playing (Agnew, 1999). This may take the burden of believability off the polygonal shoulders of the NPCs. Currently, NPCs are non-questing characters (NQCs), which means that they become far too predictable.

With a quest that is too difficult for one player on a certain level, the quest could allow for the player to wait until another player appears and helps them to solve it, or they might have to wait until another player solves a related quest before they can complete theirs. Or, depending on their race and profession, players could meet other players on different quests. If a player finds that someone else has solved a quest such as stealing a magical stone, perhaps their own quest could then change to bringing back the magical stone.

The solitary player travels through the 'Oblivion' game world, solves quests, perhaps buys houses and fills them with acquired weapons, clothing, books and artefacts, but that is the limit of inhabitation. On the other hand, 'Skyrim' features NPC followers and various mods allow all sorts of new NPC commands.

Another option is the online multiplayer version. I don't know if 'Elder Scrolls Online' offers this, but if there were multiple players entering the game world at different times and engaging in different quests, they could decide to settle in a town, learn a local role and slowly try to fit into the local AI-directed culture. When these 'settled' players discover human-directed characters, they could decide to enrich or divert the human players' world-knowledge or play an elaborate game of confusing them as to whether they are an NPC or not.

Figure 6.2   Egyptian Archaeology Using Morrowind

Humorously, there is a blogger who 'inhabits' rather than plays 'Oblivion'; he has documented his day-to-day existence and his attempts to fit in as an ordinary inhabitant rather than as a player (see http://www.screencuisine.net/aboutlivinginoblivion). He has also undertaken a similar ethnographic task with 'Skyrim' (see http://www.screencuisine.net/the-elder-strolls).

'Skyrim' has also been used to teach concepts of geography (see http://geoskyrim.blogspot.com.au). There have been articles on how to mod 'Skyrim' for history and education (Mummert, 2014) and discussions on the design of archaeology-oriented mods (see http://theskyrimblog.ning.com/group/character-building/forum/topics/character-build-the-archaeologist). It has even been deployed in an American university classroom (Donnelly, 2014) in a course 'aimed predominantly at students interested in psychology, politics, and history'.

Learning Tools

Using 'Elder Scrolls III: Morrowind' (the version of the game that pre-dated 'Oblivion'), a group of students created an archaeological learning tool: the player develops Egyptian god-like powers through exploring and decoding Egyptian hieroglyphs while avoiding the rather grumpy skeletons (Figure 6.2). The four undergraduate students completed the research and design of the temple in six weeks in 2006. The construction set that is included with 'Elder Scrolls V: Skyrim' allows for even more powerful and accessible modding and scripting.

However, to create genuine cultural worlds, such games need to afford the sensation that the NPCs are inscribing the game world with their social agency, or that their social beliefs are made material, or players need to be able to express their socially held beliefs in the game world in a way that is remembered and interpretable.

Potential Criticisms

It could be said that the cultural is but an aspect of the social and hence is not significant in highlighting differences. However, in virtual heritage environments, the lack of cultural presence despite obvious social presence suggests to me that the same issue could affect a rich and deep experience of thematic 'world' as it is experienced through role-playing in a CRPG.

The experience that one is not alone does not logically necessitate that one has the sense of being in a distinct and invigorating culture. When these 'settled' players discover human-directed characters, they could decide to enrich or divert their world-knowledge or play an elaborate game of confusing them as to whether they are an NPC or not.

Second, perhaps using 'Oblivion' as a case study is mistaken; after all, it is not multiplayer. Yet this is what makes its shortcomings and opportunities so interesting. I suggest that even though it is a single-player game, turning it into a multiplayer game does not automatically address the issues that I raised. Yet some features of 'Oblivion' could be easily adopted to help create a sense of 'role' and 'world' as they relate to not just to social identity but also to cultural emergence, while other features are still to be explored, and it is worthwhile doing so. So I am not attempting to review a game; I aim to develop a theory that can be tested against commercial CRPGs, and 'Oblivion' has enough traits of the genre and enough sheer size and scale to act as a test scenario.

That said, I agree that the issue of how a computer can take the place of a human judge is truly difficult (so much of role-play in the real world requires another social agent of human intelligence as judge and co-actor). Yet exploring how a computer program (or a computer game) can act as a social judge is still a bona fide research question (Tychsen et al., 2005), for such an investigation may also illuminate how human actors perform and judge social roles, and which aspects can be simulated or are inimical.

Third, it could be argued that the above theory is not relevant to commercial game developers. Yet if I am correct to suggest that there is a paucity of CRPGs that allow genuine curatorial role-playing, and if curatorial role-play encourages players to remain in the virtual world, surely this is of great benefit to commercial game designers. This aspect of role-play may also help improve gameplay and user testing through the player actively developing and enriching both the features and the challenges of sustaining and establishing social roles.

I also have a second audience in mind: those interested in using games and game editors to immerse and educate students and the public in virtual learning environments. A single-player game has some advantages here – for example, it does not need to worry about students or unwanted visitors distracting other students from authentic situated learning. In addition, it is easier to design, distribute and maintain in relation to specific learning outcomes. 'Oblivion' has a great deal of potential in this regard (Greeff and Lalioti, 2001), especially compared to other commercial games that feature editors. It is relatively straightforward to import 3D assets and to script events, and has a built-in terrain and weather system.

Rituals

At least as far back as 13,000 years ago, our ancestors appeared to have fed the dead or dying a last supper, with specially shaped or laid stones and with plants, food offerings and dedicated flowerbeds (Shapira, 2014). So rituals have been part of human culture for many thousands of years, but how do we know when they are enacted, how do we simulate them and how do we know when they have been performed correctly to an engaged and suitably appreciative audience?

Well there have been several papers about rituals in computer games (Gazzard and Peacock, 2011), but the ones I have read have so far missed the mark. They have been too accommodating, too willing see all personal habit as rituals. Yet rituals do not happen anywhere and everywhere. They are not repeated personal habits. Even if ritual exists on a spectrum with daily habits, there must be some distinguishing features for the term to have any relevance. For example, Roskams et al. (2013) describe ritual objects as 'ceremonial, deliberate, formal, formalised, intentional, non-utilitarian, odd, peculiar, placed, ritual, selected, special, symbolic, token and unusual'. Scott Kilmer (1977) wrote that 'ritual consists of sacred ceremonies and their routines, with the routines being seen as consecrated acts which contain great mystical powers'. He added that rituals contain 'stylized acts' which are adhered to rigidly.

Role-based action in rituals is typically performative and other people often judge the action (but not necessarily during the ritual itself). So a ritual is culturally specific and socially arbitrated. The ritual is typically in a specially designated space, with an introduction ceremony, and attendance is not open to all. While the objects and settings of ritual events can vary enormously, there is typically a sense that rituals can go wrong and that something is lost from society when rituals disappear.

For audience and performer, there may be specific physiological and postural requirements. Mossière (2012), for example, wrote that: 'Various sensorial techniques are used to commit and stimulate the participants' body, senses and spirit.' The head and body are directed; there are conventions on where one can look and for how long. By specific physiological requirements, I mean that that body has to be controlled, directed and time-regulated; it typically has to be set in repose or rhythmically controlled.

The ritual itself may happen on specific dates in specific places for specific events. There could be progression, framed or choreographed against a landscape that thematically relates to the event (such as the deliberately meandering path that leads up to the Acropolis complex of Athens). There needs to be a critical mass of believers. There are demanding levels of attention required from both the spectators and from the performers. The ritual is typically part of a wider system of belief based on mythic causality (the belief that certain actions trigger certain responses at a scale different from the human one). And the ritual is traditional in that it is typically inherited from the past and carries clues as to how it should be performed by future generations.

According to essays inside the edited book *Understanding Religious Rituals* (Hoffmann, 2012), rituals typically frame events. According to essays inside the edited book and proceedings *The Study of Play: Problems and Prospects* (Lancy and Tindall, 1977), mythology requires rituals to communicate their message and importance to the wider group. This book also raises the interesting issue that play must be unstructured. This stipulation creates an interesting tension for game definitions, especially for theorists who believe that games are systems of rules. A particularly interesting essay by Fredericka Oakley (1977) lists five elements of play (for primates):

A reordering of ordinary behavioral sequences

Exaggeration of movements

Repetition of movements or behavioral patterns

Incomplete behavioral sequences, and

Increased tempo in movements

These features of primate play are akin to simple ritual behaviour! The distinction that some theorists make between ritual, game and play may also not be as strong a distinction as they have stated. Extrapolating to humans, the distinction between play and ritual may be not as strong as I had thought; there can be elements of play inside rituals (Kilmer, 1977). For example, in *Religion as Play: Bori, a Friendly 'Witchdoctor'*, Frank Salamone (1977) argued that 'both play and the sacred suggest the game-like quality of socio-cultural life … Play and scared ritual suggest the possibility of change … New games can be played with different rules'. This is an interesting counter-proposal; rituals allow us to see that social structures are flexible and short-lived, but they are also a reminder that if we see games as a system of rules, when we try to simulate cultural activities, we risk losing the anthropological insights into the relationships between rituals, play, games and society.

Rituals do not necessarily share all of the above features, but they are certainly not features of personal habits. And we can see that rituals require more than just physical (or virtual) attendance. They require complicit engagement and adherence and, on the part of the performers, either care, dedications through years of training and/or complete frenzy.

We also seem to have inside our heads an inclination to situate through rituals and habits of going about our daily lives. Tilley (1999) noted that: 'Rituals not only say something, they do something.' Hodder attempts to show how hermeneutics (the study of interpretation, originally of historical texts) could be used in archaeology, and he explains that 'ritual regulates the relationship between people and environment' (1986) and artefacts indicate the shared intentions of their creators.

Place-making is not the capturing of an evocative image of a mysterious temple; it is more the triggering of placeholders, symbols that aid and define our daily activities. A place can also carry cultural indications of inhabitation driven by a cultural perspective similar to or different from our own. So a virtual heritage environment should allow us to see through the eyes of the original inhabitants, or at least feel that this place once belonged to someone else.

Rituals may help us in this endeavour. Rituals aid our memory; they commemorate important cyclic observations, changes in season, tides and constellations. They allow us to connect back to nature and to wider family groups for both symbolic and practical reasons. They can also function as a rite of passage or as social control. Most importantly for our purposes, they are a way of preserving and passing on cultural knowledge.

Yet how does one design for a cultural ritual taking place in a particular cultural place in virtual heritage environments? Digital environments typically lack an in-world social authority or audience to ensure that rituals are practised correctly; participants are not fully physiologically immersed in the digital space; they lack the means to fully teach ritualistic practice; and they also lack reasons and incentives to develop and refine rituals through long-term practice.

There are certain clues in the above paragraphs that might help us use technology to simulate the staging, process and reception of rituals. To ensure that the required people 'are in the moment', we need camera tracking of their faces or gaze detection (or to use head-mounted displays). Camera tracking can also show their posture and level of repose. We could also use biofeedback to keep track of their physiological levels of excitement and calm.

To ensure that performers take care, we can also exaggerate the scene-destroying affordances if their attention wavers. If their avatar moves or looks around too often, perhaps the voice of the performing character becomes muffled. Outside noise becomes apparent and increases in volume, NPCs shuffle away or the screen dims.

To clearly demarcate differences between sacred/ritual space and profane or mundane space, we can transfer the lessons developed in building sacred architecture. There are quite a few historical heuristics in the design of architecture. For example, where movement is required, such as along a path, ornamental design is kept to a minimum. By contrast places of repose (centres) are richly decorated. Create sightlines to line up sacred objects from certain vantage points. Design different textures and apparent cleanliness to demarcate sacred and profane space, as well as to raise and heighten floors and levels and ceiling heights to spatially distinguish between the two. Use symmetry for sacred spaces and asymmetry for functional spaces.

We can program interactive events to only trigger when certain events (such as the passing of cosmological bodies) take place. We can have events, textures and 3D objects triggered or transformed depending on the level of user engagement (determined from gaze detection, head tracking, biofeedback, movements or other behaviours of the avatars). We could also deliberately exaggerate sounds inside certain areas or spaces in order to make the breaking of ritual all the more obvious.

Summary

I have suggested three components of role-play that need to be incorporated into a rich role-playing game and three aspects of virtual worlds that may help enhance role-playing:

- A virtual world should enable freedom of choice and individuality, but also a complex fate. An important part of role-play is role-selection, and a world rich in such affordances would allow a multitude of possible paths.
- A virtual world has the capacity to afford the social jockeying of position. Roles are socially defined, shifting and often challenged by other social agents.
- A virtual world allows us to act as curators of tradition, for role-playing allows society to carry forward its goals, values, structure and messages.

I also suggested three dimensions of presence that all help virtual worlds afford a sense of role-play. With environmental presence, the individual affects and is affected by the outside world. If there is social presence, we affect others in a virtual world. If there is cultural presence, we should be able to detect a distinctly situated sense of inhabitation, of social values and behaviours preserved and transmitted through ritual, artefact and inscription.

Social presence does not necessarily require multiple players (although single-player social presence is definitely much more difficult) and cultural presence does not have to be alive (active). One thing that is required is hermeneutic richness – the depth of interpretation available to understanding oneself or others through artefacts and other cultural remains. Here ritual can play an important part if it does not become too tiresome, if observing and performing it provides in-game benefits, and as long as it does not seem laboured or 'cheesy'.

What of 'Oblivion'? Even though it is a single-player game, several key features allow 'Oblivion' to be considered as a social world. Despite these promising features, 'Oblivion' fails as a rich cultural world. Roles are designed for game-balance, and act more as initial affordances and concrete templates than as social profiles that allow and record differences between social expectations and individual behaviour. In other words, while certain performances can lead to expulsion from guilds, there is little if any curatorial responsibility; roles are really attribute parameters – they are not made, they are followed and maximised.

The later versions of the game ('Elder Scrolls Online' and 'Skyrim') do not yet appear to have addressed these issues apart from featuring enhanced graphics, the ability to control via voice on the Xbox Kinect and the multiplayer nature of 'Elder Scrolls Online'. 'Skyrim' also allows the player to discover preferred skills rather than basing them on racial characteristics, which was how 'Oblivion' chose to set the base individual skills.

So it could be argued that the limitations that I discussed above are the inevitable consequences of single-player computer games. I would counter this by saying that CRPGs in general could be further improved as a social world and perhaps even as a cultural world. The suggestions included enhancing the sense of embodiment, incorporating differences between active and reactive player and hero behaviour (perhaps through biofeedback), creating dynamic cognitive artefacts, allowing for social role mimicry and (if multiplayer) staggered questing. I hope that the issues I have raised will help designers understand how cultural presence is much more difficult to attain than social presence, but that it is a valuable pursuit. In addition, if these issues can be remedied, CRPGs (and their in-game editors) can be employed more effectively as a learning tool for educators in history, heritage and cultural studies.

However, such virtual worlds would not be secondary worlds (imaginary worlds that are separate from our real-world), as defined by Tolkien and expanded on by Mark Wolf (2014). If they are to be more than static models, they must be simulations of the past through present remains, contemporary scholastic imagination and evidence-based hypotheses. These virtual worlds are thus conjectural worlds. As they combine historical situations, conflict, social agents and cultural beliefs, these conjectural worlds require their own ethical dimensions and attention paid to how their story can be told, while engaging the player and contextualising their actions. Morality and narrative will thus be the focus of the next two chapters.

References

Agnew, J. 1999. Place and Politics in Post-war Italy. In K. Anderson and F. Gale (eds), *Cultural Geographies*. Melbourne: Addison Wesley.

Anonymous. 2006. Oblivion: Sneak. Available at: http://www.uesp.net/wiki/Oblivion:Sneak.

Bartle, R. 2003. *Designing Virtual Worlds*. Indianapolis: New Riders.

Bethesda Softworks 2006. The Elder Scrolls IV: Oblivion (Official Game Guide). Roseville: Prima Games.

Boess, S.U. 2008. First Steps in Role Playing. *CHI'08 Extended Abstracts on Human Factors in Computing Systems*, Florence, Italy. ACM, 2017–2024.

Celentano, A. and Nodari, M. 2004. *Adaptive Interaction in Web3D Virtual Worlds. Web3D'04: Proceedings of the Ninth International Conference on 3D Web Technology.* ACM Press, 41–50.

Champion, E. 2005. Interactive Emergent History as a Cultural Turing Test. In M. Mudge, N. Ryan and R. Scopigno (eds), *VAST 2005.* Pisa: Eurographics Publications, 120–125.

———. 2010. *Playing with the Past.* London: Springer.

Crang, M. 1998. *Cultural Geography.* London: Routledge.

Darken, R.P. and Silbert, J.L. 1996. Wayfinding Strategies and Behaviors in Large Virtual Worlds. *Proceedings of the SIGCHI Conference on Human Factors in Computing Systems: Common Ground.* Vancouver: ACM Press, 142–149.

Dekker, A. and Champion, E. 2007. Please Biofeed the Zombies: Enhancing the Gameplay and Display of a Horror Game Using Biofeedback. *DiGRA: Situated Play Conference 2007.* Tokyo, Japan: DiGRA.

Donnelly, J. 2014. How Skyrim is Teaching University Students about the Decline of US Empire. *New Statesman.* Available at: http://www.newstatesman.com/culture/2014/11/how-skyrim-teaching-university-students-about-decline-us-empire.

Dornan, J. 2007. Us Being Human. Available at: http://terranova.blogs.com/terra_nova/2007/02/us_being_human.html

Edwards, R. 2010. GNS and Other Matters of Roleplaying Theory. *The Forge: The Internet Home for Independent Role-Playing Games.* Available at: http://www.indie-rpgs.com/articles/2.

Fabri, M., Moore, D.J. and Hobbes, D.J. 2002 Expressive Agents: Non-verbal Communication in Collaborative Virtual Environments. Embodied Conversational Agents – Let's Specify and Evaluate Them! Workshop in conjunction with the *First International Joint Conference on Autonomous Agents & Multi-agent Systems*, 16 July, Bologna, Italy.

Gazzard, A. and Peacock, A. 2011. Repetition and Ritual Logic in Video Games. *Games and Culture*, 6, 499–512.

Goins, E.S., Egert, C., Phelps, A., Reedy, C. and Kincaid, J. 2013. Modding the Humanities: Experiments in Historic Narratives. *Journal of Interactive Humanities*, 1, 2.

Greeff, M. and Lalioti, V. 2001. Interactive Cultural Experiences Using Virtual Identities. *Proceedings of iCHIM2001*, Politecnico di Milano, Italy, 455–465.

Hallford, N. and Hallford, J. 2001. *Swords & Circuitry: A Designer's Guide to Computer Role Playing Games.* Prima Tech.

Herold, C. 2006. So Many Rackets, So Little Time. Available at: http://www.nytimes.com/2006/04/20/technology/20game.html?ex=1185076800&en=82f426956ef91ac1&ei=5070.

Hodder, I. 1986. *Reading the Past: Current Approaches to Interpretation in Archaeology.* Cambridge: Cambridge University Press.

Hoffmann, J.P. (ed.) 2012. *Understanding Religious Ritual: Theoretical Approaches and Innovations.* Oxford: Routledge.

Huizinga, J. 1955. *Homo Ludens: A Study of the Play Element in Culture*. Boston, MA: Beacon Press.

Johnson, S. 2005. *Everything Bad is Good for You: How Popular Culture is Making Us Smarter*. London: Allen Lane.

Kilmer, S. 1977. Sport as Ritual: A Theoretical Approach. In D.F. Lancy and B.A. Tindall (eds), *The Study of Play: Problems and Prospects: Proceedings of the First Annual Meeting of the Association for the Anthropological Study of Play*, 2nd edn. New York: Leisure Press, 44–49.

Klastrup, L. 2002. Towards a Poetics of Virtual Worlds: Multi-user Textuality and the Emergence of Story. PhD thesis, IT University of Copenhagen.

Kroeber, A. and Kluckhohn, C. 1952. *Culture: A Critical Review of Concepts and Definitions*. New York: Vintage Books.

Lancy, D.F. and Tindall, B.A. (eds) 1977. *The Study of Play: Problems and Prospects: Proceedings of the First Annual Meeting of the Association for the Anthropological Study of Play*, 2nd edn. New York: Leisure Press.

Mateas, M. 2003. Expressive AI: Games and Artificial Intelligence. *Digital Games Research Conference*, 4–6 November, University of Utrecht, The Netherlands. DiGRA.

Mossière, G. 2012. Experience, Subjectivity, and Performance. In J.P. Hoffmann (ed.), *Understanding Religious Ritual: Theoretical Approaches and Innovations*. Oxford: Routledge, 54–72.

Mummert, J. 2014. Modding Skyrim: The Value of Myth and Metaphor. *Playing the Past*. Available at: http://www.playthepast.org/?p=4333.

Nareyek, A. 2007. Game AI is Dead. Long Live Game AI! *IEEE Intelligent Systems*, 22, 9–11.

Okada, M., Tarumi, H., Yoshimura, T. and Moriya, K. 2001. Collaborative Environmental Education Using Distributed Virtual Environment Accessible from Real and Virtual Worlds. *SIGAPP Applied Computing Review*, 9, 15–21.

Ondrejka, C. 2006. Finding Common Ground in New Worlds. *Games and Culture*, 111–115.

Onyett, C. 2006. Oblivion Impossible Wishlist. Available at: http://au.xbox360.ign.com/articles/710/710179p1.html.

Paulsen, J. 2006. MultiTES4 – Oblivion Multiplayer Mod. Available at: http://download.boomtown.net/en_uk/articles/art.view.php?id=11795.

Perlin, K. 2005. Between a Game and a Story? *Electronic Book Review*. Available at: http://www.electronicbookreview.com/thread/firstperson/formal.

Pujol, L. and Champion, E. 2012. Evaluating Presence in Cultural Heritage Projects. *International Journal of Heritage Studies*, 18, 83–102.

Riva, G., Waterworth, J.A. and Waterworth, E.L. 2004. The Layers of Presence: A Bio-cultural Approach to Understanding Presence in Natural and Mediated Environments. *Cyberpsychology & Behavior*, 7, 402–416.

Riva, G., Castelnuovo, G., Gaggioli, A. and Mantovani, F. 2002. Towards a Cultural Approach to Presence. In F.R. Gouveia (ed.), *Proceedings of the Fifth Annual International Workshop PRESENCE*, October, Porto, Portugal, 305–309.

Roskams, S., Neal, C., Richardson, J. and Leary, R. 2013. A Late Roman Well at Heslington East, York: Ritual or Routine Practices? *Internet Archaeology*. Available at: http://intarch.ac.uk/journal/issue34/5/2–2.html.

Rozak, M. 2006a. The NPC-Conversation Wall. Available at: http://www.mxac.com.au/drt/NPCConversationWall.htm.

——. 2006b. Un-designing Oblivion. Available at: http://www.mxac.com.au/drt/UndesignOblivion.htm.

Ruberg, B. 2007. Clint Hocking Speaks Out on the Virtues of Exploration. *Gamsutra*. Available at: http://www.gamasutra.com/features/20070514/ruberg_01.shtml.

Salamone, F. 1977. Religion as Play: Bori, a Friendly 'Witchdoctor'. *Journal of Religion in Africa* 8(3): 201–211.

Schiffer, M.B. and Miller, A.R. 1999. *The Material Life of Human Beings: Artifacts, Behaviour and Communication*. London: Routledge.

Schroeder, R. 2002. Copresence and interaction in virtual environments: an overview of the range of issues. In F. Gouveia (ed.), *Proceedings of the Fifth Annual International Workshop PRESENCE*, October, Porto, Portugal, 274–295.

Shapira, R. 2014. Carmel Cavemen Used Plants in Rituals 13,000 Years Ago, Archaeologists Find. *Haaretz*. Available at: http://www.haaretz.com/archaeology/1.570106.

Steinkuehler, C.A. 2006. Why Game (Culture) Studies Now? *Games and Culture*, 1, 97–102.

Tilley, C. 1999. *Metaphor and Material Culture*. Oxford: Blackwell.

Tringham, R. 1994. Engendered Places in Prehistory. *Gender, Place and Culture: A Journal of Feminist Geography*, 1, 169–203.

Tychsen, A. 2006. Role Playing Games: Comparative Analysis across Two Media Platforms. *Proceedings of the 3rd Australasian Conference on Interactive Entertainment*, Perth, Australia.

——. 2008. Role Playing Games: Comparative Analysis across Two Media Platforms. *Proceedings of the 3rd Australasian Conference on Interactive Entertainment*, Perth, Australia. Perth: Murdoch University, 75–82.

Tychsen, A., Hitchens, M., Brolund, T. and Kavakli, M. 2005. The Game Master. *Proceedings of the Second Australasian Conference on Interactive Entertainment*, Sydney: Creativity & Cognition Studios Press, 215–222.

Wittgenstein, L. 1963. *Philosophical Investigations*. Oxford: Blackwell.

Wolf, M.J.P. 2014. *Building Imaginary Worlds: The Theory and History of Subcreation*. Hoboken, NJ: Taylor & Francis.

Writers, A.S. 2006. Multiplayer Oblivion – Mod Developer Interview. *Atomic*. Available at: http://www.atomicmpc.com.au/article.asp?SCID=25&CIID=57221.

Chapter 7

Joysticks of Death, Violence and Morality

We have seen that computer games can be considered to be *cultural*. Jesper Juul has written of literature revealing the importance of games as cultural artefacts and cultural traditions. Games can also be considered acultural in the sense that their elements and the outcomes are not taken seriously or considered by the players when playing as having serious long-term effects.

Games can also be considered anti-cultural either in the sense that they are escapist (they waste valuable time that could be spent on more socially acceptable activities) or demean public institutions (religious values, the police, other cultures, valuable possessions, important dignitaries or icons). I could even argue that games could be acultural in the sense that our interaction with a digital game as a modifiable artefact is not generally shareable.

The social or anti-social leaning of individual computer games is important when we consider whether computer games are genuine cultural artefacts. Gamers can create their own personal game levels and sometimes add in homemade script. However, our personal ludic experience of playing the game is not richly shared back into the environment for future relived experiences or as experiences to be shared with others. Non-digital experiences are created by erosion, wear and tear, and other forms of personalization. The imperfection of a homemade table becomes part of the life history of that table as a cultural artefact. Wine reveals its origins, where it is stored and the body temperature of the person who holds it in a glass. A book becomes a holder of not just text, but also of a 'reader', each page becomes intended, margins annotated and spines take on the deformation of a personal history.

So the digital game is a curiously stillborn cultural artefact. It reveals shared social ideas via genre and market reception, and it is obviously the product of one or more artistic creators. Yet it resists enculturation. The market life of games and the length required to develop and beta test game versions makes for a product that resists the personalization of its participants. In that sense at the very least, I suggest that games are anti-cultural.

Self-evidently, games encapsulate artefacts, goals, challenges, strategies, competitors, collaborators, meta-views, metaphorical imagination and play. Games are cultural in the sense that they are codified; they contain knowledge frameworks, social roles, historical beliefs and situated ways of learning. So it is no surprise that games are seen as potentially rich learning environments, by academics (Atkins, 2003; Squire and Barab, 2004; Gee, 2007). In that sense, they would surely appear to have ethical value – they can help the knowledge acquisition of today's generation, a generation that has grown up on *explicit* images and sound rather than on books and *implied* special effects.

We do learn from games, but we don't necessarily learn meaningfully. Some games already encourage world building as systems, or as collated or created artefacts, or as the exchange of social roles and social possessions. They could do more. Games could encourage players to develop ethical decision-making perspectives, cooperation, understanding of cultural alterity, meta-views and an understanding of situations not previously foreseen or typically ignored.

Can games act as moral learning environments? Gamers often talk about 'Deus Ex' as an example of player choice and 'Black & White' as an environment where the avatar reflects the player's morality (Gee, 2003; Zagal, 2009; Hogle, 2012). And there are now quite a few papers reflecting on ethical questions raised by games. Zagal, for example, suggests four ways for talking about ethics in computer games:

1. Value of Artifact: is it ethical for this game to exist? Should a particular game have been created in the first place?
2. Business Ethics: how do we create, produce, market and sell games ethically?
3. Ethics of Play: what does it mean to play ethically? What is sportsmanship? How do we understand the meaning of cheating?
4. Framework: what in-game actions are defined as 'good' by the game?

Zagal's 2009 paper ranges from a discussion of games like 'Ultima IV: The Quest of the Avatar (UIV)', 'Manhunt', 'Fire Emblem: Radiant Dawn (FE:RD)', 'Grand Theft Auto (GTA)' and 'Fable'. Zagal argues – convincingly in my opinion – that the moral dilemmas in the games add dramatic tension and that they can help engender ethical reflection and critical discussion. They may not be moral learning environments and they may not all be ethically commendable games, but they are ethically notable and are worthy of classroom discussion for the moral dilemmas they create.

As to violence, many games express or require some aspect of force, but they are not necessarily unthinking in the way in which they ask players to deal with the violence. Gee (2007) notes that even violent games typically have a large amount of strategy. However, the amount of strategy and the amount of brainpower that a game could generate do not require moral decision making to take place.

I suggest that games are amoral learning environments if only because they have not fully developed their potential to act as a socially valuable communication medium. Now that we all recognize that games are here to stay, we must also work out ways to make them more meaningful. I believe it is not enough to trumpet 'serious games'. Educators need to own up to the serious issues confronting those of us attempting to combine education and entertainment. We need to outline the issues and not just the vague potential of games to afford a meaningful learning experience.

Games can be serious learning environments, but we still lack examples of meaningful interaction and morally desirable outcomes. To attract the maximum 'repeat offenders' segment of the market, the genres of 'serious games' slogans, popular e-games are typically too homogeneous and too limiting to be not just engaging but also edifying. In too many commercial games, the content is destroyed rather than developed (understanding is enriched by creating), competition hinders understanding due to the brutality of interaction, while collaboration is shallow and enforced rather than complex and intriguing.

One particular issue is that of violence and its potential effect on its young audience. I suggest that there are two main issues: the depiction of violence and the cajolement of the player to interact using thoughts of violence without serious consequences. In the real world, and in archaeology in particular, there is a further problem – the past was often bloody; knowledge, cultural traditions and expansion of civilization was often based on the use of force on others. Can we avoid the encouragement of violent imagery and interaction in computer games, and can we use these ideas to develop new virtual environments and game levels?

Interaction in digital heritage projects is commonly inspired by or directly based on computer games. Computer games have recently been put under the microscope in their depiction of violence, their suggestion or at least tacit support of simulations of violence to achieve personal yet destructive goals, and their alleged responsibility for either desensitizing young players to simulated and sometimes real acts of violence or pushing them to explode into frenzied and bloody violence. This chapter will not concentrate on whether computer games do create or cause or exacerbate violence; the literature (Postlethwaite, 2014) is extensive yet contradictory (Karkov, 2012; Bushman, 2013; Jaslow, 2013; Vitelli, 2013; Rose, 2014) and the clearest outcome of the research seems to be that psychological research should itself be more rigorously implemented (Ferguson, 2008).

However, I do personally sympathize with the view that computer games may be associated with either desensitization to violence or a tendency to follow interaction themes that are simulations of violent acts. Yet, if games are amoral learning environments, it is due in great part to their failure to speedily develop their potential to act as a socially valuable communication medium. So even if games are immoral or do lead to violence, that is not necessarily inescapable.

That said, the most commercially popular game franchises are not necessarily the most violent ones. The Video Games Wikia lists versions of 'Mario', 'Pokémon', 'Wii Series' and 'Wii Sports' games as the most popular franchises (http://vgsales. wikia.com/wiki/Best_selling_game_franchises). So 'Mario' dominates games sales if the figures are accurate (and as the data seems to be compiled from many different sources and is anonymous, caution is advised). 'Mario' can hardly be called an explicitly violent game.

As David Ewalt (2006) remarked: 'The most powerful person in the videogame industry isn't a CEO – he's a plumber.' However, this does not negate the overall issue of the huge amount of time and effort and marketing spent on first-person shooters. So how can we create alternatives to the mainstream game mechanic of shoot, frag and strafe?

Parameters to the Argument

Games are Here to Stay

It would be a sign of great optimism to believe that more appropriate and authentic learning environments will quickly and easily replace mainstream computer games and their more violent examples. Computer games are unlikely to be replaced anytime soon by rich and meaningful and effective yet peaceful learning environments. Yet they are also challenging, players learn via failure (something other forms of education fail to understand), they are more intuitive in terms of interaction even for a non-playing audience (Champion, 2008), and they provide for a large range of cheap but effective interaction modes and peripherals, and general technical and interaction design-related innovation (many references to literature listing their advantages can be found in *Playing with the Past* (Champion, 2010)).

Most significantly, their income rivals the movie industry in many countries. Yet, they are not seen by cultural critics such as the late Roger Ebert (2010) as a medium of great artistic value. Most importantly for cultural heritage professionals, we typically learn about our own cultural traditions and expectations through playing traditional games. Yes, we cannot say the same about computer games, but we can say they are entrenched in social communities; computer game motifs are now used to advertise all sorts of consumer products. So even if they are not cultural agents (arguably they do not allow us to directly and collectively transform our material cultural identities), computer games feature heavily in certain social circles and as 'downtime' recreation in many households.

Due to the above factors, especially when considering their huge and loyal market, profitability and amount of resources, computer games are here to stay. So the question is rather can we leverage the successful elements of computer games while either replacing the violent modes of interaction or engaging the player with how digitally simulated acts of violence have consequences and how there are alternatives to violence?

Violence and Game Design

Research papers on computer games do mention the 'grey' area of depicting violence. The online article 'Ethics of Game Design' by Dean Takahasi (2004) provides a pithy two-page review of the opinions facing game designers, but in general he leaves readers to make up their own minds. His reporting on the thoughts of game designers can be summarized as follows:

1. The more realistic a world, the more dangerous the consequences of simulated violence.
2. Designers of war simulations endeavour to re-create as realistically as possible without creating evocative environments that remind families

of particular individuals. Any violence that does not suit the simulated environment is gratuitous. However, Takahashi (2004) notes that: 'In some ways, that suggests the creators of games with horrific plot lines have the most artistic license.'

3. There are variations between considering the audience who actually play the games (as opposed to who buy it) and the marketing of games to children who are not old enough to officially buy these games.

4. Some game designers and producers appear to believe that violence is dictated by market needs. It also appears that it is easier to create viable game mechanics out of violence than from socially oriented ideas. 'If designers just create "fun" games, but the buying trends are heading toward more realistic and violent games, then the designers that refuse to move along will likely be left behind', says Lorne Lanning, President of Oddworld Inhabitants in San Luis Obispo, California. 'It's also true that it is easier to create viable game mechanics out of violence than from socially oriented ideas. Socially oriented ideas and cooperative play that doesn't end in violence are extremely challenging to achieve.'

5. Designers disagree amongst themselves as to whether violence is cathartic and good, or non-cathartic, or easily acquired by the wrong age group. There are even books on videogame violence that argue it can affect players positively (Jones, 2002).

Digital Simulations versus Enactments

At no point am I suggesting that simulations of violence cannot happen in non-digital re-enactments. Popular historical re-enactments often involve the depiction and demonstration of weapons of war and quite often involve also simulated acts of war, bloodletting or sacrifice (Figure 7.1).

Violent Games and Re-enactments

Are computer games more violent than games and re-enactments? Arguably yes, but why is this so? If we follow the theory of a French sociologist, Roger Caillois (2001), games (but not necessarily computer games) must contain one or more of four elements. They must contain an element of competitive play, play via the sense of vertigo or falling, playing via mimicry and/or play via chance.

Of all these themes, playing via mimicry seems most difficult in computer games, because non-human opponents lack the range of rich expressions in lying, cheating or trying to send the wrong message. And in computer games it is easier to cater for reflex-based challenges, stopping the player from thinking, from having time to reflect, but challenging them to both move and aim (coordinate) at the same time. So computer games typically involve an element of competition (challenge), sometimes an element of chance and sometimes an element of vertigo

Figure 7.1   Annual Viking Re-enactment at Moesgaard Museum, Aarhus, Denmark

or kinaesthetic instability (such as a game mechanic where one has to aim and shoot at the same time).

In addition, the keyboard easily allows for the metaphor of direction (the arrow keys) and shooting (buttons on a mouse or the space bar). The keyboard also affords near-instant feedback (someone dies if you shoot quickly and accurately) in a clear, non-textual and intuitive fashion. And the paths of imagined bullets are easy to calculate via a computer; it is a point, click and shoot (between two points) metaphor.

Factors Leading to Violence

Computer games typically appear to have the following factors that lend themselves to violent shooting motifs:

1. There is no realistic human opponent, so expressive and rich forms of interaction are not available.
2. As there is no human opponent, the richness and variety of human-derived judgment is also missing. As such, the judgment of the success or failure of the gamer must be mechanically calculated (or, more precisely, mathematically calculated). Judgment lacks a human touch.
3. Early games had limited content, crude graphic fidelity and limited spatial variety, so the brain was deliberately confused in order to prevent the player

from realizing that content and situations were constantly being recycled. Due to this, games typically prevent the gamer from having time to relax and reflect.

4. The idea of a gun sight, and trigger, is an easy interface metaphor, avoids requiring gamers to use different cognitive parts of their brain (for text and for visual images), and a 2D gun image planted over a 3D background is much easier for the computer to continually calculate and update on the screen.

5. The use of guns (and other weapons) can easily add to the apparent seriousness of the challenge. In addition, their difficulty of use can be easily adjusted from self-evident to expert in order to cater for different levels of players and vastly improving performance of players.

6. Many of the early computer users were teenage boys.

7. Many violent computer games can be played as single player and can be played anonymously via the Internet. There is no required personal accountability or responsibility on the computer game player.

Digital Heritage – Specific Requirements

The above seven observations as to why violent computer games are popular is not desirable when seen from the point of view of cultural heritage professionals. When used for virtual heritage purposes, computer games may also have specific extra risks to consider. First, a so-called scientific reconstruction could add to the apparent weight of authority to digitally simulated events or artefacts of a violent nature.

Second, the interaction possibilities inherent in the medium could cajole the visitor into viscerally participating in and enjoying the spectacle and the violence associated therein.

Third, the artefacts found, preserved and digitally simulated are often related to war and to sacrifice, and hence are often digitally reconstructed more graphically, which could persuade some viewers or players to see their use as the main focus of the culture portrayed.

Fourth – and this is almost certainly due to the typical interaction found in computer games – the interaction often involves players using weapons to destroy virtual characters, yet in re-enactments only actors or semi-trained hobbyists are allowed to directly fight each other.

The Indiana Jones Dilemma

Where games have been used in an archaeological setting, from 'Castle Wolfenstein' to 'Tomb Raider', they seem to run into what earlier writers have called an 'Indiana Jones Dilemma'. The Indiana Jones films (and the related games) make archaeology seem exciting to the general public, but the protagonist typically destroys what they are supposed to be preserving and studying or, worse, the archaeological items extracted are only to be added to their own collections, or the apparent magic be used to control kingdoms and destroy mortal enemies!

And here it may be opportune to list a simplified description of violence in digital heritage simulations:

1. The player can create simulated violence, affecting the externs (the wider external environmental factors, such as in the game 'Black and White'.
2. The player's moral decisions can control the overall game characters and potentially the environment).
3. Simulated violence could affect representations of people (either computer-scripted agents or avatars of actual players).
4. Simulated violence could affect the beliefs or practices of people either playing in the game or represented by the game. This last type of violence is not typically described in the literature on violent games, but it is a real problem in cultural heritage simulations.

Alternatives to Violence in Digital Heritage Projects

Digital heritage projects are typically inspired to communicate unique cultural values and significance. They may also include representations of intangible cultural heritage, so point three in the above list is of particular importance.

From the above list of factors that influenced computer games to use interactive metaphors of violence, we can see that digital heritage projects could consider the following factors.

Reflexivity

Projects could contain a reflective space where players are encouraged to relax and consider the consequences of their actions. How do we create spaces where players have time to think without being bored? Do we require moral dilemma-thinking spaces?

Performativity

The player, if in a class situation, could be asked to perform or orate and present their experience of the digital heritage environment, their decisions taken, and where information and decision making was similar or dissimilar to how past inhabitants may have behaved, and where and what sort of information appeared to be missing from the reconstruction or was misleadingly added. One example might be the Drama in the Delta project (http://dramainthedelta.org). Led by Emily Roxworthy, students re-enact the experiences of a Japanese-American girl in the American internment camps during the Second World War. The objective is to encourage empathy ('historical empathy') and discussion about inter-racial discrimination (Losh, 2011).

Role-playing Virtue Ethics

Players could take on characters in role-playing games and see how their characters change in relation to perceived development of virtue ethics. One example might be the early 1990s Blaxxun Community 3D digital simulation of a seventeenth-century Renaissance book of manners.

Fateful Consequentialism

Players could be allowed to be violent, but the consequences of their actions could affect their future pathways through the game. Possibly, other players could see the consequences of individual actions (even if the individual players could not) and could use this to their own advantage. The results of their decisions could be discussed after the game. Biofeedback could easily be used here.

Alternative Strategies

Violence could be offered as a strategy, but it could be offered as a long-term destructive strategy. This is similar to fateful consequentialism, but the alternative offered modes of interaction could be considered and then chosen in the game, and the consequences could also be viewed while still playing the game. Games like 'Deus Ex' exemplify this approach. One could use the avatar of the player to either indicate alternative strategies and their effect on player character, or the avatar could graphically express the consequences or personal viewpoint of player decisions.

Creative Uses for Weapons

The violent game 'Half-Life 2' and its associated game engine Source has extensive modding capability; one modded community version called 'SourceFort' allows players to build forts using the 'gravity gun' in teams. So in some game engines, weapons of war can also be used creatively and for communal purposes. This is similar to the alternative strategies option given above.

NPC Distaste and Disparagement

Recent games such as 'Elder Scrolls IV: Oblivion' have NPCs that can tell the character of the player by their past actions, decisions and choice of skills. As 'Oblivion' and its successor 'Elder Scrolls V: Skyrim' can be modded, it may be possible to engender social discouragement of violence through scripting the non-playing characters to react disagreeably or withhold vital information from player characters that appear to be too violent or ignorant of local cultural practices. As in alternative strategies, the player's avatar could also be a barometer of social regard.

Biofeedback

Knowledge could be linked to calmness via biofeedback. In the last decade or so, there has been an explosion in reliable, convenient and affordable biofeedback devices for gaming in particular and for computer usage in general. I will explore this idea in Chapter 9.

Expressive and Embodied Modes of Interaction

We no longer have to rely on point-and-click hard surface interfaces. We can interact via breathing, scent, sound and touch, and via drawing. We could use calligraphic and sketching interfaces to allow players to navigate and explore based on how well they learn, remember and simulate cultural icons. If interaction is more embodied, the player may also feel more directly associated with both interaction and consequence, and less desensitized.

Emphasis on Non-violent Competition

Some game design teachers refuse to let the student designers in the class feature bullets (projectiles) of any kind in their games. Where the element of competition must be used, it could involve competing against time, against past scores and performances, or for the development of new winning strategies. Competition could also be shifted from between players to between player communities and non-human foes. Research does suggest that cooperation can lessen aggression (Zack, 2014); the issue is how to design for it so that confrontation and aggressive competition between teams does not become an issue.

Moral Accountability

To design games so that players take on moral accountability for their actions is perhaps the most valuable yet most difficult aim to implement. A fragmented start is given in Sicart (2005) and is elaborated upon in Sicart (2009), but it needs to be further developed in the case of digital heritage. Who judges and who decides if the player has been honourable, and what is honour in past or extant cultures?

Summary

Now that we all recognize that games are here to stay, we must also develop ways to make them more meaningful. I believe it is not enough to trumpet 'serious games'. Educators need to own up to the serious issues confronting those of us attempting to combine education and entertainment. We need to outline the issues and not just the vague potential of games to afford a meaningful and authentic learning experience.

They can be serious learning environments, but we still lack examples of meaningful interaction and morally desirable outcomes in e-games. To attract the maximum 'repeat offenders' segment of a market, the genres of 'serious games' slogans, popular e-games are typically too homogeneous and too limiting to be not just engaging but also edifying. And this homogeneity does not augur well for the development of disseminating specific and unique cultural heritage.

This chapter has attempted to explain why computer games are typically violent, but it has also attempted to explain the extra requirements of digital heritage projects, even if they are based on game-style interaction. My suggestion is to view violence not so much as a black or white decision, but rather as an issue of choice and reflection. If a violent interaction mode is hard to avoid, possibly there could be an alternative non-violent mode so that people could choose, and they would be made aware of the consequences of their action. Hopefully the suggested alternatives will be critiqued and extended by designers of future digital heritage environments.

References

Atkins, B. 2003. *More Than a Game: The Computer Game as Fictional Form*. Manchester: Manchester University Press.

Bushman, B.J. 2013. The Effects of Violent Video Games. Do They Affect Our Behavior? *Psychology Today, Media Spotlight*. Available at: http://www.ithp.org/articles/violentvideogames.html.

Caillois, R. 2001. *Man Play and Games,* Champaign, IL: University of Illinois Press.

Champion, E. 2008. Otherness of Place: Game-Based Interaction and Learning in Virtual Heritage Projects. *International Journal of Heritage Studies*, 14, 210–228.

———. 2010. *Playing with the Past.* London: Springer.

Ebert, R. 2010. Video Games Can Never Be Art. *Roger Ebert's Journal*. Available at: http://www.rogerebert.com/rogers-journal/video-games-can-never-be-art.

Ewalt, D.M. 2006. The Best-Selling Videogame Franchises. *Forbes*. Available at: http://www.forbes.com/2006/08/02/bestselling-video-games-cx_de_0802mario.html.

Ferguson, C.J. 2008. The School Shooting/Violent Video Game Link: Causal Link or Moral Panic? *Journal of Investigative Psychology and Offender Profiling*, 5(1–2), 25–37.

Gee, J.P. 2003. What Video Games Have to Teach Us about Learning and Literacy. *ACM Computers in Entertainment*, 1, 1–4.

———. 2007. *Good Video Games Plus Good Learning.* New York: Peter Lang.

Hogle, J. 2012. Deus Ex Ludos: Representation, Agency, and Ethics in Deus Ex: Invisible War. *Well Played: A Journal on Video Games, Value and Meaning*, 1, 49–69.

Jaslow, R. 2013. Violent Video Games and Mass Violence: A Complex Link. *CBS News.* Available at: http://www.cbsnews.com/8301-204_162-57569948/ violent-video-games-and-mass-violence-a-complex-link.

Jones, G. 2008. *Killing Monsters: Why Children Need Fantasy.* New York: Basic Books.

Karkov, R. 2012. Violent Computer Games Cleared by Researchers. *Science Nordic.* Available at: http://sciencenordic.com/violent-computer-games-cleared-researchers.

Losh, L. 2011. Role-Playing Racial History through Digital Games. *Dml Central Digital Media + Learning: The Power of Participation.* Available at: http:// dmlcentral.net/blog/liz-losh/role-playing-racial-history-through-digital-games.

Postlethwaite, J. 2014. Video Game Violence. Available at: http://ludodemia. pbworks.com/w/page/67789950/Video Game Violence.

Rose, M. 2014. Video Games and Gun Violence: A Year after Sandy Hook. *Gamsutra.* Available at: http://www.gamasutra.com/view/feature/210322/ video_games_and_gun_violence_a_.php.

Sicart, M. 2005. Game, Player, Ethics: A Virtue Ethics Approach to Computer Games. *International Review of Information Ethics*, 4. Available at: http:// www.i-r-i-e.net/inhalt/004/Sicart.pdf.

———. 2009. *The Ethics of Computer Games.* Cambridge, MA: MIT Press.

Squire, K. and Barab, S. 2004. Replaying History: Engaging Urban Underserved Students in Learning World History through Computer Simulation Games. *Proceedings of the 6th International Conference on Learning Sciences.* International Society of the Learning Sciences, 505–512.

Takahasi, D. 2004. Ethics of Game Desgin. Available at: http://www.gamasutra. com/view/feature/130594/ethics_of_game_design.php.

Vitelli, R. 2013. Can Video Games Cause Violence? *Psychology Today, Media Spotlight.* Available at: http://www.psychologytoday.com/blog/media-spotlight/201304/can-video-games-cause-violence.

Zack, M. 5 February 2014. Video Games and Violence: What Does Academia Say? *Gamemoir.* Available at: http://gamemoir.com/2014/02/05/video-games-and-violence-what-does-academia-say.

Zagal, J.P. 2009. Ethically Notable Videogames: Moral Dilemmas and Gameplay. Breaking New Ground: Innovation in Games, Play, Practice and Theory. *Proceedings of DiGRA 2009.* London.

Chapter 8

Intelligent Agents, Drama and Cinematic Narrative

In this chapter I will outline some interesting aspects of narrative theory, issues regarding intelligent agents and AI characters, and the problem of virtual environments, interactive cinema and art. These three issues may not seem relevant to interactive heritage and digital history, but I will put forward five main arguments to make the case that actually they are important, and that understanding and resolving these issues will help improve both the scholar's awareness of the education potential of agents and narrative, and the designer's understanding of how narrative, cinematography and artificial intelligence (AI) can be better integrated into their projects.

Theories of Drama

Aristotle's *Poetics* (Aristotle, 1997) is widely considered to be the earliest surviving example of Western dramatic theory. In this work, Aristotle defined tragedy and outlined its rules and six-part composition (the second book, on comedy, has been lost). Tragedy must have plot (plot structures story), character, thought, diction, melody and spectacle (set, costume and props). These elements have also been described as 'Character, Thought, Language, Pattern and Enactment (spectacle) – Muthos (plot) and Mimesis (mimetic activity) being the two main concepts'. According to Louchart and Aylett (2004), mimesis is the 'representation or portrayal of action and behaviours – a dramatic enactment'.

Yet for Aristotle, in an era where tragedy was the highest form of art and was controlled by the Fates, muthos is most important. Muthos is 'the arrangement of the incidents or the organisation of the events that form the overall plot structure of the narrative'. Aristotle also discussed the construction of epics and distinguished genres of poetry (which for the Ancient Greeks meant 'making') in terms of matter (language, rhythm and melody), subject (agent) and method. Despite being the first example of narrative theory in the West, Aristotle's theory has influenced contemporary theorists and practitioners in interactive narrative such as Brenda Laurel and Michael Mateas (Louchart and Aylett, 2004). However, I agree with Louchart and Aylett that Aristotelian theories of drama have two major issues when used in virtual environments: their plot-driven focus conflicts with a desire for player agency, and their narrative tends to be author-driven rather than character-driven. Due to these features, Cavazza and Pizzi (2006) have also remarked that Aristotelian theories may need to be modified for interactive drama.

Formalism is another historical school of narrative theory. The most famous figure, Vladimir Propp (1895–1970), could also be called a functionalist. He analysed the plots of 100 Russian folktales and determined there were 31 functions (or elements) common to all (Propp, 1968). He also wrote that every narrative had eight different dramatis personae ('persons of the drama', which can be more simply referred to as character types). He also proposed four main premises (Burke, 2014):

1. The functions of characters serve as stable, constant elements in a tale, independent of how and by whom they are fulfilled.
2. The number of functions known to the fairy tale is limited.
3. The sequence of functions is always identical.
4. All fairy tales are of one type in regard to their structure.

Propp can be criticized for the application of his theory to folktales worldwide and to other narrative forms that are dissimilar to Russian folktales. But this would be unfair – Propp's publisher changed the title of his book *Morphology of the Wondertale* to *Morphology of the Folktale*. Propp had intended the book to be about Russian wondertales rather than folktales per se (Propp, 1984) and he was not responsible for the use of his theory to create narrative, let alone digital narratives. Propp's theory was also criticized for being suitable only for quest-driven narratives and for reducing the importance of the characters themselves (Louchart and Aylett, 2004).

A more recent taxonomy classified Multi-User Dungeon (MUD) players into four types (Bartle, 1996):

1. Achievers, who 'are interested in doing things to the game'.
2. Explorers, who 'are interested in having the game surprise them' and 'delight in having the game expose its internal machinations to them'.
3. Socializers, who 'are interested in interacting with other players'.
4. Killers, who 'demonstrate their superiority over fellow humans'.

While the above simple taxonomy of the players of these has been widely cited, others have criticized the theory for being derived from specific examples and thus hard to extrapolate generally, and for discussing player motivations without in-depth qualitative data (Dixon, 2011; Richard, 2014). A more empirically grounded player taxonomy has been created by Nick Yee, which listed the following:

1. Achievement: Advancement, Mechanics and Competition.
2. Social: Socializing, Relationship and Teamwork.
3. Immersion: Discovery, Role-Playing, Customization and Escapism.

Why are there only three types of player motivations? According to Yee, 'the analysis revealed that the correlation between Achievers and Griefers (Killers) is too high for these types to be truly distinct. The analysis also revealed that role-playing is a distinct motivation that is uncorrelated with the desire to socialize' (Yee, 2005). The above taxonomies are described in more detail in a chapter by Richard (2014) and there is another interesting taxonomy of generic player motivations given by Vandenberghe (2012):

1. Novelty: the newness of the experience.
2. Challenge: the amount of effort or self-control that the player is expected to use.
3. Stimulation: the engagement of the play experience.
4. Harmony: the relation of the rules to social and player-to-player accord in the game.
5. Threat: the presence and strength of negative emotional triggers.

Implications for virtual heritage and digital history are not readily apparent, as these interactive environments are typically not so competitive and not so orientated towards role-playing as MUDs. However, if we design narrative settings to engage different types of player motivations, rather than providing a standard array of characters according to a Propp-type structure, we may find it easier to provide a setting for emergent narrative. While such player typologies express more clearly what certain types of players like to do, they are less helpful for designing narratives that engage and affect these different types of players.

Mythical Narrative

Apart from Propp's theory of folktale morphology, Joseph Campbell's (2008) concept of the Hero's Journey has received attention in game design circles, including by Dunniway (2004), who defined a Hero's Journey as simply a 'trip that a central character goes on in order to resolve a problem'. This theory is very person-centric and suits third-person games that involve heroism. Campbell structured the Journey into 25 stages, but this was simplified by Vogler (2007) into 12 stages: The Ordinary World; The Call to Adventure; The Reluctant Hero; The Wise Old Man; Into the Special Fantasy World; Tests; Allies & Enemies; The Inmost Cave – Second Threshold; The Supreme Ordeal; Seizing the Sword – Reward; The Road Back; and Resurrection and Return – Ending.

There has been widespread criticism of Campbell's monomyth theory – while it was inspired by Jung's notion of archetypes and has been applied to many cultures, does that mean it is universal and not gender-biased (Manganaro, 1992)? Does it provide enough details to create rich contextual stories and is there rigorous scholarly evidence to support it? The theory can be over-simplified and lead to repetitive plots. The Hero's Journey necessitates a substantial length of time and considerable effort in setting up and requires a more linear world to ensure that all stages are experienced in a suitable sequence (although not all stages are required, and some argue that these stages can be re-ordered).

Player Archetypes

Following Campbell and simplifying his theory of the monomyth, Vogler's book *The Writer's Journey* (2007) also listed seven player archetypes ('the function or role a character plays in a story'):

1. Hero 'to serve and sacrifice'.
2. Mentor 'to guide'.
3. Threshold Guardian 'to test'.
4. Herald 'to warn and challenge'.
5. Shapeshifter 'to question and deceive'.
6. Shadow 'to destroy'.
7. Trickster 'to disrupt'.

Vogler's book influenced both Hollywood (for examples, see http://www. thewritersjourney.com) and game criticism (Cassar, 2013), but as a descendant of Campbell's theory, it is also open to the same criticisms, and as a simplification it is also open to criticism by those who prefer Campbell's more extensive theory. As Corey Mandrell (2010) has remarked, a formula for structure does not actually create an engaging story. Chris Huntley (2007) has also reviewed six famous theories, including Vogler's, and he has remarked that most theories are from the audience's standpoint rather than from the writer's viewpoint.

Belief-Desire-Intention Agents

Belief-Desire-Intention (BDI)-based agents are the result of another theory of intelligent agent design, based on the writings of Michael Bratman (Georgeff et al., 1999), that what is required for designing AI is a method to trifurcate beliefs, desires and intentions so that an intelligent agent can separate stored plans for current and activated plans. The agent must have beliefs about the world, itself and others. Desires motivate the agent, and goals are desires that are actively being sought. Intentions are what the agent has chosen to do and are commitments based on the agent's desires, and plans (or sequences of plans) are also based on intentions, but are not necessarily complete in detail. The final part of the theory is the notion of an event, which is a trigger for the agent to react to. Triggers can be external or internal to the agent.

Critics might argue that it is a method for planning rather than designing AI and that there is no description of how the agents would communicate with each other or even how an agent would learn from mistakes or past experiences. However, there are some other advantages: a BDI agent can have beliefs that are actually wrong and a BDI agent has some leeway in changing plans according to changing circumstances.

Intelligent Agents as Dramatic Characters

Interactive drama is the Holy Grail for many academics in game design and AI research, and could be of huge benefit to historical simulations and virtual heritage projects. In this section, I wish to provide a critical overview of at least one of the competing theories, how its success could impact digital humanities and why I think some of the philosophical underpinnings are, to some extent, questionable. I will concentrate in particular on an article by Selmer Bringsjord (2001) and will outline why I believe some of these theories are too strict, and why simpler and more achievable forms of interactive narrative could be of immense help to digital humanists in the dissemination of humanities themes and ideas, and heightened public engagement.

Selmer Bringsjord (2001) has raised some interesting questions for interactive narrative. Simply put, he did not believe (at least at the time of writing) that artificial characters are currently advanced enough to provide interactive narrative. I believe that he mistakes engagement for AI narrative – that he does not understand that a sense of another is as important as the story itself. He has also created too high a requirement for interactive narrative on the level of creative genius. There are alternatives to having to develop (or, more accurately, waiting some decades for the development of) highly sophisticated AI characters.

Bringsjord believed that games can be compelling, but that they are not dramatically compelling – that, unlike some films, they do not have captivating narrative, engaging characters and they have 'zero literary power'. He also said that massively multiplayer online role-playing games (MMORGs) are 'demographically one-dimensional'. The last characterization is either so woeful or horrifically out of date (after all, the article was written in 2001) that I will not respond to it, but I would like to question what he means by 'captivating narrative', and 'engaging characters'. He has created a dangerous criterion for many classic and masterly films or books if judged by an expansive demographic: I am not sure whether the great majority of children will always be captivated or engaged by such old-fashioned works of art. These classics are still canonical works of art, even if current generations do not appreciate them.

Next, Bringsjord seems to equate interactive digital narrative with huge advances in AI:

> Interactive digital narrative will need to be crafted and massaged *as the story is unfolding*, computers, not slow-by-comparison humans, will need to be enlisted as at least decent dramatists – but getting a computer to be a dramatist requires remarkable AI.

Bringsjord believed (and as far as I know, still does) that we have compelling interactive digital entertainment and dramatically compelling interactive entertainment (for example, improvisational theatre). However, he said we have no 'dramatically compelling interactive digital entertainment'. As such, he probably would not appreciate Façade (http://www.interactivestory.net), which is, to my mind, one of the closest things to dramatically compelling interactive digital entertainment with intelligent-seeming avatars.

Matt Barton (2005) described Façade as:

> quite exhilerating [sic] for several hours because I had never felt such 'emotional realism' in a game before … However, it soons [sic] becomes apparent why the game is called Façade: It's all just a clever ruse. Soon enough, I figured out how the game was reacting to my inputs. Bizarre comments resulted in automatic responses ('My, you're a kidder') ('Uh, Yeah …') and such. I had a similar experience as a kid playing Eliza. Unfortunately, these programs work by tricking us. Trip and Grace don't learn.

> … Bringsjord argues that games like Façade won't succeed until they are able to convince players that the characters are 'autonomous', that is, free-willed. Thus, I would have to be convinced that Trip and Grace aren't automatons programmed to respond a certain way to various inputs.

Emotional realism and experiential realism are fascinating concepts, but it does not appear that Façade (or a modification of it) would appeal to Bringsjord. Could something similar be sufficient for museum displays and virtual heritage projects? Given different conditions, yes I think so. It could also have a simple 'filibuster' detector, catching out people who are trying to catch it out. An even simpler objection could be whether it really needs to feature remarkable AI to do its job? By the way, I believe Façade was developed after Bringsjord's article was written, so I don't know if he has even seen it, but the creators certainly know of his work (Mateas and Stern, 2003).

There are other concepts that Bringsjord believed AI would have to master. These were: immemorial themes; story mastery ('if genuine drama is desired, then something or someone must ensure that what happens is dramatically interesting'); robust, autonomous characters ('literature and drama exploits [sic] the central properties of being a person … great stories come to be remembered in terms of great characters'); and personalization ('if virtual characters are going to react intelligently to you as user or gamer, they must, in some sense, understand you').

Even in 2001, Bringsjord conceded that it might be possible to build virtually intelligent animals, but we could not build virtual personhood. He defined personhood as linguistic ability, autonomy ('free will'), creativity, phenomenal consciousness and 'robust abstract reasoning (e.g., ability to create conceptual schemes, and to switch from one to another)'. For Bringsjord, anything that passes the Turing Test but only passes the Turing Test was 'only on the strength of clever but shallow trickery'.

Bringsjord created another test, 'The Lovelace Test', but what most interests me is his overall argument, especially premise 1: 'Dramatically compelling interactive digital entertainment requires the presence in such entertainment of virtual persons, and therefore requires the presence of autonomous virtual characters.'

Other writers seem to agree that human characters are needed. For example, Luppa and Borst (2007, p. 122) wrote: 'No matter how much progress is made, the "human storyteller" will stay central to the conception, creation, and composition of immersive story experiences.' It may well be true that we still do not have the ability to produce the autonomous virtual character that Bringsjord stipulated is necessary. This does not mean that such a character is necessary for compelling interactive entertainment or for compelling interactive drama. Drama is itself a complicit illusion, an actor is in a way cheating us, so I don't believe that we use the same criteria of personhood for an actor or narrator as we do for ascribing personhood to another apparently human being.

However, for drama, there are other issues. We have trouble creating interactive engaging drama, because the actor does not experience the drama, we experience the apparent inner emotional turmoil of the actor. Drama is a story or chain of related events that expresses change in a character or unexpected actions, as well as a range of attempts to control the situation. A character that passively accepts all adversity does not make for great drama.

Drama is the externally revealed interplay of Character 1 and Character 2 against changing conditions. Drama exposes and reveals and analyses, and revels in inner turmoil and how people respond to inner conflict by attempting to change themselves or their surrounds. So drama is a study of characters' mental models of the external world conflicting with the world as it is and of basic desires being thwarted.

In a sense, then, drama necessitates engaged characters with some perception of their inner turmoil offered or at least expressing that turmoil. And drama features unexpected events, which often seem triggered, although only in retrospect, from features of the characters portrayed. Character-revealing drama advances the story and reveals character depth.

Thus, Bringsjord's problem is really as follows: can computer agents become engaging improvisational theatre actors and dramaturgical masterminds on the level of the greatest performers, writers and directors of history? According to his Lovelace Test, we would have to be engaged by their creative spontaneous synergy and we know all about their internal circuitry, but we don't know how they do it. This seems a difficult challenge though, as we don't know the internal workings of human actors! And is not the title of his paper 'Is it Possible to Build Dramatically Compelling Interactive Digital Entertainment (in the Form, e.g., of Computer Games)?'

Following Bringsjord's model, an agent has desires that are thwarted and has inner conflict, and tries to resolve this inner conflict by changing external conditions. Games typically do not feature (or require) inner conflict and clumsiness rather than doubt is represented. Drama is typically an external spectator sport. We want to see the inner conflict in others and we want to see them fight against the odds and then we want to perceive a change in the expression of emotions, of doubt turning into bravery. Drama is a study of reason and optimism overcoming fear and flight, of control over passion, of stubbornness over indecision or cowardice. A character wants to be happy, destroying indecision and overcoming negative conditions, so cognitively we want to resolve or force an ending that appears to be novel and yet appropriate or even destined in when considered in hindsight!

And is more than one character needed? For example, can stand-up comedy qualify as drama? In most situations, stand-up comedy cannot qualify as drama – you need two characters for conflict. One needs an idea of a character pitted against external forces, conflicts, etc. Audio-visual cues and memories in one-act plays can be used instead of other players, but this requires great skill and is possibly beyond the bounds of 'dramatically compelling' interactive digital entertainment.

As such, I will turn away from the issue of personhood and explore whether we could have drama in historical simulations and virtual heritage, and whether AIs could have any role to play. Do they need to be totally believable and incredibly smart?

First, though, we have another issue – the forcefulness of drama might destroy the voluntary nature of the magic circle. You can be engaged in a task (it holds your attention), but you are compelled to watch a drama unfold (you are persuaded or forced to do so). The former is a measure of the undividedness of your attention, while the latter is a measure of the lack of autonomy from the desire to do something. So the two concepts require attentiveness and desire. These are two different things. Yes, drama can be compelling – you feel pushed along by the momentum of the narrative – but engagement is subsidiary. You can be engaged in a game, but a game is still a *flight* of imagination. So drama is more than a game, for it is so wound up with destiny and momentum that you feel forced to confront something.

There is the potential danger that an audience becomes so enchanted by the drama that it misses the point of the simulation. Game-based digital history and virtual heritage projects run the risk of the participants ignoring the environment in order to win the game (finish tasks, etc.), so an interactive drama might run into similar problems. While such a forceful and fate-driven interpretation of drama favours Aristotelian drama theory, it leaves little room for player agency.

And what are universal themes? Perhaps games reduce the impact of universal themes; I know I experience them less often and less profoundly in games than I do in other media. Perhaps it is because game characters have questionable mortality; they can often be resurrected. If drama can be seen as a heightened feeling of the significance of events through the perception of potential conflict between autonomous or seemingly autonomous characters (the more dramatic the event, the more portentous the outcome, and the more compelling the motivation to be engaged in the virtual environment), then I will have to feel the fear and duty of the artificial actors, I will have to have an investment in their sacrifice. If I can replace Lara Croft version 1 with Lara Croft version 2, the investment I lose with the death of the first character is relatively inconsequential.

Emergent Narrative

According to Szilas (1999, p. 151), there are four principles for creating emergent narrative:

1. A character's actions are motivated by narrative constraints rather than [by] emotional, psychological or social reasoning.
2. A story can be broken down into a succession of generic processes.
3. The conflict is the core of dramatic narrative.
4. Any narrative assumes an intention of the author towards the user; this intention is supposed to be part of the conflict itself and how it is solved.

Earlier in this chapter I argued that some of the above principles are actually core parts of drama, especially the third, that 'conflict is the core of dramatic narrative'. However, I would replace 'conflict' with tension and would suggest that for our purposes, the narrative does not have to be intentions of the author towards the user, as some of our narrative intentions are in fact extrapolated from history or from cultural heritage such as myths and epics. So are we trying to design emergent agents? For digital heritage and interactive history, I would suggest that our main aim would be to create information-providing and context-setting agents. We are lucky in that some of our narratives are already made for us; however, we are constrained in that we do not necessarily want any form of gameplay or any interpretations and reflections to arise from the interactive narrative. Perhaps we require a new form of intelligent agent?

Cultural Agents

There have been many virtual heritage projects involving some form of intelligent agents. Some agents are based on the BDI model and perform social roles such in the 'City of Uruk' project (Bogdanovych et al., 2012); some agents are guides (Roussou, 2001; Song et al., 2004; Lim et al., 2005) or even route-planners (Costantini et al., 2008); some agents tell stories (Ibanez et al., 2003) or are virtual augmented characters in a dramatic retelling of Pompeii (Papagiannakis and Magnenat-Thalmann, 2007); while in many other projects, agents are employed to create a sense of inhabitation and enact crowd simulations (Bogdanovych et al., 2009; Lim et al., 2013; Sequeira and Morgado, 2013; Sequeira et al., 2014). There have also been a few papers covering crowd simulation agents with brain-controlled interfaces such as the 'Roma Nova' project, which was designed to improve learning about historical simulations (Vourvopoulos et al., 2012).

When we compare the agents used in the above and similar projects with the use of AI and NPCs in computer games, we find in digital heritage and interactive history projects that intelligent agents are usually designed for limited forms of conversation. Sometimes they are used as guides, leading players to important landmarks, revealing past events and appropriate behaviour. In larger environments, intelligent agents can appear to humanize the content and provide a sense of scale and inhabitation. In computer games, they typically provide challenge and competition. In some of the more advanced computer games, they complete requests from players, such as carrying or finding specific objects, as well as spreading information on behalf of the player or providing feedback on the player's action back to the player.

As noted earlier, culture can exist and be transmitted to some extent independently of people. Culture is a framework for the shared remembering of the past, but can also be seen as the material inscription and embodiment of projected social values into a shared potential future. Culture identifies groups of people in an attempt to defeat the passing of time, but it must also be maintained and continually kept in circulation.

My suggestion here is that our field needs to develop the concept of cultural agents. A cultural agent recognizes, adds to or transmits physically embedded and embodied aspects of culture. Culture is itself heritage-biased towards both past and future, unlike society's focus on now. Recognizing culture independently of social agents is possible, but cultural agents modify cultural knowledge (culture managed by infrastructure or institution) using past knowledge, current frameworks of shared understanding and projected visions of the future.

Cultural agents are not merely conversational agents, for a cultural agent should be able to:

1. automatically select correct cultural behaviours given specific events or situations;
2. recognize in/correct cultural behaviours given specific events or situations;
3. transmit cultural knowledge;
4. modify, create or command artefacts that become cultural knowledge.

So our challenge is to develop agents that can pass on information about a past or distant culture without disrupting historical authenticity or player engagement. Our aim should then to be to develop an evaluable proof of concept leading to realized projects that incorporate and integrate historical situations, face tracking, speech to text or biofeedback and game-themed situations. New technological opportunities include developments in biofeedback and realistic avatars, as well as camera tracking, but conventions and theories in theatrical and more generic performance design may also be of great assistance.

Storyspaces

Storyspaces are possibility spaces according to Will Wright (2006): 'Games usually start at a well-defined state (the setup in chess, for instance) and end when a specific state is reached (the king is checkmated). Players navigate this possibility space by their choices and actions; every player's path is unique.' According to Michael Joyce (see Ritchie, 2013), there are exploratory spaces (which 'only allow the audience to choose paths, links or lexia') and constructive space ('empowers the audience to create content as well as navigate the object').

In previous writings I have distinguished between observation-based, activity-based and hermeneutic (through their actions, players either leave interpretations of themselves or discover interpretations of others). Thus, I would suggest that although I have only ever mentioned virtual environments as stage sets in passing and have not explored the notion of storyspaces, Joyce fails to separate this third type of space – interpretable space (or hermeneutically enriched space). However, Ritchie does discuss interpretable space and suggests:

> The audience attempts to understand a storyworld through exhausting the possibilities of its storyspace. To do so requires that the audience understand the storyspace in their explorations and mental mapping of many, most or all of the conceptual blank spaces in the work. This interpretation's distinguishing between the spatial representation of a story, the audience's mapping and understanding of the space in which a story takes place and the audience's achieving narrative closure underscores the narrative possibilities of digital, interactive forms and poses several problems for designers and audiences.

Ritchie suggests that we need to create prompts, affordances and constraints, and he calls this a 'rhetoric of interactivity'. So we need to find solutions that are engaging like other games, expose the interesting workings of character motivations and personality, help the gameplay and perhaps the narrative of the game (if games can have narrative), and to some extent design the virtual geography to reflect the effort required in maintaining social relationships and unique identities.

In an online interview with Henry Jenkins (2009), Michael Nitsche talks about his book on story maps (Nitsche, 2008), which is 'a form of imaginary map that we form in our mind as we play our way through a virtual environment'. In this interview, Nitsche states that virtual worlds are typically designed to be dramatic environments replete with 'extraordinary events and opportunities'. He also provides examples of games (such as 'Doom' and 'Silent Hill') that are not only navigable virtual architectures but also create dramatic situations that are highly engaging. In both spatial and thematic terms, a video game is a 'dramatic positioning of a protagonist, antagonist and spatial opportunities'.

Some Possible Design Solutions

One possible design option might be to use indirect biofeedback and the contributions or even attention of other people to create compelling interactive drama between the player and other characters or between the player and the virtual environment. Biofeedback could reveal inner knowledge and conflict to others; other people could try to use this knowledge to manipulate us. The computer does not need to be an actor, it does not need to be a director and it does not need to be super-smart; it only needs to help us.

A second option might be to re-stage the idea of humanity on a spectrum of mortality-immortality. If we view dramatic characters as heroes, and narrators as gods, humans and other humans and computer agents can all act as heroes or gods – the permutations are plentiful. There could even be a range of mortal or beyond-mortal powers, or points in the story when agents and heroes lose godliness or gain it (to some degree). Many cultures feature myths of mortals becoming immortal or immortals losing their immortality. The dynamic environmental conditions could be random, actual (based on real-world dynamic data) or historical or theorized potential pasts (or all of the above!)

A third option might be to try to evoke engaging drama by playing on the nature of truth. Imagine yourself as a psychologist who sits behind a one-way glass window. In front of you are prisoners with varying mannerisms. You have to work out which person is lying from their mannerisms. In a sense, you are being challenged to accurately match behavioural patterns with lying; you have to know external expressions of inner turmoil and conflict. I don't think it would be very engaging in its current form and, really, the description above is not very interactive (perhaps you have tools to make them nervous). Yet it could arguably be dramatic.

Perhaps we could increase our chances if we create phobic-charged environments. Imagine you are questioning a suicidal witness while they stand teetering on the edge of a building. You need to be able to ask them worrying questions to solve a murder, but you know that too many questions will literally push them over the edge. A caveat: this is a purely hypothetical suggestion – I would have some moral qualms about actually designing such a scenario. Perhaps a less ethically challenging version could work in its place.

I find all of the above interesting design ideas, but they do not seem to advance the potential aims of interactive digital history or virtual heritage environments. Perhaps we could amalgamate their most promising features?

A Cultural Turing Test

While some writers on virtual place, such as Kalay and Marx (2001), initially argued that cultural immersion requires the perceived presence of other real social beings, we do not have contextually based evaluation data on how embedded and culturally constrained visitors to a virtual heritage site need to be. For example, if we use our own language to communicate, we will not be fully embedded in the recreated culture. Other visitors will almost certainly distract from the contextually situated embedded and embodied cultural experience. The premise that visitors require other real people in the virtual environment in order to feel cultural presence is thus unsubstantiated and highly problematic.

However, it occurred to me that we could solve the social presence problem and the believable agents problem by creating a situation where the authenticity of the player (and not the NPCs) is called into question. In order to satisfy the NPCs that the player is a 'local', the player has to satisfy questions and perform like the actual local characters (the scripted NPCs). Hence, the player has to observe and mimic these artificial agents for fear of being discovered. I have called this a cultural Turing test, but in fact it is a reversal of the Turing test, where a questioner has to determine from written answers if the writer is a human or a computer. Here the computer (through the artificial characters) is trying to determine if the human player is sufficiently artificial character-like.

A promising scenario to help people learn about culturally situated behaviour is to evaluate a multi-user virtual environment game where the task is to imitate local inhabitants' behaviour and dialogue in order to move up the social ladder without being caught (by scripted agents or by other users). A mix of scripted characters and other real-world users all try to detect and catch out inappropriate behaviour, interaction or dialogue (inappropriate in terms of space, time or social encounter). Progression could be achieved by the advancement through a social hierarchy that in return offers more power and freedom of interaction.

Such a scenario requires a 'believably' intelligent AI that appears to have agency, *agon* (competition) and alterity (otherness). However, as a cultural Turing test, this scenario may allow the integration of historical fact, cultural behaviours, embedded multiple users and goal-based motivation that relies on acquiring contextually appropriate cultural knowledge, not destroying it. The Turing test asked people to decide if something behind a wall answering questions was human or an AI. Here in this scenario, the participant is instead trying to stop the AI from realizing that she or he is actually human and an interloper.

Such a scenario could be highly competitive and puts the onus to perform authentically on the participant, not the virtual environment. A changing mix of scripted characters and real-world users adds a form of mystery and engagement, and helps to ensure that a reasonable level of challenge persists after the initial learning period. I believe that this scenario addresses some of the problems of social presence and cultural presence.

On the one hand, multi-user environments are inherently engaging; on the other hand, we may wish to restrict users' contextual interaction and dialogue so that they learn about the local culture and do not use the setting as a mere chatroom. By asking users to imitate inhabitants and avoid detection (by agents or other users), we introduce challenging game elements while at the same time allowing them to learn contextually relevant behaviour and local knowledge.

Further, this scenario starts to address how users can play against each other without destroying notions of a past authentic world, but rather work towards that world. It also requires them being accepted by others, and not to just observe, but also to emulate the behaviours and rituals of others. Suspicious locals could ask the human 'imposters' to show their local knowledge, which the 'imposters' could accumulate by either asking the correct questions or snooping around the site. Perhaps some of these encounters could even be inserted as random or place-triggered or event-triggered cut scenes in the gameplay of future players.

Is this a useful new direction? Other researchers have reviewed frameworks for a rich interactive narrative (Takeda et al., 2012), but I know of no research in developing any variant of the cultural Turing test for virtual heritage. There is, however, a game called 'SpyParty', involving 'subtle behavior, perception, and deception' (a beta version is available at http://www.spyparty.com).

Cinematic Narrative: Machinima as Reflection or Interpretation

In a DiGRA 2009 conference paper, I asked the following question: 'Is Machinima a Form of Art?' (Champion, 2009). For MIT's book *The Machinima Reader*, I tried to answer the question in another way, suggesting that the strength of machinima lies in the challenge to define it (Champion, 2011). My main point was inspired by Roger Ebert's provocative comment that games could never be works of art because they lack an authorial voice. This is a topic that seems quite popular in classroom discussions, but I suggest that the much longer and more elaborately argued book chapter in *The Machinima Reader* would be more relevant.

So what is machinima? What is art? How do the two overlap? Are there essential differences between machinima, games, mods and art? How is authorial content a critical issue? Is the discussion of any relevance to the main subject areas of this book?

Machinima is typically defined as using real-time, interactive (game) 3D engines to produce videos, as a genre using these engines or as emergent gameplay. Paul Marino declared that machinima could be explained as 'animated filmmaking within a real-time virtual 3D environment' (Marino, 2004, p. 1). However, it is important to note that machinima here is defined by how it is made, not by what it is capable of.

What machinima is capable of is revealing our ingrained default responses to apparent game content. For although machinima's content is often that of the games associated with the engines that it uses, machinima can reveal the 'genre baggage' of the host game, and how it helps or hinders narrative and reflection. Hence, one purpose of machinima may be to reveal the behavioural triggers of games and how they affect us or mix cinematic genres with digital media tropes.

In a *Gamasutra* article, John Hopson (2001) also mentioned how the computer game is a behavioural skinner box, a reward system consisting of reinforcers, contingencies and responses. Machinima often uses or evokes images and associations created by playing a game, and because these resources are such powerful triggering mechanisms, the game-player as spectator is caught between viewing the machinima as film and reaching for a keyboard mouse or joystick to shoot the bad guys, strafe to avoid danger, rotate the camera view or run towards a portal. Computer games have their own acquired language of perceived affordances and reacting to these perceived affordances becomes second nature to the experienced gamer (Van Vugt et al., 2006).

Machinima is typically created from the camera functions of game engines. However, they are also typically made from resources associated with the game engine and hence they carry genre attachments. The repetitive nature of games conditions us to automatically respond by enacting game-behaviours, dodging, shooting, running, strafing, etc. So there are triggers, but there are also 'things' that stimulate the player vocabulary. In another *Gamasutra* article, Brett Johnson (2001) has explained how game level designers deliberately develop a 'player vocabulary' so that the game player instinctively acts: 'As designers, we can carefully build a vocabulary of game mechanics and shape what the player knows about the environment, and when they know it.'

To say that the power of machinima is derived from its refocusing on what we have previously taken for granted, or previously adopted without reflection, relies on previous gaming knowledge. I agree with Steven Johnson (2005) – I believe that the way in which games are designed to trigger and overload certain cognitive processes is deliberate, intricate and difficult. To trigger behavioural responses while at the same time causing the player/observer to reflect upon them and still stay engaged is sophisticated and skilful. It is not easy to play on our Pavlovian tendency to reach for an all-so-shiny gun that a 'Halo' character is toying with while he recounts how he survived severe teenage acne and a dominating mother.

So could we consider machinima and games to be a story-telling form of art? Anthony Breznican (2004) reported that Steven Spielberg and Robert Zemeckis believed 'video games are getting closer to a storytelling art form – but are not quite there yet'. Spielberg sets down a benchmark for reaching this level:

> 'I think the real indicator will be when somebody confesses that they cried at level 17 … It's important to emphasize story and emotion and character. This is one of the things that games don't do', Spielberg said … 'Is the player in charge of the story, or is the programmer in control of the story?' Spielberg asked. 'How do you make those two things reconcile with each other? Audiences often don't want to be in control of a story. They want to be lost in your story. They come to hear you be the storyteller, but in gaming it's going to have to be a little bit of both, a little bit of give and take.'

I partially agree with Spielberg that computer games will be hard-pressed to reach the expressive and controlled level of films. Game characters are simplified in form and in movement; they have a limited range of animation. The typical plot is skimpy at best, for the player has to concentrate on surviving as well as on what to do next. The camera is limited and lighting is limited, restricted and reduced in order to save on rendering time and processing power. The games that use game engines that in turn are used for machinima are also geared towards panic and hurry, not towards viewing picturesque scenes and contemplating the universe.

Game engines have trouble approximating the emotional impact and aesthetic beauty of film; they simply lack the control and finesse in character expression, setting and cinematic tools (cameras, filters and lighting). On the other hand, in the same article, Zemeckis admits that films have borrowed from game techniques: 'In the '80s, cinema became influenced by the pace and style of television commercials ... I think the next decades are going to be influenced greatly by the digital world of gaming.'

So if games cannot be art and if machinima does not have to refer to games, must we consider machinima as art only whenever and if it ever creates cinema-standard work (Reimer, 2005)? How can it be or become an artistic medium that is distinct from film? Second, do video games require authorial control in order to be *potentially* classified as art? Roger Ebert (2005) seemed to think so:

> Video games by their nature require player choices, which is the opposite of the strategy of serious film and literature, which requires authorial control. I am prepared to believe that video games can be elegant, subtle, sophisticated, challenging and visually wonderful. But I believe the nature of the medium prevents it from moving beyond craftsmanship to the stature of art. To my knowledge, no one in or out of the field has ever been able to cite a game worthy of comparison with the great dramatists, poets, filmmakers, novelists and composers. That a game can aspire to artistic importance as a visual experience, I accept. But for most gamers, video games represent a loss of those precious hours we have available to make ourselves more cultured, civilized and empathetic.

A major part of the problem of whether games or machinima can be considered art can be laid at the feet of this issue: that we do not have a clear concept of what art actually is, let alone a clear and coherent concept and definition that people can agree on. Our theories of art also tend to suit our own tastes in art, and a film critic's definition of art is likely to have a bias towards the cinematic. So a film critic might appreciate, say, 'Myst', but is it advancing the *art* or even *craft* of computer game design?

For the public, or the spectator or end-user (and hopefully the former is merging into the latter), to enjoy experiencing a self-reflective jolt when their gaming impulses or genre- detection facilities are provoked, challenged or questioned by machinima is surely a worthy (if difficult) challenge. And interactive media has a long way to go to achieve this. Machinima can act as a catalyst for students to question their own opinions and conventions. Their tacit acceptance of game conventions becomes self-evident, for example, when they are asked to create or reflectively critique and challenge mediums or genres which their compatriots value.

Allowing students to use their favourite game engines and game genres does not necessarily encourage them to build fresh and innovative new games. Yet encouraging their ambitions of a cinematic-quality experience in such a way that they are confronted with the practical limitations of current machinima and game engines in particular could prove to be a far more valuable experience. Although students are often attracted to the latest and most advanced game engines, the constraints of earlier (and probably more stable and accessible) game engines can actually aid creativity rather than merely stymie it.

If there are no hard-and-fast rules, machinima could potentially be partially or entirely real-time (just as the early demo recordings of games were) rather than fully pre-rendered. Bots may be controlled by actors or by script or may alternate between the two. Off-scene dynamic data or even audience biofeedback could be fed into the scene or affect the environmental conditions, motivation triggers for the characters and story pathways. Even in the final presentation or exhibition, designers could layer machinima between real-time user-controlled artefacts with script triggers or commands and traditional film clips, allowing viewers to explore and play with what is interactive and what is not.

Thus, machinima could be seen as a reflective and aesthetically directed re-experience of gameplay, game genre and game-level resources that gains impact from its new take on cinematic conventions. Innocuous games like 'The Sims' could be used to parody the homogeneity and shocking plot devices of, say, a television soap opera. But a more powerful interpretation is to consider machinima as an interpretively amorphous vehicle that questions and challenges our understanding of what is static, dynamic, alive, sentient, responsive or automated and what is not.

The reason I am so interested in machinima is not just because it offers teachers and students a way of capturing, staging, choreographing and narrating canned visualizations (and that is reason enough to include it in this book), but it is also a medium which has created a great deal of critical reflection on the computer game medium by the people who love computer games themselves. Machinima can be a very interesting critical and crafted take on computer games. I noted earlier that our tendencies evolving from gameplay could be challenged by machinima when it acts as a form of procedural subversion. As virtual environments typically lack social judgment, machinima can allow us to experience a film evoking our game-taught reflexes and behaviours, and can reveal these inbuilt responses and allow us to reflect on them.

How can we apply this notion? Virtual heritage and digital history projects could use in-scene cameras to record what people do and how they make their decisions, and play this back to them, in contrast to model cinematic narratives created by historians, archaeologists, anthropologists or heritage specialists. These short user-focused movies could reveal what could be done and what should have been done or what is known, partially known or artistically created. Unlike conventional films, machinima can be interlaced with real-time gameplay, explaining or mystifying the viewer/player with what is fact or fiction, past or future.

Digital Story-telling for Heritage and History

Virtual heritage and digital history require portraying and interacting with layers of certainty and authenticity, and conveying those layers and levels of detail. We do not have to create super-creative narratives as our projects are not totally fictional, they don't necessarily have to include 'great art' experiences and, due to their typical classroom or museum settings, participant time may be severely limited. However, these projects are often helped by the use of multimodality (information and scene-setting does not need to be solely or primarily text-based).

Multimodality can help to provide multiple narratives and different types of evidence. Narrative fragments can be threaded and buried through an environment, coaxing people to explore, reflect and integrate their personal exploration into what they have uncovered. Clues can be provided to uncover stories, or stories can in turn be the clues to help people find certain objects or complete tasks. Story aids are not just aids or rewards for exploration; they can also help to convey the fragility of specific sites, their situated cultural significance and the underlying universality of their content.

Second, formal characters (that are plot-driven and set the scene) might be useful, as completely emergent narrative is not required and is sometimes an obstacle to the aims of the project. Characters can do more than simply advance a plot; they can also convey a specific theme to an audience. Social roles specify historical significance and local situated challenges, they provide motivation to explore and understand the simulated environment.

Third, conversational agents can provide site-specific or activity-specific information more conveniently than through game interaction and may help reduce the risk that players will leave the virtual environment to read background material. They can provide a sense of inhabitation, can help draw attention, may help direct or reveal mannerisms and social behaviours, can highlight specific places spots and times, are useful affordances for competition or can act as external memory devices and tools for players.

Human-like agents can provide a sense of inhabitation and human scale; they are easy to find and easy to mimic. They can highlight specific goals, places or sports, important times or events, and can provide information and feedback on particular ways to behave. They are also typically used in games to create competition, but they can also be employed to evoke empathy and develop leadership skills (by following and commenting on the decisions of the player), and can also be seen as aids to help the player.

Cultural agents are of particular interest here in terms of conveying situated cultural behaviours and values, conveying cultural change or transmitting elements that create cultural change. There may be an important distinction between AI's notion of intelligent agents and cultural agents. Cultural agents are not necessarily logical or even reasonable (by our standards); they might not even understand us. So the aims of much AI research may be less important and relevant here.

There is also another potential type of agent, which can create directorial coherence and filtering of events so that it can be viewed as a story. This type of agency can control plot or flesh out a story, but they are not necessarily just conversational agents and they might not necessarily be cultural agents. Their goals might be to select and emphasize important or evocative moments, and weave them into dramatic narratives, allegories or cinematic experiences.

Fourth, storyspaces portray a thematic way of inhabiting and behaving; they contain action affordances and help to focus the audience. Storyspaces might be the overall virtual stage on which actions and events take place, they might trigger certain stories or snippets or clues of narrative, they might afford certain types of actions and events or they might be the space which memorializes and evokes these actions and events in retrospect.

In-game stories are not just created by the deployment of conversational agents or by the use of artificial actors. Game-based stories are also cinematic stories. Director algorithms can help recognize important story elements and create coherent explanations and interpretations of activities and events. Machinima software can record player actions, allow them to reflect on these actions, and filter interpretations and levels of certainty. Cut-scenes can also be used to provide specific knowledge either in terms of place, plot or back-story. They can also provide clues and feedback or indicate expected actions. In-game camera footage can be mixed with past gameplay or with pre-recorded sequences. Using cinematic techniques, we can imply narratives and dramatic motivations, but we also create time for reflection.

Summary

This chapter has outlined four contentions and then disputed them in part or in full. These contentions are as follows:

1. Formalist narrative theory extrapolated into algorithms is of central importance to virtual heritage and digital history.
2. Stories must follow a formal pattern of narrative with a certain number of sequences.
3. Narratives require incredibly intelligent and creative intelligent agents.
4. Game environments are closer to film than to theatre – they require authorial control to be art, but this stymies the required agency for them to be truly interactive media.

Is it possible to generate dramatic entertainment via computers? Drama requires conflict and engagement, and agents are a quick way to create a sense of challenge and competition. Are characters enough to create a story? Do they require a highly sophisticated form of AI? For our purposes, this does not seem to be necessary. What may be necessary (at least for built heritage) is a developed spatial setting as a 'storyspace'. Cultural agents are interesting and I have suggested one example scenario, a cultural Turing test, which has a variety of advantages and does not force programmers to develop a highly sophisticated AI.

I have also critiqued the notion that an interactive narrative would not be able to employ cinematic techniques in general and machinima in particular to help create moments of dramatic engagement. In order to understand engagement, we need to understand drama. In order to create engaging drama, we need to improve the apparent humanness of other avatars – NPCs. And in order to provide more accessible critical expositions depicting historical and heritage events and situations, machinima has the potential to be used in critical debates to visualize and stage alternative interpretations.

What about the debate over whether games can be art? Well if games cannot be considered art because they lack an authorial viewpoint, then this has consequences for depicting historical narratives. And if games cannot be considered art because they lack the range of refined emotions that art apparently can evoke, then we may have problems in creating games that afford empathy and critical thinking. The issue of whether games can be art may seem to be an irrelevant question for those who research and design interactive history and digital heritage. Without empathy, we will not understand other cultures through eyes and minds other than our own, and without critical thinking, we will not question and ponder how the technologies powering digital illusion and virtual entertainment can lead us to an improved understanding of the past.

References

Aristotle 1997. *Aristotle's Poetics.* Montreal: McGill-Queen's University Press.

Bartle, R. 1996. Hearts, Clubs, Diamonds, Spades: Players Who Suit MUDs. MUSE Ltd, Colchester, UK. Available at: http://mud.co.uk/richard/hcds.htm.

Barton, M. 2005. Review: Façade. *Gameology.* Available at: http://www.gameology.org/reviews/review_facade.

Bogdanovych, A., Ijaz, K. and Simoff, S. 2012. The City of Uruk: Teaching Ancient History in a Virtual World. In Y. Nakano, M. Neff, A. Paiva and M. Walker (eds), *Intelligent Virtual Agents.* Santa Cruz: Springer, 28–35.

Bogdanovych, A., Rodriguez, J.A., Simoff, S. and Cohen, A. 2009. Virtual Agents and 3D Virtual Worlds for Preserving and Simulating Cultures. In Y. Nakano, M. Neff, A. Paiva and M. Walker (eds), *Intelligent Virtual Agents.* Santa Cruz: Springer, 257–271.

Breznican, A. 2004. Spielberg, Zemeckis Say Video Games, Films Could Become One. *U-T San Diego.* Available at: http://www.signonsandiego.com/news/features/20040915–1336-ca-games-spielberg-zemeckis.html.

Bringsjord, S. 2001. Is it Possible to Build Dramatically Compelling Interactive Digital Entertainment (in the Form, e.g., of Computer Games)? *International Journal of Computer Game Research*, 1(1).

Burke, M. 2014. *The Routledge Handbook of Stylistics.* London: Routledge.

Campbell, J. 2008. *The Hero with a Thousand Faces.* San Francisco: New World Library.

Cassar, R. 2013. God of War: A Narrative Analysis. *Eludamos. Journal for Computer Game Culture*, 7. Available at: http://www.eludamos.org/eludamos/index.php/eludamos/article/viewArticle/vol7no1–5/7-1-5-html.

Cavazza, M. and Pizzi, D. 2006. Narratology for Interactive Storytelling: A Critical Introduction. In S. Göbel, R. Malkewitz and I. Iurgel (eds), *Technologies for Interactive Digital Storytelling and Entertainment.* Berlin: Springer, 72–83.

Champion, E. 2009. Keeping it Reel: Is Machinima A Form of Art? DiGRA 2009 Conference, 1–4 September, Brunel, UK. Available at: www.digra.org/dl/db/09291.09190.pdf.

——. 2011. Undefining Machinima. In M. Nitsche and H. Lowood (eds), *The Machinima Reader.* Cambridge, MA: MIT Press, 219–238.

Costantini, S., Mostarda, L., Tocchio, A. and Tsintza, P. 2008. DALICA: Agent-Based Ambient Intelligence for Cultural-Heritage Scenarios. *IEEE Intelligent Systems*, 23, 34–41.

Dixon, D. 2011. Player Types and Gamification. *CHI 2011 Workshop on Gamification*, Vancouver, BC, Canada.

Dunniway, T. 2004. Using the Hero's Journey in Games. *Gamasutra*. Available at: http://www.gamasutra.com/view/feature/131527.

Ebert, R. 2005. Why Did the Chicken Cross the Genders? Available at: http://www.rogerebert.com/answer-man/why-did-the-chicken-cross-the-genders.

Georgeff, M., Pell, B., Pollack, M., Tambe, M. and Wooldridge, M. 1999. The Belief-Desire-Intention Model of Agency. *Intelligent Agents V: Agents Theories, Architectures, and Languages.* New York: Springer, 1–10.

Hopson, J. 2001. Behavioral Game Design. *Gamasutra*, 1–2. Available at: http://www.gamasutra.com/view/feature/131494/behavioral_game_design.php.

Huntley, C. 2007. How and Why Dramatica is Different from Six Other Story Paradigms. *Dramatica® The Next Chapter in Story Development.* Available at: http://dramatica.com/articles/how-and-why-dramatica-is-different-from-six-other-story-paradigms.

Ibanez, J., Aylett, R. and Ruiz-Rodarte, R. 2003. Storytelling in Virtual Environments from a Virtual Guide Perspective. *Virtual Reality*, 7, 30–42.

Jenkins, H. 2009. Computer Game Spaces: An Interview with Georgia Tech's Michael Nitsche (Part One). *Confessions of an Aca-Fan.* Available at: http://henryjenkins.org/2009/02/what_architecture_and_urban_pl.html.

Johnson, B. 2001. Great Expectations: Building a Player Vocabulary. *Gamsutra.* Available at: http://www.gamasutra.com/resource_guide/20010716/johnson_01.htm.

Johnson, S. 2005. *Everything Bad is Good for You: How Popular Culture is Making Us Smarter.* London: Allen Lane.

Kalay, Y.E. and Marx, J. 2001. The Role of Place in Cyberspace. *Proceedings on the IEEE Seventh International Conference on Virtual Systems and Multimedia*, 770–779.

Lim, C.-K., Cani, M.-P., Galvane, Q., Pettre, J. and Zawawi, T.A. 2013. Simulation of Past Life: Controlling Agent Behaviors from the Interactions between Ethnic Groups. Digital Heritage Congress 2013.

Lim, M.Y., Aylett, R. and Jones, C.M. 2005. Affective Guide with Attitude. *Affective Computing and Intelligent Interaction.* New York: Springer.

Louchart, S. and Aylett, R. 2004. Narrative Theory and Emergent Interactive Narrative. *International Journal of Continuing Engineering Education and Life Long Learning*, 14, 506–518.

Luppa, N.V. and Borst, T. 2007. *Story and Simulations for Serious Games: Tales from the Trenches.* Oxford: Elsevier.

Mandrell, C. 2010. Why Story Structure Formulas Don't Work. *Corey's Blog.* Available at: http://coreymandell.net/blog/screenwriting-advice/why-story-structure-formulas-don%E2%80%99t-work-part-one.

Manganaro, M. 1992. *Myth, Rhetoric, and the Voice of Authority: A Critique of Frazer, Eliot, Frye, & Campbell.* New Haven: Yale University Press.

Marino, P. 2004. *3D Game-Based Filmmaking: The Art of Machinima.* Scottsdale, AZ: Paraglyph Press.

Mateas, M. and Stern, A. 2003. Façade: An Experiment in Building a Fully-Realized Interactive Drama. *Game Developers Conference*, 4–8.

Nitsche, M. 2008. *Video Game Spaces: Image, Play, and Structure in 3D Game Worlds.* Cambridge, MA: MIT Press.

Papagiannakis, G. and Magnenat-Thalmann, N. 2007. Mobile Augmented Heritage: Enabling Human Life in Ancient Pompeii. *International Journal of Architectural Computing*, 5, 396–415.

Propp, V.I. 1968. *Morphology of the Folktale.* Austin: University of Texas Press.

———. 1984. *Theory and History of Folklore.* Manchester: Manchester University Press.

Reimer, J. 2005. Roger Ebert Says Games Will Never Be as Worthy as Movies. *Ars technica.* Available at: http://arstechnica.com/news.ars/post/20051130–5657.html.

Richard, G.T. 2014. Designing for the Audience: Past Practices and Inclusive Considerations. In K. Schrier (ed.), *Learning, Education and Games, Volume One: Curricular and Design Considerations.* Pittsburgh: ETC. Press, 199–223.

Ritchie, J. 2013. V6N1: Navigation the Gap: The Rhetoric of Digital Space and Interactive Narratives. *iDMA-International Digital Media and Arts Association.* Available at: http://idmaa.org/?post_type=journalarticle&p=520.

Roussou, M. 2001. The Interplay between Form, Story, and History : The Use of Narrative in Cultural and Educational Virtual Reality. *Virtual Storytelling Using Virtual Reality Technologies for Storytelling*, 181–190.

Sequeira, L.M. and Morgado, L.C. 2013. Virtual Archaeology in Second Life and Opensimulator. *Journal for Virtual Worlds Research*, 6.

Sequeira, L.M., Morgado, L. and Pires, E. 2014. Simplifying Crowd Automation in the Virtual Laboratory of Archaeology. *Procedia Technology*, 13, 56–65.

Song, M., Elias, T., Martinovic, I., Mueller-Wittig, W. and Chan, T.K. 2004. Digital Heritage Application as an Edutainment Tool. *Proceedings of the 2004 ACM SIGGRAPH International Conference on Virtual Reality Continuum and its Applications in Industry*. ACM, 163–167.

Szilas, N. 1999. Interactive Drama on Computer: Beyond Linear Narrative. *Proceedings of the AAAI Fall Symposium on Narrative Intelligence*, 150–156.

Takeda, K., Earl, G., Frey, J., Keay, S. and Wade, A. 2012. Enhancing Research Publications Using Rich Interactive Narratives. *Philosophical Transactions of the Royal Society A*.

Van Vugt, H.C., Hoorn, J.F., Konijn, E.A. and De Bie Dimitriadou, A. 2006. Affective Affordances: Improving Interface Character Engagement through Interaction. *International Journal of Human-Computer Studies*, 64, 874–888.

Vandenberghe, J. 2012. The 5 Domains of Play. *Game Developers Conference 2012*. San Francisco.

Vogler, C. 2007. *The Writer's Journey: Mythic Structure for Writers,* Studio City, CA: Michael Wiese Productions.

Vourvopoulos, A., Liarokapis, F. and Petridis, P. 2012. Brain-Controlled Serious Games for Cultural Heritage. *18th International Conference on Virtual Systems and Multimedia (VSMM)*. IEEE, 291–298.

Wright, W. 2006. Dream Machines. *WIRED*. Available at: http://archive.wired.com/wired/archive/14.04/wright.html.

Yee, N. (2005). Motivations of Play in MMORPGs. Paper presented at *DiGRA 2005 – 'Changing Views – Worlds in Play'*, Vancouver, Canada. Available at: http://www.digra.org/digital-library/publications/motivations-of-play-in-mmorpgs.

Chapter 9
Biofeedback, Space and Place

Introduction

This chapter explains the potential benefits of indirect biofeedback used within interactive virtual environments and reflects on an earlier study that allowed for the dynamic modification of a virtual environment's graphic shaders, music and AI based on the biofeedback of the player. The aim was to determine which augmented effects aided or discouraged engagement in the game. Conversely, biofeedback can help calm down rather than stress participants and can attune them to different ways of interacting within a virtual environment. Other potential advantages of indirect biofeedback include increased personalization, thematicized object and interaction creation, atmospheric augmentation, customized filtering of information, and tracking of participants' understanding and engagement. These features may help designers to create more intuitive virtual environments with more thematically appropriate interaction while reducing cognitive loading (the total amount of mental activity imposed on working memory at any one moment) on the participants.

Embodiment, Empathy and Virtual Worlds

Twenty years ago, Novak described future virtual worlds as 'liquid architecture' (Novak, 1991). In this chapter I will argue for alternatives to 'liquid architecture'. Rather than a liquid realm, we may wish for vague digital media boundaries that congeal or even solidify on interaction in order to direct people into different cognitive realms, and through their more indeterminate nature afford a wider and richer range of interactive modes and contextual information. Unfortunately, the built environment has too often been viewed as an art form that relies on its aesthetic value in terms of being an immovable and immutable object.

For example, in the nineteenth and twentieth centuries, according to Leech (1979), Malgrave and Ikonomou (1994), Newman (1995) and Morgan (1996), empathy theorists viewed architecture as little more than sculptural objects that we can create associations for. In a similar manner, the philosopher Anthony Savile (1993) argued that Foster's buildings treated the essence of architecture as sculptural form.

For Savile, architecture also involves interior spaces, the linking of spaces (e.g. from inner to outer and vice versa), and the placing or locating, using and imagining of symbolic objects (as well as the self and other people) in order to create a significant sense of place. Whether Savile was or was not correct in his criticism of a modernist architect, it is clear that many famous architectural critics (Huxtable, 1999; Wolfe, 1999; Tilley, 2009) believed that the experiencing of architecture involves an understanding of how environments affect the psychology and physiology of the inhabitant, the visitor and the passer-by.

Even though there is undoubtedly a great deal of literature concerning how buildings and the environment are experienced, and a substantial body of research and debate into the experience of presence in virtual environments, this research does not seem to have found its way into the design of virtual environments for architectural and environmental visualization. For if it had found its way into the design of virtual environments for architectural visualization, then surely critics would not describe virtual environments as sterile or boring. In his inaugural address, Richard Coyne (1999) stated: 'It is a common lament against contemporary architecture that it has lost touch with the body ... Some see the incursion of the computer, computer-aided design and the invention of digital architecture, as the last step in this transformation. The computer also takes us away from engagement with each other at a bodily level.'

The experiencing of the built environment in a virtual environment typically lacks the richly embodied and visceral experience of visiting and moving through the real-world equivalent situated on changing terrain and visited during changes of light, heat, atmosphere and sound. Technical limitations may be part of the issue, but a further factor is the inability of current virtual environments to adapt meaningfully to the participants.

At this point, you might be compelled to ask why this chapter is so predicated on built environments. In my earlier chapters I have written about how culture and place are in a feedback loop, at least in the real world. In order to create a sense of cultural presence and convey cultural significance, I believe that we need to understand and simulate the built and natural environments as experiences rather than not just as objects. I realize this means a modification of a view that suggests games are foremost simulations. For heritage and history purposes, I am now suggesting that serious games need to be both simulation and model, although I also stress that architectural experiences are interactive and embodied. Given this, could biofeedback help to address this lack of rich embodiment in digital environments?

Defining Biofeedback

I will use my colleague Andrew Dekker's term for biofeedback. Biofeedback represents a real-time two-way feedback loop between the machine and the user: the user reacts to an action initiated by the system, and the system can then react based on the participants' physical/emotional reaction (and so forth). Biofeedback interaction does not necessarily form the primary mode of interaction, but augments existing interaction. This is an important point: human–computer interaction (HCI) researchers have warned us that direct biofeedback control is difficult and variable for many users, but they do not seem to have fully scoped the potential of indirect biofeedback to avoid these issues.

Biofeedback in Computer Games

For first-person shooter (FPS) computer games, biofeedback can help in the visual and audio adjustments of the avatar and heads-up display (HUD). Manipulation of the game environment and events, and enhancement of generalized gameplay can be affected (player speed, strength and avatar abilities). Low galvanic skin response helps with the aiming of weapons and the ability to collect and retain inventory items. High heart rate might also assist with agility and movement.

There are also stealth games, which could require the player to remain calm while walking through the city, avoiding suspicion, and monitor their breathing and heart rate when using a weapon to perform, say, an assassination. They may have to raise their heart rate to move faster during an escape, but also keep their skin response low in order to remain focused. Similarly, for jail breaking, when speaking with NPCs or when hiding objects, the player must remain calm to be inconspicuous. Traditional game interfaces designed to accomplish these kinds of interaction do not help break down the barrier between the player and their avatar.

In the developing world of social player games, biofeedback can also help to provide other players with information on the trustworthiness of the player. After all, the lie detector is a simple form of biofeedback. Biofeedback can also be used to trigger automatic facial behaviours or physical gestures in the avatar responding to the physiological state of the human player. We could also send information about the player's physiological states to NPCs to help them portray more empathic and believable behaviour. Conversely, information about the player could be sent to bots controlled by the computer to either help or hinder the player, potentially also creating more strategically responsive and perspicacious enemies.

Boredom could trigger certain avatar characteristics so that other players realize this player is not fully engaged, but this could also be accomplished with eye tracking, which was part of the CALLAS research project (Bertoncini and Cavazza, 2007). However, eye tracking is of interest to evaluation and visualization, for it can help us understand which features and spaces people are interested in, where they tarry, and (with biofeedback results) which spaces and events and encounters they most enjoyed and were attentive to. Evaluation results could in turn change the design or presentation of the digital environment: attractive features could have higher resolution or more enticing lighting of sound effects, while less desirable features could be hidden entirely or could appear at lower resolution.

Past Work: Case Study

In the following case study (Dekker and Champion, 2007), Andrew Dekker and I investigated how commercial biofeedback devices could be integrated into existing computer game environments. The audience for the project was derived from data drawn from the then-existing audience for PC FPSs, particularly players who had previously played 'Half-Life 2'. The case study used a simple device within a commercial gaming environment mod to create indirect biofeedback. While the initial implications are for games, there is also widespread potential for many forms of digital interaction (Fairclough, 2009).

We hoped to address the following questions:

- By augmenting existing gaming environments with biofeedback, can the system be aware of users' reaction to game content?
- Can we successfully tailor game content to create a more engaging experience than with traditional environments?

Andrew Dekker sought out an appropriate existing gaming environment that would have a high chance of eliciting emotional reactions from the player throughout the gaming experience. A variety of game engines and game environments were examined informally and through literature in order to choose an appropriate setting. Although my initial reason for creating the project brief was to develop interaction suitable for reflection and meditation in Buddhist temples, we decided that FPSs were the most likely to provide a visceral emotional reaction (tension, action, etc.). RPGs did appear to provide more of an emotional change over time, but it was more at the reflective level (visceral, behavioural and reflective stages being part of Norman's (2004) theory of Emotional Design). Horror was chosen as the theme of the game because it provides a physical reaction that is relatively easy to measure (stress and tension) and something that is controllable.

The design, development and evaluation were conducted throughout an iterative design process. Scenarios and events drew inspiration from various entertainment mediums. The event (or ability) was designed and developed in the game engine. The event was tested in order to examine two things:

(a) What sensory readings were appropriate to trigger the event?
(b) How did the event change the users' sensory readings?

The study evaluation was a qualitative process, not quantitative. Interviews and observations of the 14 participants were used to determine the success or failure of each event, but for anything other than a pilot study, given the subjective nature of biofeedback, I suggest at least double this number of participants.

Test Equipment

This study utilized the 'Wild Divine' sensor technology, which includes a device that clips onto the fingers. The Lightstone measures the Electrocardiogram Heart Rate Variability (ECG HRV) and the galvanic skin response (GSR) of the user in real time. While these measurements do not give enough information to make a

Figure 9.1   'Wild Divine' Lightstone Biofeedback Sensor

complete biometric analysis, they provide insight into participants' reactions to specific game events.

The Lightstone device (Figure 9.1) has the potential to measure anxiety and stress, relaxation and meditation, tension, sudden changes in mood and breathing variability. The electroencephalogram (EEG) was not used due to ethical considerations.

Andrew Dekker developed sockets for the 'Wild Divine' biosensor, enabling us to use them for a wider range of commercial games and for virtual environments.

Software Design

For our experimental design, we modified an existing zombie horror level developed in the 'Half-Life 2' source game engine by connecting 'Wild Divine' sensors. Invisible boxes placed in the game level detected the player's biofeedback. Depending on whether the biofeedback registered calmness or excitement, it triggered changes in apparent time (bullet time effects), music and visibility (a calmer participant could see through walls or their avatar could even become invisible to their enemies).

Figure 9.2   'Half-Life 2' and Biofed Shaders

Filters (Figure 9.2) were also applied to the game if the player's heartbeat was faster or slower than average. If the user's heartbeat and GSR was over three times their average, the screen became bright red, the field of view of the avatar would change to 130 degrees and the speed of the avatar would dramatically increase (to simulate a 'berserker'). A calmer heartbeat turned the display black and white or faded it to white, while an excited heartbeat caused the display to fade to red or further, to shake, to represent a lack of control.

Most of the data of the experiment has already been published (Dekker and Champion, 2007), so I will only briefly mention the demographic factors. In short, the qualitative evaluation of the prototype was performed with 14 participants, who were aged between 15 and 50. The gender split was 25 per cent female, 75 per cent male. They were both experienced and not experienced in FPSs and 'Half-Life'. They had not previously been involved in the project and had not participated in earlier informal evaluations.

To compensate for possible problems associated with this method of analysis, readings were averaged at two-second intervals. The average of the participants' biometrics was compared against the calibration average in order to create a multiplier. The three multipliers (HRV, GSR and heartbeat) dynamically changed the game environment.

The prototype was designed to support the structure of the evaluation. Two game levels (named Level A and Level B) were developed for the evaluation. Level A re-created a level from the FPS 'Half-Life 2'. Level B was created as an extension to Level A, where added game events were triggered from biometric information.

Participants were required to read the information sheet supplied and give consent to be evaluated and have their experiences video-recorded. First, the participant played a level (either the standard or enhanced level) for five minutes and then the played the alternate level (the level that was not previously played) for five minutes. After playing the levels, each participant was given a short interview, where they answered questions about the game and discussed their experiences.

It was important to identify and eliminate where possible variables that might influence results. Both levels were created to limit the amount of variables within the evaluation. The variables that were anticipated as possible influences on the evaluation results were:

- user preferences for game genre, theme and style of game;
- learning curve of the interaction method;
- HCI problems associated with the Lightstone device;
- preconceptions of the prototype with influence from commercial computer games;
- issues with the design and pace of the enhanced game;
- the learning curve of the level structure (e.g. where to go);
- dynamic events within the environment;
- being killed and other immersion breaking events;
- the Hawthorne effect (placating the interview);
- the placebo effect (from wearing the biometric device);
- external environment and technical inconsistencies.

These variables were either controlled and removed for the evaluation or taken into consideration when analysing evaluation results. We would also suggest changing and/or randomizing the sequence order of the environments visited, as the order in which they are experienced may affect the results. The most apparent variable within the evaluation process was the learning curve associated with the game level. Aspects to the gameplay including exploration and triggering objects within the world were influenced by users playing through the base game level twice (once in the control (Level A) and once in the biofeedback environment (Level B)).

Events that affected gameplay in the prototype were considered to be a variable that should be taken into account during evaluation. Generic game events such as being killed or escaping to the game menu have the ability to break the users' sense of immersion. The evaluation analysis also considered the Hawthorne effect (where users are inclined to agree with the interviewer) by structuring interview questions in a way that creates a discussion. The biometric device was required wearing in both the standard level (A) and the enhanced level (B) to avoid any influence based on the interaction influence of the Lightstone device.

In our paper (Dekker and Champion, 2007), we noted that the participants' changes in facial expressions were easily comparable to the change in biometric information (we also used video cameras to track both the participants and the onscreen action). Audio effects had a considerable influence on participants' biometric information and reactions. The computer game's dynamic shaders clearly affected the participants, while black and white visualization calmed them. The red filter visualization did not affect biometric information significantly, but the white screen visualization confused them. Participants seemed more engaged in the enhanced biofeedback version (over the control environment), especially when sounds were played. Participants also reacted strongly when the screen shook. Participants realized when there was biofeedback, but did not try to adjust their breathing or heart rate to see how it affected gameplay. In short, indirect biofeedback seemed effective and more engaging than the control (a game level with no biofeedback).

In general, the participants appeared to appreciate the addition of biofeedback. However, we were reluctant to recommend further use of the 'Wild Divine' technology (although the sensors and the software seem to be more robust now). The sensors interfered with hand control, required continual recalibration and occasionally gave unreliable data. While for our research these limitations were acceptable (although some might disagree, such as Kuikkaniemi et al. (2010), more recent hardware such as 'NeuroSky' and 'Emotiv' offers more promise in terms of stability and ease of use. Having said that, I seem to have trouble with the Bluetooth connection for 'NeuroSky', while the 'Emotiv' device at the time of writing uses wet sensors, which require constant cleaning.

I note in passing that the 'Half-Life 2' source game engine also had implementation issues, but one advantage of using the source game engine is that the parent company Valve also researches the use of biofeedback in its games (Ambinder, 2011), so the current iteration of the engine is probably more user-friendly. That said, with our new middleware, now we can connect to easier-to-use game engines/real-time rendering engines, such as 'Unity'. This middleware allows the evaluator to attach commercial biofeedback devices to commercial or self-created game engines and virtual environments, but we are yet to fully test the software. Soon there will hopefully be better systems for correlating video and eye tracking with biofeedback and there are already biofeedback arduino kits. I also hope, via the new Kinect and similar technology, to evaluate the suggestion that postural changes (in the spine) could be related to changes in engagement in virtual environments (Friedman et al., 2005).

Biofed Possibilities

There are various papers and projects on using biofeedback or phobic triggers in virtual environments to either expose (and cure) phobias or to develop understanding of oneself or of others, and biofeedback seems to be of increasing concern at HCI conferences (Kuikkaniemi et al., 2010; Fairclough et al., 2011; Nacke et al., 2011; Pan et al., 2011), but we have not encountered substantial discussion on how biofeedback can be used to enhance (digital) built form appreciation and understanding.

One potential use is for personalization. Digital environments have been criticized for being sterile and empty, and for lacking personality, individuality or warmth (Green, 1996; Minocha and Reeves, 2010). Biofeedback could augment and provide individual personalization, adding in unique lighting effects, sounds or other details relating directly and dynamically to the participant's physiological states.

Biofeedback could also personalize social virtual environments, where multiple people (such as stakeholders in urban design projects) are simultaneously immersed in a virtual environment. They could view or hear how others are reacting to the virtual space. Or perhaps where the virtual world is based on a real-world place, biofeedback from real-world passers-by and inhabitants could be fed into the virtual world in real time.

If walking through a virtual environment triggers participants' memories or emotional attachments of the real-world place being simulated, it may be possible to colour or otherwise tag these locations in the virtual environment in relation to the biofeedback being generated. However, this does not seem to be accurate or reliable. Bored mental states that arise independently of the virtual environment may affect results. There may be useful applications in the evaluation of engagement via virtual environments being automatically tagged by the biofeedback of visitors (chairs, rooms or graspable objects could retain a metaphorical aura, for example), but this would be hard to evaluate in small experiments.

There is also the notion of architectural empathy. In a book entitled *Empathy and its Development* (Eisenberg and Stronyer, 1987), a clear distinction is made between empathy and sympathy (concern for people). Despite various definitions of empathy, there is a tendency for empathy to be divided into empirical empathy (by association) or empathy through feeling (also called personal empathy). Empirical or aesthetic empathy involves attributing personal qualities to people and to objects, such as columns, etc. So one may be able to create differing architectural spaces and evaluate with biofeedback as to whether they elicit certain responses, but this at least initially appears a highly involved and complex situation to evaluate.

Atmospheric augmentation was carried out in the 'Ravensholm'/'Wild Divine'/'Half-Life 2' study; uniquely personalized and augmented environments could be created from varying rates of biofeedback. However, how the environment is modified might not necessarily augment the experience during play and might not even be recognizable (let alone be considered evocative) by the participants. Another problem is that this may gamify and adrenalize the architectural experience. In other words, enjoyment comes from visceral augmentation and a rewards system, which does not necessarily relate to the architecture as designed and may not help any meaningful experience of the surroundings themselves apart from as a backdrop or as ludic affordances.

Perhaps more effectively, biofeedback may be used to augment the overall atmosphere or even climate. Recent technology has seen the development of real-time interactive weather simulation and could also be controlled by biofeedback. However, although this external environmental data may add to user engagement, this information is not necessarily relevant to the individuals' goals and emotional state. A more architecturally appropriate interaction metaphor might be linking visual signs of pollution and decay to the overly excited biofeedback; the more excited the player, the more quickly the building decays.

Extrapolating from game mechanics, we could leverage biofeedback states that are generated from excitement (or boredom) in games to colour or otherwise alter digital spaces as a reward and feedback system. Architecture can be seen as a complex symbolic relationship of path and centre, of detail at places of rest (such as in formal seating areas), and subdued detail where circulation is important (such as corridors and staircases). If the participant understood that a space was designed more for rest than for activity and acted accordingly (such as slowed down their heartbeat and GSR to appropriate levels), the environment could change to reflect their physiological harmony with their surrounds.

Such a scenario might not work so well in a game environment where it would not be clear how activity-based biofeedback would give either the participant or the viewer a better idea of how the participant is affected by the architectural quality of the space itself and not just by responses to located events. However, it may be appropriate for sacred or mythical spaces, where the calmer the participant is, the richer the interaction that is afforded. Biofeedback could also be used to determine the amount of detail in an environment, avatars could develop supernatural and mystical powers, or religious beliefs could take virtual form.

It is also possible to use biofeedback as an evaluation mechanism, such as evaluating spatial awareness and detecting potential differences between spatial designers and the public. This technology might be able to detect developing spatial awareness in student designers, and where and when spatial awareness impinges on general awareness in virtual environments.

Biofed virtual environments could track phobias (also known as negative engagement in VR literature). Where people encounter phobias near points or areas in time and space, their negative phobias can be visibly recorded and aggregated. The digital environments could be 'sprayed' with an aggregated spray of phobia colour. We note here that it may be difficult to aggregate phobic areas or even locate the spatial or symbolic phobic triggers. Furthermore, trained psychological help may be required to create, calibrate and adjust the environments as well as ensure that the test environments pass ethical and medical clearance and are used safely and effectively.

Conversely, positive engagement could also be tracked: significant points of interest (indicated by pauses and by heightened or lowered rates of biofeedback, and perhaps camera tracking of postural change or tracking of eye gaze) could be recorded.

Finally, filtering environmental detail through biofeedback may aid both virtual and augmented reality projects. For example, the *lifeClipper* project (Torpus and Bühlmann, 2005), was a commercial tourism and mixed reality urban heritage product and research project in Switzerland. Through the HMD, participants saw vague and cultured video characters as they walked through Basel, but through oddly shaped stencils. Biofeedback could affect the perimeter and clarity of the augmented reality objects. For example, the relative calmness of the walker could affect the resolution clarity or viewing window shape or size of the augmented reality (AR)-displayed object or video. This project also featured pressure sensors incorporated in soles to wear in one's own shoes for tracking walking behaviour, but it could also be used to augment the excitement level in the augmented environment. For example, if the participant is more excited, less or more detail could be added to the augmented projection, or shader effects could be triggered.

At a simpler level, biofeedback can be used to affect territorial awareness – for example, more excited states could increase or diminish the field of view, and this could have significant benefits for large-scale projected environments such as CAVEUT (Jacobson et al., 2005).

Brains and Virtual Worlds

Facebook bought Oculus for a reputed $2 billion in March 2014 (Hern and Stuart, 2014; Souppouris, 2014); Oculus is famous for the Oculus Rift (an HMD), while Facebook is known as a social media company. However, Philip Rosendale, the creator of 'Second Life', has been working with the Oculus Rift and brain-scanning (MRI and EEG) to show how when people are inside a VR shown on an Oculus Rift, the brain-scanning can show which parts of their brain are activated. I have spoken to researchers in neuroscience and visualization who believe that the findings are extremely unreliable, and I know from personal experience that subjective differences, personal preferences and calibration issues prevent researchers from stating with certainty that one can evaluate specific emotional states. Regardless, this is still an exciting area of research.

To give you an idea of what may be possible with brain-scanning technology, a consortium of University of California research labs (the UCSF Neuroscape Lab, the UCSF Gazzaley lab and the UCSD Swartz Centre for Computational Neuroscience) have created a 'glass brain' proof of concept visualization (Figure 9.3). Neuroscape Lab (http://neuroscapelab.com/projects/glass-brain) describes it as follows:

> This is an anatomically-realistic 3D brain visualization depicting real-time source-localized activity (power and 'effective' connectivity) from EEG (electroencephalographic) signals. Each color represents source power and

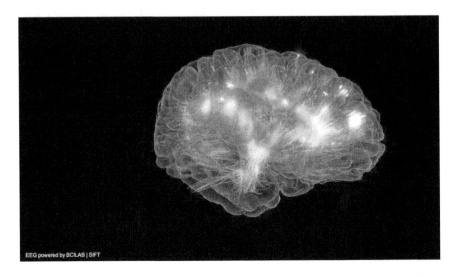

Figure 9.3   The Glass Brain
Source: Gazzaley Lab, UCSF: Swartz Center, USCD

connectivity in a different frequency band (theta, alpha, beta, gamma) and the golden lines are white matter anatomical fiber tracts. Estimated information transfer between brain regions is visualized as pulses of light flowing along the fiber tracts connecting the regions.

The modeling pipeline includes MRI (Magnetic Resonance Imaging) brain scanning to generate a high-resolution 3D model of an individual's brain, skull, and scalp tissue, DTI (Diffusion Tensor Imaging) for reconstructing white matter tracts, and BCILAB/SIFT to remove artifacts and statistically reconstruct the locations and dynamics (amplitude and multivariate Granger-causal interactions) of multiple sources of activity inside the brain from signals measured at electrodes on the scalp (in this demo, a 64-channel 'wet' mobile system by Cognionics/BrainVision.

The final visualization is done in Unity3D and allows the user to fly around and through the brain with a gamepad while seeing real-time live brain activity from someone wearing an EEG cap.

If we combine neuroscience research, biofeedback, brain-scanning technology and social media applications (such as Facebook or Rosendale's new and improved alternative to 'Second Life'), the future could be both exhilarating and very worrying. While the evaluation possibilities are exciting, the privacy issues could be daunting.

Heritage and Biofeedback

In terms of heritage, I know of one major research project undertaken at Coventry University (Fairclough et al., 2011; Vourvopoulos et al., 2012; Liarokapis et al., 2013). Using either 'Neurosky Mindset' headgear or 'Emotiv' headgear, the target audience (children) would navigate through 'Roman Nova' (built on 'Rome Reborn'), a Unity recreation of ancient Rome. The children controlled the navigation of their avatar via EEG. There were also predefined 'intelligent' avatars that walked along pre-selected paths. The writers mention calibration issues (as one would expect), but I am unclear as how the brain–computer interface helped participants to understand the history and the cultural heritage and significance of the digital simulation.

Methodological Issues

Are there currently accessible, effective and accurate devices to measure biofeedback? What can we measure, react to and creatively leverage when implementing individual and group biofeedback that is appropriate to the architectural domain? Are there any advantages or disadvantages to the use of biofeedback and can we ascertain them by trial evaluations?

The 'Neurosky', 'Emotiv', and 'Wild Divine' products seem to be the most commonly used and accessible biofeedback devices for research into virtual worlds and digital games. Indirect biofeedback can be applied in terms of understanding the self, the environment or other (fictional or real) participants' reactions to the environment. An audience could see in a very immediate and vivid manner how different market segments experience and react to biofeedback-augmented digital visualizations. So a digital place can be layered or otherwise augmented by the biofeedback of past or current visitors. However, the variety of responses possible, the lag, the calibration required, and the indirect and vague nature of biofeedback necessitate that care must be taken with how the level of detail of the test environment and how rich the interaction should be.

Second, I suggest that indirect biofeedback used to increase the sense of trepidation or excitement of the environment is best employed in games (or perhaps in social worlds). However, there is the potential to assess serenity and contemplation in sacred spaces such as digital simulations of churches and meditation spaces. Biofeedback can be used to artificially or thematically increase powers, or provide more opportunities the calmer or more excited the player becomes. With gaze tracking or other methods, we could also reward the player for concentration or increase the challenges if they become distracted. In terms of mythology, biofeedback has great potential to provide the players with thematic god-like powers.

Third, using indirect biofeedback to personalize the environment and recognize the attitude through physiological state of others is interesting but difficult to evaluate in smaller test environments of shorter duration. For measuring subjective responses, using a control group to test comparative results in task performance does not seem appropriate.

Designers may be more interested in whether participants find the modified environment to be more responsive (in a positive way), with more character, more appropriate to what is simulated and more interesting. They may also be interested in whether the modified environment has a more engaging sense of territoriality. Do certain seated views or standing positions create a sense of unease? For example, changes between calm and excited biofeedback states could affect the field of vision and the lighting condition. The participants could also be asked which of these biofeedback-influenced factors has the most natural mappings (where the interaction metaphors are most appropriate).

Summary

I have suggested five main areas of applications for the above type of biofeedback (indirect biofeedback based on changes in physiological states) for virtual environments:

- Participants' biofeedback could indirectly colour their surroundings, affording them more insight into the world around them, their interactions with it or the progress and experience of other participants.
- More uniquely personalized and engaging environment objects (also known as externs) directly or indirectly created or modified by aggregated biofeedback recorded from virtual visitors.
- Atmospheric-affecting biofeedback that augments and enhances a sense of inhabitation (popular places could have a biofed 'aura').
- Biofeedback could filter and display relevant information so that a user is not overloaded with extraneous information or, conversely, more empathic and observant participants could be rewarded with more information.
- Indirect biofeedback could track participants' phobias and their changing levels of engagement and disengagement.

These ideas may be of interest to those keen to create more engaging virtual worlds, those interested in whether digital simulations can better approach the experiential richness of real world places, and those curious about indirect interaction metaphors for experiencing places. Biofeedback may help those who wish to create not just simulations of religious, revered and historical sites, but also those who also wish to convey a sense of the experience of various audiences who have visited them.

The 'Roman Nova' project aside, as far as I know, there is as yet no convincing and thorough review of how biofeedback, and indirect biofeedback in particular, could be usefully applied to historical simulations and virtual heritage. While there are increasing numbers of explorative papers on biofeedback applied to games, such research must be critically reviewed before being applied to digital simulations of history and heritage, for the aims of the two fields can differ significantly.

Despite the lack of relevant research to heritage and history, I am convinced that biofeedback could be successfully applied to digital heritage, if calibration, accuracy and equipment robustness are improved. Biofeedback can help users to understand their own physiological states and phobias, or the physiological states and phobias of other people. So biofeedback can help people to understand themselves and understand others, but it can also be used to indirectly enrich the background and create a more personalized atmosphere, or to create more empathic and believable NPCs (computer-controlled non-playing characters designed to aid the story or gameplay) or more aware bots (computer-controlled opponents). Responses can also be used to evaluate engagement without disrupting the user experience.

References

Ambinder, M. 2011. Biofeedback in Gameplay: How Valve Measures Physiology to Enhance Gaming Experience. Available at: http://www.gdcvault.com/play/1014734/Biofeedback-in-Gameplay-How-Valve.

Bertoncini, M. and Cavazza, M. 2007. Emotional Multimodal Interfaces for Digital Media: The CALLAS Challenge. *Proceedings of HCI International.* Available at: https://www.academia.edu/2853399/Emotional_Multimodal_Interfaces_for_Digital_Media_The_CALLAS_Challenge.

Coyne, R. 1999. The Embodied Architect in the Information Age. *Arq: Architectural Research Quarterly*, 3, 175–186.

Dekker, A. and Champion, E. 2007. Please Biofeed the Zombies: Enhancing the Gameplay and Display of a Horror Game Using Biofeedback. In B. Akira (ed.), *DiGRA 2007: Situated Play Conference*, Tokyo. DiGRA, 550–558.

Eisenberg, N. and Stronyer, J. (eds) 1987. *Empathy and its Development.* New York: Cambridge University Press.

Fairclough, S.H. 2009. Fundamentals of Physiological Computing. *Interacting with Computers*, 21, 133–145.

Fairclough, S.H., Gilleade, K., Nacke, L.E. and Mandryk, R.L. 2011. Brain and Body Interfaces: Designing for Meaningful Interaction. *Proceedings of the 2011 Annual Conference: Extended Abstracts on Human Factors in Computing Systems.* Vancouver, BC: ACM, 65–68.

Friedman, D., Brogni, A., Antley, A., Guger, C. and Slater, M. 2005. Sharing and Analysing Presence Experiments Data. *PRESENCE 2005*, 111.

Green, M. 1996 Animation in the Virtual world. *Proceedings of Computer Animation '96*, Geneva, 5–12.

Hern, A. and Stuart, K. 2014. Oculus Rift: Facebook Sees Virtual Reality Future in $2bn Deal. *The Guardian.* Available at: http://www.theguardian.com/technology/2014/mar/26/facebook-buys-oculus-virtual-reality.

Huxtable, A.L. 1999. *The Unreal America: Architecture and Illusion.* New York: New Press.

Jacobson, J., Kelley, M., Ellis, S. and Seethaller, L. 2005. Immersive Displays for Education using CAVEUT. *World Conference on Educational Multimedia Hyoermedia & Telecommunications*, Montreal, Canada. AACE.

Kuikkaniemi, K., Laitinen, T., Turpeinen, M., Saari, T., Kosunen, I. and Ravaja, N. 2010. The Influence of Implicit and Explicit Biofeedback in First-Person Shooter Games. *Proceedings of the SIGCHI Conference on Human Factors in Computing Systems.* ACM, 859–868.

Leech, P. 1979. Aesthetic Representations of Mind: The Critical Writings of Adrian Stokes. *British Journal of Aesthetics,* 19, 76–80.

Liarokapis, F., Vourvopoulos, A., Ene, A. and Petridis, P. 2013. Assessing Brain-Computer Interfaces for Controlling Serious Games. *2013 5th International Conference on Games and Virtual Worlds for Serious Applications (VS-GAMES),* 11–13 September, Bournemouth University, 1–4.

Mallgrave, H.F. and Ikonomou, E. (eds) 1994. *Empathy Forme & Space: Problems in German Aesthetics 1873–1893.* Santa Monica: Getty Center for the Humanities.

Minocha, S. and Reeves, A.J. 2010. Design of Learning Spaces in 3D Virtual Worlds: An Empirical Investigation of Second Life. *Learning, Media and Technology,* 35, 111–137.

Morgan, D. 1996. The Enchantment of Art: Abstraction and Empathy from German Romanticism to Expressionism. *Journal of the History of Ideas,* 57, 317–341.

Nacke, L.E., Kalyn, M., Lough, C. and Mandryk, R.L. 2011. Biofeedback Game Design: Using Direct and Indirect Physiological Control to Enhance Game Interaction. *Proceedings of the SIGCHI Conference on Human Factors in Computing Systems,* ACM, 103–112.

Newman, G. 1995. Adrian Stokes and Venice. *British Journal of Aesthetics,* 35, 254–261.

Norman, D.A. 2004. Emotional Design. *Ubiquity,* 1.

Novak, M. 1991. Liquid Architectures in Cyberspace. In M. Benedikt (ed.), *Cyberspace: First Steps.* Cambridge, MA: MIT Press, 225–254.

Pan, M.K.X.J., Chang, J.-S., Himmetoglu, G.H., Moon, A., Hazelton, T.W., Maclean, K.E. and Croft, E.A. 2011. Now where was I?: physiologically-triggered bookmarking. Proceedings of the SIGCHI Conference on Human Factors in Computing Systems, Vancouver, BC, Canada. ACM, 363–372.

Savile, A. 1993. *Kantian Aesthetics Pursued.* Edinburgh: Edinburgh University Press.

Souppouris, A. 2014. John Carmack Breaks Silence on Facebook's Oculus Acquisition. Available at: http://www.theverge.com/2014/3/30/5563440/john-carmack-facebook-oculus-rift-purchase-comments.

Tilley, J. 2009. *Architecture Depends.* Cambridge, MA: MIT Press.

Torpus, J.L. and BüHlmann, V. 2005. LifeClipper. *VSMM 2005 Proceedings of the Eleventh International Conference on Virtual Systems and Multimedia,* Belgium.

Vourvopoulos, A., Liarokapis, F. and Petridis, P. 2012. Brain-Controlled Serious Games for Cultural Heritage. *18th International Conference on Virtual Systems and Multimedia (VSMM)*, Milan. IEEE, 291–298.

Wolfe, T. 1999. *From Bauhaus to Our House.* New York: Picador.

Chapter 10
Applying Critical Thinking and Critical Play

Can we take the preceding ideas and theoretical concepts, and employ them in practice in the classroom and in projects for the public? I will endeavour to explain where these or similar ideas are already being employed, which areas are the most controversial, unproven or in need of more work, and I will end with speculation on which areas of game studies and DH are most likely to intersect for maximum benefit to both parties.

Arguably, my first chapter is the most controversial. Do some people think DH is about text, foremost, primarily and most significantly? In Chapter 1 I gave a rather lengthy critique on this point. Is this of relevance to critical gaming? Yes, I believe it is, because until this point is refuted, computer games as a critical medium will be relegated to arcades and living rooms. I may be preaching to the converted, but I am worried that I still have not shown the usefulness of visualization in particular, and design in general, to traditional humanities scholars. Of even more importance is that I really think I should have spent more time showing how and where these technologies are accessible or can be made even more accessible.

In Chapter 2 I have questioned whether we meaningfully learn by playing computer games. My personal opinion is that we do, but that it is not highly transferrable. And I suspect that many of the more famous theories about game-based learning, serious gaming, gaming by stealth, procedural rhetoric, persuasive games, playful learning and learning by stealth confuse prescription with description. Many times they do not clarify whether they are talking about games or computer games. Too often they appear to be talking about games in general, but instead they are actually talking about the potential of games. Well, in digital history and cultural heritage, we really have to say whether the potential of games is worthwhile. Game development costs time, resources and money – couldn't that go towards the direct preservation of the documents, sites or artefacts in question?

As I said in Chapter 2, the issue of procedural rhetoric is so complex that I need to give more thought to it. I apologize unreservedly for not being to give a more sustained and in-depth critique on this subject in this book.

Chapter 3 gave a brief whirlwind tour of some of the more significant items of migration from VR projects to consumer-based entertainment. As my book is aimed at humanities scholars more than visualization experts and computer scientists, I apologize for any simplifications. I am sure that this chapter is very open to debate, especially on where the technology is going to, and even if technology is leading in a certain direction that offers no guarantee that it will be taken up by the public. The rise, fall and death of VRML and other related software, as well as the huge white elephants of many well-funded VR centres, should give us pause for concern. The control of interface technology and peripherals by social media and advertising companies is also worthy of more than the raising of eyebrows. Data is power. Personal data is money and power and control.

Chapter 4 is a summary of various projects and potential design techniques to address some specific issues of simulating history. My background in architectural history no doubt biases me. Archaeologists specializing in the prehistoric have cautioned me that I concentrate on the historical side of archaeology and I take their criticism to heart!

Chapter 5, on virtual heritage, is central to this book, but I have published rather extensively on this subject elsewhere. To avoid the risk of self-plagiarism, I have only given the broadest of brushstrokes here. The term could be viewed as self-contradictory, there is a surprising lack of archival practice associated with the area and there are sizeable gaps between content, learning and technology in many virtual heritage projects. How can we develop more useful and robust criticism in this field when so many projects are based on large-scale research grants that do not reward learning from failure? At the very least, we need to improve the way we evaluate the learning benefits of virtual heritage. If it is heritage, then it cannot be only to impress people – it has to motivate but also educate people.

Chapter 6 contains three key concepts. I question the use of 'world' in much of the literature. I have not even partially covered the numbers of publications that use the term as if it is self-explanatory. The concept of 'role' is also problematic, but is of great potential to, for example, historical simulations. There is a great deal of scope for researchers to explore how role-playing can be better employed in serious games. Likewise, the concept of 'ritual' is problematic even in the traditional literature (only some of which I could include in this book). My tentative steps in explaining the various attributes of rituals are really only to show that this term has been used clumsily and too broadly in the literature about games and virtual worlds. I also hope to improve the design of cultural rituals in simulations without insulting either the original cultural shareholders or the intelligence of the players and the wider audience.

Chapter 7 attempted to explain that violence must sometimes be employed in historical simulations and virtual heritage projects, but how it is addressed could be articulated and resolved more beneficially by considering whether violence is required in the representation, interaction or understanding. Even if violence needs to be depicted or performed, what is most important is to ensure that the background, context, alternatives and consequences have all been investigated and explained to the participant. It would have greatly helped this chapter if I had had the time and space to investigate concrete examples, problems and solutions. Perhaps part of the problem is that so few virtual heritage projects feature violence not because they have successfully resolved the issue, but because they are widely accessible, contextually comprehensive, highly immersive or thematically interactive!

Chapter 8 is a can of worms. At a shallower level, I am suggesting that various AI researchers might say they are interested in interactive drama, but really they are interested in creating writers at the level of Shakespeare. I am also saying that drama and engagement are terms that have been thrown around, while the narrative advantages and disadvantages of games still need to be explored, poked and prodded. The above may get me into serious polemical trouble, but the next part is also contentious.

I have also taken the additional step of examining machinima to see if it has some interest in relation to the design and critique of historical simulations and digital heritage. I suggest that it is worth exploring, that it can be much more accessible at a design level, does not necessarily require programming skill and can help provide visualizations in a relatively short period of time that can be critiqued in class by teachers and students. At a deeper level, while I briefly borrow and explain some cinematic devices to account for exploring across time and space even when historical knowledge is patchy, I concede there is a huge amount of work to do.

Chapter 9 was more experimental, suggesting ways in which biofeedback and sensors and interaction that more fully involve the brain and the body may be creatively and appropriately employed to convey the visceral and less immediately visual potential of historical simulations, and to convey the more embodied and contextually embedded features of heritage sites and artefacts. This is such a nascent area that I am sure that researchers can greatly add to the suggestions in this chapter. However, I also find it immensely exciting and capable of addressing other issues of accessibility, health, and collaborative interaction, and it may well extend the reach of history and heritage into public spaces.

In this final chapter (Chapter 10), I will leave you with the following suggestion as to how to spot a good or bad theoretical argument about computer games, I will also suggest that a good argument in this area is not just sound and valid, but is also aware of *and maximizes* the rhetorical implications.

Criticism and Gaming

How can we ensure that our critical positions, theories and arguments about gaming have merit? This is a work-in-progress checklist that may help identify weak points in an argument.

Ideally, a critical position/argument about computer games should be the following:

1. Falsifiable and verifiable – not such a common feature in the humanities and not always relevant, but in my opinion a good argument should be saying where and when it is contestable, and where and when it can be proven or disproven.
2. Extensible and scalable – we should be able to add to it, extend it, apply it to more research questions and research areas or add it to current research findings or critical frameworks.

3. Reconfigurable – components are more useful than take-it-or-leave-it positions.
4. Useful even if proven wrong in terms of data, findings, methods, or argument (possibly this heuristic should be combined with point 3).
5. Helpful to the current and future design of computer games, and having the potential to forecast future changes in design, deployment or acceptance.
6. Not in danger of conflating *describing* computer games with *prescribing* how computer games should be – several of the arguments cited in this book appear to make this mistake.
7. Aware of the distinction between methods and methodology – the selection or rejection of methods should always be examined and communicated.
8. Lucid and honest about the background, context and motivations as factors driving it – the parameters of the argument should also be disclosed.
9. Constantly aiming for validity and soundness of argument.
10. Motivated by the attempt to provide in a long-term and accessible way for the data, output and results of any experiment or survey to be examinable by others.

Do I use the above steps when reviewing grants or student applications? It depends. With student project or thesis applications, I often see an extremely broad research question. Aims are not clearly separated from objectives. Many proposals lack criteria that explain exactly who (or what) determines whether the project or experiment was a success or failure. Care in showing what has been already proven or disproven will impress potential supervisors. But a good research project should go further and should explain why it expects to employ the methods it has chosen, how it can test its ideas and which audience in particular would find the results significant and useful.

To put it even more simply, it would be great if a thesis or research project proposal was created by *working backwards* – for example, in three years I will have proven this, it will take me x years to learn the steps to arrive at this final proof (or finding), and this is what I need to learn or use in order to arrive at each of these steps.

My suggestion appears to be backed up by the method employed in a recent journal article and survey on serious games (Connolly et al., 2012) that determined 'high-quality' publication by:

1. the appropriateness of the research design for addressing the research question;
2. the appropriateness of the methods and analysis;
3. how generalizable the findings were (with respect to sample size and representativeness);
4. the relevance of the focus of the study;
5. the extent to which the study findings can be trusted in answering the study question(s).

This last criterion is very important and is easier to address if a research proposal works backwards from the intended final findings to create the focus, scope and parameters of the research question.

The Next Step

How can the public communicate to each other opinions, memories, stories and reflections of place, but when they are visiting or designing virtual worlds? Tagging both personalizes and contextualizes, yet this use of imaginative, dynamic and creative user-based infill is often not made available in digital media projects. New interfaces and game engines can help the personalization of the environment by an active viewer; 'tagging' place could increase engagement and insight into the socio-cultural elements of urban and rural and imaginative spaces, and could also enrich virtual heritage environments.

For example, student projects re-created environments from historical sources using commercially available game engines. Inspired by a scenario called a cultural Turing test, the game levels re-create not only the tangible surroundings but also rule-based social behaviour using impostor-detecting avatars, and by creating communication channels between players in the form of diary entries that record contextual historical and cultural information. The diary entries can take the form of text, or there can be dynamic capture of external data such as videos of people inserted into the virtual environment as narrators or collaborators. New technology in the form of biometrics, dynamic sound, dynamic textures, and user-driven geo-data can augment and update static and lifeless virtual environments with communal memories and personal experiences.

Through the game itself, we can also create our own levels that bend space and time. Could we also bend or invert conventional notions of historical narrative? Is it possible to meaningfully do so and personalize a virtual environment through the interactions that take place within it, even if that interaction initially appears to be destructive? Can we share these meanings within a community or reveal meanings about a community that is typically removed from us? Given improvements in technology, will these environments improve or hinder a sense of authenticity?

More than just for visualization, though, this technology can also help educate through self-directed learning. Possible features include: learning by resource management; learning about social behaviour (chat, observation, mimicry); visualization of scale, landscape or climate; depicting varying levels of uncertainty; allowing the visitor to filter or reconfigure reconstructions; immersion in the excitement of the times; selecting correct objects or appearance to move about the 'world' or to trade or to advance the social role or period of time; deciphering codes and language and avoiding traps; and online walkthroughs by expert guides.

References

Australia ICOMOS Incorporated. 2013. The Burra Charter, The Australia ICOMOS Charter for Places of Cultural Significance.

Connolly, T.M., Boyle, E.A., MacArthur, E., Hainey, T., and Boyle, J.M. (2012). A Systematic Literature Review of Empirical Evidence on Computer Games and Serious Games. *Computers & Education*, 59(2), 661–686.

Wolf, M.J.P. (2014). Building Imaginary Worlds: The Theory and History of Subcreation. Available at: http://CURTIN.eblib.com.au/patron/FullRecord.aspx?p=1211703.

Index

Printed in the United States
by Baker & Taylor Publisher Services